PRINCE SHŌTOKU'S
COMMENTARY ON THE
ŚRĪMĀLĀ SUTRA

BDK English Tripiṭaka Series

PRINCE SHŌTOKU'S COMMENTARY ON THE ŚRĪMĀLĀ SUTRA

(Taishō Volume 56, Number 2185)

Translated from the Chinese

by

Mark W. Dennis

Bukkyō Dendō Kyōkai America, Inc.
2011

First Printing, 2011
ISBN: 978-1-886439-43-6
Library of Congress Catalog Card Number: 2011918396

Published by
Bukkyō Dendō Kyōkai America, Inc.
2620 Warring Street
Berkeley, California 94704

Printed in the United States of America

A Message on the Publication of the English Tripiṭaka

The Buddhist canon is said to contain eighty-four thousand different teachings. I believe that this is because the Buddha's basic approach was to prescribe a different treatment for every spiritual ailment, much as a doctor prescribes a different medicine for every medical ailment. Thus his teachings were always appropriate for the particular suffering individual and for the time at which the teaching was given, and over the ages not one of his prescriptions has failed to relieve the suffering to which it was addressed.

Ever since the Buddha's Great Demise over twenty-five hundred years ago, his message of wisdom and compassion has spread throughout the world. Yet no one has ever attempted to translate the entire Buddhist canon into English throughout the history of Japan. It is my greatest wish to see this done and to make the translations available to the many English-speaking people who have never had the opportunity to learn about the Buddha's teachings.

Of course, it would be impossible to translate all of the Buddha's eighty-four thousand teachings in a few years. I have, therefore, had one hundred thirty-nine of the scriptural texts in the prodigious Taishō edition of the Chinese Buddhist canon selected for inclusion in the First Series of this translation project.

It is in the nature of this undertaking that the results are bound to be criticized. Nonetheless, I am convinced that unless someone takes it upon himself or herself to initiate this project, it will never be done. At the same time, I hope that an improved, revised edition will appear in the future.

It is most gratifying that, thanks to the efforts of more than a hundred Buddhist scholars from the East and the West, this monumental project has finally gotten off the ground. May the rays of the Wisdom of the Compassionate One reach each and every person in the world.

NUMATA Yehan
Founder of the English
Tripiṭaka Project

August 7, 1991

Editorial Foreword

In January 1982, Dr. NUMATA Yehan, the founder of Bukkyō Dendō Kyōkai (Society for the Promotion of Buddhism), decided to begin the monumental task of translating the complete Taishō edition of the Chinese Tripiṭaka (Buddhist canon) into the English language. Under his leadership, a special preparatory committee was organized in April 1982. By July of the same year, the Translation Committee of the English Tripiṭaka was officially convened.

The initial Committee consisted of the following members: (late) HANAYAMA Shōyū (Chairperson), (late) BANDŌ Shōjun, ISHIGAMI Zennō, (late) KAMATA Shigeo, (late) KANAOKA Shūyū, MAYEDA Sengaku, NARA Yasuaki, (late) SAYEKI Shinkō, (late) SHIOIRI Ryōtatsu, TAMARU Noriyoshi, (late) TAMURA Kwansei, URYŪZU Ryūshin, and YUYAMA Akira. Assistant members of the Committee were as follows: KANAZAWA Atsushi, WATANABE Shōgo, Rolf Giebel of New Zealand, and Rudy Smet of Belgium.

After holding planning meetings on a monthly basis, the Committee selected one hundred thirty-nine texts for the First Series of translations, an estimated one hundred printed volumes in all. The texts selected are not necessarily limited to those originally written in India but also include works written or composed in China and Japan. While the publication of the First Series proceeds, the texts for the Second Series will be selected from among the remaining works; this process will continue until all the texts, in Japanese as well as in Chinese, have been published.

Frankly speaking, it will take perhaps one hundred years or more to accomplish the English translation of the complete Chinese and Japanese texts, for they consist of thousands of works. Nevertheless, as Dr. NUMATA wished, it is the sincere hope of the Committee that this project will continue unto completion, even after all its present members have passed away.

Dr. NUMATA passed away on May 5, 1994, at the age of ninety-seven, entrusting his son, Mr. NUMATA Toshihide, with the continuation and completion of the Translation Project. The Committee also lost its able and devoted Chairperson,

Professor HANAYAMA Shōyū, on June 16, 1995, at the age of sixty-three. After these severe blows, the Committee elected me, then Vice President of Musashino Women's College, to be the Chair in October 1995. The Committee has renewed its determination to carry out the noble intention of Dr. NUMATA, under the leadership of Mr. NUMATA Toshihide.

The present members of the Committee are MAYEDA Sengaku (Chairperson), ICHISHIMA Shōshin, ISHIGAMI Zennō, KATSURA Shōryū, NAMAI Chishō, NARA Yasuaki, SAITŌ Akira, SHIMODA Masahiro, Kenneth K. Tanaka, WATANABE Shōgo, and YONEZAWA Yoshiyasu.

The Numata Center for Buddhist Translation and Research was established in November 1984, in Berkeley, California, U.S.A., to assist in the publication of the BDK English Tripiṭaka First Series. The Publication Committee was organized at the Numata Center in December 1991. In 2010, the Numata Center's operations were merged into Bukkyō Dendō Kyōkai America, Inc. (BDK America) and BDK America continues to oversee the English Tripiṭaka project in close cooperation with the Editorial Committee in Tokyo.

MAYEDA Sengaku
Chairperson
Editorial Committee of
the BDK English Tripiṭaka

Publisher's Foreword

On behalf of the Publication Committee, I am happy to present this contribution to the BDK English Tripiṭaka Series. The initial translation and editing of the Buddhist scripture found here were performed under the direction of the Editorial Committee in Tokyo, Japan, chaired by Professor Sengaku Mayeda, Professor Emeritus of Musashino University. The Publication Committee members then put this volume through a rigorous succession of editorial and book-making efforts.

Both the Editorial Committee in Tokyo and the Publication Committee in Berkeley are dedicated to the production of clear, readable English texts of the Buddhist canon. The members of both committees and associated staff work to honor the deep faith, spirit, and concern of the late Reverend Dr. Yehan Numata, who founded the BDK English Tripiṭaka Series in order to disseminate Buddhist teachings throughout the world.

The long-term goal of our project is the translation and publication of the one hundred-volume Taishō edition of the Chinese Buddhist canon, plus a few influential extracanonical Japanese Buddhist texts. The list of texts selected for the First Series of this translation project is given at the end of each volume.

As Chair of the Publication Committee, I am deeply honored to serve in the post formerly held by the late Dr. Philip B. Yampolsky, who was so good to me during his lifetime; the esteemed late Dr. Kenneth K. Inada, who has had such a great impact on Buddhist studies in the United States; and the beloved late Dr. Francis H. Cook, a dear friend and colleague.

In conclusion, let me thank the members of the Publication Committee for the efforts they have undertaken in preparing this volume for publication: Senior Editor Marianne Dresser, Dr. Hudaya Kandahjaya, Dr. Carl Bielefeldt, Dr. Robert Sharf, Reverend Kiyoshi Yamashita, and Reverend Brian Nagata, President of Bukkyō Dendō Kyōkai America, Inc.

John R. McRae
Chairperson
Publication Committee

Contents

Contents

Translator's Introduction

This book is a translation of the *Shōmangyō-gisho* (*Commentary on the Śrīmālādevīsiṃhanāda-sūtra*), one of three Buddhist commentaries written in classical Chinese that have been attributed to Japan's Prince Shōtoku (574–622).[1] The *Shōmangyō-gisho* offers an interpretation of the *Śrīmālādevīsiṃhanāda-sūtra* (*Sutra of the Lion's Roar of Queen Śrīmālā*), more commonly known as the *Śrīmālā-sūtra*.[2] In this text, Queen Śrīmālā of Ayodhyā receives a letter from her parents, King Prasenajit and Queen Mallikā, extolling the superiority of the Mahayana, or "Great Vehicle." The letter prompts Śrīmālā to speak the Buddha's name in praise and request him to appear to her. The Buddha responds to her request by appearing before Śrīmālā and her court attendants in the sky in front of the palace. Much of the text describes Śrīmālā's explanation of central Mahayana doctrines through the eloquence granted her by the Buddha. The central teachings of the text include the *tathāgatagarbha,* "storehouse of the Tathāgata"; the *ekayāna,* "One Vehicle"; and the conditioned and unconditioned forms of the Four Noble Truths.

The *Śrīmālā-sūtra*

The *Śrīmālā-sūtra* is considered one of the key early Mahayana sutras that espouse the *tathāgatagarbha*—a Sanskrit compound term that combines "*tathāgata,*" an epithet of the Buddha (literally, "thus gone"), and "*garbha,*" meaning the "storehouse," "matrix," "womb," or "seed" of enlightenment that is present in all sentient beings. While the *tathāgatagarbha* is closely related to the notion of buddha-nature, the *Shōmangyō-gisho* describes the former at length but refers to the latter just once. Indeed, both doctrines were more fully developed in later Mahayana texts, particularly the *Ratnagotravibhāga-śāstra,* the *Laṅkāvatāra-sūtra,* and the *Awakening of Mahayana Faith.*

Ekayāna, the second of the sutra's central teachings, is a Sanskrit term meaning the "One Vehicle" that encompasses all Buddhist paths. It appears in a number of Mahayana Buddhist texts and has been understood as an attempt to harmonize divergent Buddhist interpretations and paths, particularly those of the three vehicles—the bodhisattva, *pratyekabuddha,* and *śrāvaka.* The *Shō-mangyō-gisho* also refers to the *ekayāna* in contrast to the two vehicles; some of these references point to the paths of the *pratyekabuddha* and *śrāvaka,* while others refer to *pratyekabuddha*s and arhats. The term *ekayāna* is also used in reference to the five vehicles, which adds those of the *deva*s (gods) and humans to the other three.

Pratyekabuddha means "self-enlightened one" or "solitary realizer," while *śrāvaka* ("hearer") originally referred to a direct disciple of the Buddha—those who had heard him teach. Later, the term *śrāvaka* came to mean a monastic whose goal was to become an enlightened master, or arhat (literally, "one who is worthy of respect"). All three figures—*pratyekabuddha*s, *śrāvaka*s, and arhats—are often criticized in Mahayana polemics, with the arhat coming under particular criticism for "selfishly" focusing on his own enlightenment. This lack of selflessness is contrasted to the altruistic and superior goal of the bodhisattva, who becomes the ideal practitioner of the Mahayana. This "Great Vehicle," when understood through the lens of the *ekayāna,* teaches ultimate truth, unlike the lower vehicles it encompasses, whose teachings are described as provisional—taught by the Buddha as a form of "skillful means."

The *Śrīmālā-sūtra* also discusses at length the Four Noble Truths, commonly rendered as: life is characterized by suffering; suffering is caused by desire; remove desire and thereby eliminate suffering; follow the eightfold path to remove suffering. In the translation, however, these four truths are often abbreviated as suffering, origination, cessation, and path. The *Śrīmālā-sūtra* is noteworthy in this regard because it distinguishes the "conditioned" from the "unconditioned" forms of these truths. The four conditioned truths are the realm of the disciples, self-enlightened ones, and arhats, while the unconditioned truths are understood only by the Buddha and bodhisattvas of high spiritual attainment. While the four conditioned truths are provisional, the four unconditioned truths represent ultimate truth. Among the latter set, however, the truth of the cessation of suffering is described as the ultimate refuge for Buddhist practitioners.

Early Accounts of Shōtoku and the *Shōmangyō-gisho*

The earliest surviving written records describing Prince Shōtoku were not composed until some one hundred years after his death. Perhaps the most important of these early accounts is the *Nihon shoki,* compiled in 720 C.E. Modeled on the Chinese dynastic histories, the *Nihon shoki* seeks to legitimize the Japanese imperial house by describing an unbroken lineage of sovereigns that descended from Amaterasu, the Sun Goddess, a primary figure in Japan's creation mythology. This lineage is traced through the descent of the Heavenly Grandson, Ninigi-no-mikoto, to a line of human sovereigns that includes a number of Shōtoku's relatives, including his aunt, Empress Suiko (554–628 C.E.).[3]

The *Nihon shoki* describes Shōtoku as a master politician and shining figure in the imperial line. After being appointed regent by his aunt in 593 C.E., he played a leading role in the government until his death in 622.[4] During this thirty-year period, he is credited with composing a seventeen-article proto-constitution, instituting a system of twelve ranks to distinguish court functionaries, and promoting diplomatic, cultural, and religious contacts with the Sui and Tang dynasties of China as well as with the three Korean kingdoms of Goguryeo, Baekje, and Silla. The text also recounts the transmission of Buddhism from Baekje to the Japanese archipelago in the mid-sixth century and important battles fought by the Soga clan, said to have been key supporters of Buddhism, and the Mononobe clan over its acceptance.

The *Nihon shoki* also depicts Shōtoku as a devout practitioner and generous patron of Buddhism who donated land to the Buddhist community and helped build Hōryūji and other temples. His keen intellectual interest and understanding of Buddhist doctrine, honed under the instruction of continental tutors, led to lectures at court on the *Śrīmālādevī-sūtra* and the *Lotus Sutra* (*Saddharmapuṇḍarīka-sūtra*). Although the *Nihon shoki* remains silent on Shōtoku's composition of any of the three commentaries that are attributed to him, later texts describe these lectures as the source of their composition.

The *Jōgū Shōtoku hōō teisetsu*

The earliest reference to Shōtoku's composition of any of the three Buddhist commentaries appears in the *Jōgū Shōtoku hōō teisetsu,* though the author and dates of composition of this text are unknown. While the *Teisetsu* describes Shōtoku's great intellect and sagacity in terms similar to the *Nihon shoki,* it focuses to a greater degree on his Buddhist activities, noting that he promoted the Buddhist faith by supporting the sangha through building temples, sending monks abroad, and collecting texts.

The *Teisetsu* also records that in an effort to gain a deeper understanding of Buddhist teachings, Shōtoku studied with Hyeja, a Buddhist teacher from the Korean peninsula. The text notes that during his tutelage under Hyeja, and at the behest of Empress Suiko, Shōtoku offered to a number of dignitaries lectures on the *Śrīmālā-sūtra* that lasted for three days. The *Teisetsu* describes his lectures as being like those of a monk, and notes that all in attendance were greatly pleased, gained faith, and converted to Buddhism. After these lectures, Empress Suiko offered Shōtoku a substantial gift of land in the region of Harima (modern-day Hyōgo prefecture), which he pledged, in turn, to Hōryūji. But there is no mention of Shōtoku's lectures on the *Hokke-gisho* (*Commentary on the Lotus Sutra*), which are noted in the *Nihon shoki,* nor specifically his authorship of all three commentaries. Instead, the *Teisetsu* states that Shōtoku composed Buddhist texts on the *Lotus Sutra* and other unnamed sutras. Though vague, scholars who have studied Shōtoku's works have assumed this passage refers to the other two texts that make up the *Sangyō-gisho.*

The *Teisetsu* also records that Hyeja returned to his homeland with Shōtoku's commentaries, and lamented his passing when he heard of Shōtoku's death. Hyeja is said to have predicted that he himself would die on the one-year anniversary of the prince's death, and would meet his student again in the Pure Land. The text adds that, just as predicted, Hyeja took ill and died exactly one year after Shōtoku.

The *Shengmanjing shuyi sichao*

The *Teisetsu* states Shōtoku's commentaries were carried back across the sea by Hyeja, but nothing more is heard of their fate or influence on Korean Buddhist traditions. Such is not the case, however, in China. The Tang dynasty Tiantai monk Mingkong (no dates) composed a study of the *Śrīmālā-sūtra,* the *Shengmanjing shuyi sichao,* after coming across a copy of Shōtoku's *Shōmangyō-gisho* that had been brought to China by Japanese monks. The little that is known of Mingkong comes from the colophon to his commentary, which states he was a disciple of Zhanran (711–782), the sixth patriarch of the Tiantai school.

In the *Shengmanjing shuyi sichao,* Mingkong draws on the ideas of a number of Buddhist exegetes, including Kumārajīva (350–419), Zhizang (458–522), Sengzhao (384–414?), and also Shōtoku.[5] Shinshō Hanayama, a well-respected Shōtoku scholar, estimates that of the approximately one thousand seven hundred lines that make up the *Shōmangyō-gisho,* Mingkong either quotes directly from or clearly interprets about one-fifteenth of the total text. Mingkong's text was later copied and brought back to Japan by the Japanese Tendai monk Ennin (794–864), whose discovery of the *Shengmanjing shuyi sichao* in China is recorded in a postscript to a copy of it written by Enchin (814–891), which notes that Ennin entered Tang China in 838. Later figures such as Eizon (1201–1290) cited the composition of Mingkong's commentary as evidence of the *Shōmangyō-gisho*'s erudition and value, Shōtoku's greatness as a Buddhist exegete, and the sophistication and legitimacy of the Japanese Buddhist traditions that drew upon Shōtoku's thought.

Although the *Sangyō-gisho* became interwoven into the broader East Asian Buddhist exegetical tradition in this way, information about Shōtoku's texts was also transmitted through artwork (statues, mandalas, and pictorial biographies), poetry, and rituals at Hōryūji and other temples that commemorate Shōtoku's lectures on the *Śrīmālā* and *Lotus* sutras.

Shōtoku's Reincarnations

Over time, Shōtoku's image was embellished in these sources through the appearance of a body of auspicious omens, predictions, and supernatural events. These accounts claim, for example, that Shōtoku could speak at birth, faced the east and chanted "hail to the Buddha" at the age of two, and at age seven was capable of reading Buddhist texts sent from the continent. He was believed to possess the gift of clairvoyance and the ability to listen simultaneously to the claims of ten people and produce a sagacious judgment for each. Shōtoku was also connected by rebirth or other means to central Buddhist figures, including Śākyamuni Buddha, Maitreya, Avalokiteśvara, Queen Śrīmālā, Bodhidharma, and the Chinese Tiantai master Huisi (515–577). He was said to have reappeared to the faithful as he reincarnated or manifested in dreams or other forms, including Emperor Shōmu (701–756) and other prominent figures.

The Development
of an Exegetical Tradition

Evidence suggests that by the mid-eighth century the texts of the *Sangyō-gisho* were being copied by monks at Hōryūji as an act of devotion, and possibly studied by a small group of literate monks living in the temple or having access to its library. Over time, they became the objects of study for an exegetical tradition that can be traced to the work of the Tendai school's Chikō (708?–780?) and other scholar-monks of the Nara (710–794) and Heian (794–1185) periods. This tradition of exegesis became firmly established, however, in the Kamakura period (1185–1333), when the Tōdaiji exegete Gyōnen (1240–1321) composed three detailed sub-commentaries of Shōtoku's work.

Modern Scholarship

The modern period has seen an outpouring of scholarly and popular works addressing Shōtoku and his texts. Scholars have invested much intellectual effort in the study of the *Sangyō-gisho* and related materials in an effort to recover the authentic Shōtoku by proving whether or not particular events, achievements, and texts ascribed to him are credible. Although most scholars believe that Shōtoku authored the *Sangyō-gisho,* a small number of critics argue that he is not the rightful author of these commentaries. The studies of this latter group first appeared in the more open intellectual environment of the postwar period and can be traced to the work of the historian Sōkichi Tsuda.

Tsuda was instrumental in beginning a process of identifying historical inaccuracies in the *Nihon shoki* and other early accounts describing the formation of the nascent Japanese state. He challenges the veracity of a number of early records describing Shōtoku, arguing, for example, that accounts of Shōtoku's lectures on the *Śrīmālā* and *Lotus* sutras were the fabrications of pious Buddhists. He thus rejects Shōtoku's authorship of the *Hokke-gisho* and the *Shōmangyō-gisho.*[6] This position has been elaborated upon by a few other scholars, who cite a lack of contemporaneous written records describing either Shōtoku as an individual or the details surrounding the composition of the texts. These scholars note that the earliest extant records are not only filled with embellishments and inaccuracies but also postdate Shōtoku's death by at least a hundred years. Irrespective of these scholarly debates, however, the influence of the *Shōmangyō-gisho* is undeniable in both premodern and modern forms of Japanese Buddhism, and it is still a source of inspiration for many.

Conventions for the Translation

The *Shōmangyō-gisho* generally follows the *Śrīmālā-sūtra* from beginning to end, although it occasionally moves back and forth between sections. It often quotes the sutra and then offers an explanation of the passage in question. The beginning of such quotations is generally indicated by the construction, "from . . . below," but does not indicate where the passage ends. Some of these quotations are just one or two words, making it difficult in the case of common terms to determine which passage in the sutra is the referent. For example, many quotations simply begin with the question, repeated throughout the sutra, "Why?" To distinguish among these and other ambiguous passages, I have often inserted at least part of the following sentence from the sutra. These and other interpolations and additions to the *Shōmangyō-gisho* are indicated with brackets.

The structure of the text is often confusing due to its many sections, subsections, and so forth. The commentary divides the sutra into three major sections: the introduction, the main teaching, and the propagation of the sutra, with their corresponding chapters. But it also divides the sutra's fourteen chapters in other ways. For example, it distinguishes between "self-practice" and "other-practice." The former is the realm of Śrīmālā and other bodhisattvas who are at the seventh stage of bodhisattva practice and below, while the latter applies only to those bodhisattvas at the eighth stage and above. There are many other divisions that can make identifying a particular passage's location in the broader argument difficult as well. To clarify these relationships, many critical editions and translations of the text include headings and *kadan* tables, which offer a visual map of the text's structure. I have followed this tradition by inserting numbered headings and subheadings that are accompanied by short descriptions of the coming section. The *Shōmangyō-gisho* also tends to repeat material by offering a short introduction to a new section, sometimes indicated by the word *raii* ("the coming idea"), which simply lists the relevant passages to be discussed below. The text then repeats those passages when each is taken up for discussion in more detail.

I have used English translations of technical Buddhist terms whenever possible. For example, *pratyekabuddha* is rendered as "self-enlightened one," *śrāvaka* as "disciple," and *ekayāna* as "One Vehicle." I have kept "bodhisattva," "Tathāgata," and other Sanskrit terms if they are commonly used in English translations of Buddhist texts. There are a few cases where it made sense to move back and forth between languages. For example, I have used both the Sanskrit "Dharma" and the English "teaching," depending on context. This is also true of the Sanskrit terms "Mahayana" and "Hinayana," which appear in some contexts as "Great Vehicle" and "Small Vehicle." I have generally kept *tathāgatagarbha* in its Sanskrit form, but have rendered *garbha* as "storehouse" in sections that discuss the meaning of the term. Translations of other technical terms are consistent throughout the text, while I have used different words to translate key terms whose meanings overlap, for example, "afflictions" for the Japanese *bonnō* and "mental disturbances" for *waku*.

In a number of passages, the author abbreviates material by referring the reader to the *Śrīmālā-sūtra,* the object of this interpretive commentary. I have translated these references with some variation of the phrase "See the sutra." There are also frequent references to anonymous interpreters whose work is quoted, summarized, and sometimes criticized. I have translated these references as "One interpreter says," "Another interpreter argues," and so on. Scholars have debated the identity of these interpreters and their texts, particularly that of the *hongi,* which I have translated as "model text." This text served as a resource or model for the composition of the *Shōmangyō-gisho,* and much scholarly work has been devoted to identifying the *hongi* and debating the relationship between the two texts.

I have tried to minimize clutter in the translation by supplying terms without brackets that are clearly implied by the author. For example, "embracing the true Dharma," a phrase that is repeated throughout the text, is often indicated simply by the character for "embracing" but it clearly refers to the true Dharma. In this and similar cases I have supplied the entire phrase without brackets: "embracing the true Dharma" instead of "embracing [the true Dharma]."

Finally, I would like to thank Professor Noritoshi Aramaki, who generously helped me to begin work on this translation; and Laurie Dennis, whose keen editorial eye transformed it into a more coherent and smooth whole. I also wish to thank Professor Kenneth Tanaka of Bukkyō Dendō Kyōkai and Senior

Editor Marianne Dresser of the BDK English Tripiṭaka Project, who kindly and patiently assisted me in completing this project; and Professor Hiroshi Kanno, who painstakingly compared my final translation to the original Chinese. I would also like to acknowledge the value of the translations I have consulted of the *Śrīmālā-sūtra* and the *Shōmangyō-gisho* (see Bibliography), as well as the Digital Dictionary of Buddhism (http://www.buddhism-dict.net/ddb/), which I have used extensively in preparing this translation.

PRINCE SHŌTOKU'S COMMENTARY
ON THE *ŚRĪMĀLĀ SUTRA*

Introduction

[The Lion's Roar of Queen Śrīmālā: The Correct and Extensive Sutra
Proclaiming the Great Expedient Means of the One Vehicle.]

[Translated during the Liu-Song dynasty (420–479)
by the Indian Tripiṭaka master Guṇabhadra.]

This is from the private collection of King Jōgū
of the Great Land of Yamato. It is not a text from across the sea.[7]

The Contents of the Sutra

As for Queen Śrīmālā, she was originally inconceivable. No one knows   1a6
whether she was a transformation of the Tathāgata, or if she was a bodhisattva [of the tenth and highest bodhisattva stage called] the "Dharma Cloud."
Recognizing from afar that it was the proper time, she took on the form of
a woman in Ayodhyā, [a city in the kingdom of Śrāvastī]. First, she was born
to the king of Śrāvastī so that she could perform completely [the duties on]
the path of filial piety. She then became the wife of King Yaśomītra of Ayodhyā in order to fulfill the three subordinations [to father, husband, and son].
Finally, influenced by Śākyamuni, she helped him widen the path of the
Mahayana ("Great Vehicle").

The teaching [expounded in the sutra] is divided into fourteen chapters.
The sutra's essential meaning is not shallow since it establishes the far-reaching truth. Indeed, each time Śrīmālā expounds the teaching, the Tathāgata
praises her words, saying that they are the same as those of the buddhas [of
the past, present, and future], and thereby validates the teaching.

The Title of the Sutra

[The sutra's title can be broken into the following elements.] "Śrīmālā": It is
said that in the world, women adorn their bodies with the seven precious jewels. But here, Śrīmālā adorns her truth body with all the virtuous practices,

and is thus called "Śrīmālā" ("Auspicious Garland"). "The Lion's Roar": Since Śrīmālā fearlessly proclaims the great principles, she is like the lion that fears no other animal. The title thus includes [the words] "Lion's Roar." And while "Śrīmālā" is a name given based on her essential [qualities], "Lion" is a metaphor.

"The Correct and Extensive [Sutra Proclaiming] the Great Expedient Means of the One Vehicle": This phrase addresses the Dharma that will be expounded. [The word] *jing* ("sutra") means both "Dharma" (or "teaching") and "eternal." That is, the truth of the Great Sage's teaching does not change, even though time passes and customs vary. It is thus called "eternal." It is also the law for sentient beings, and so is called "Dharma." Furthermore, this [term *jing*] is a Chinese word. In the foreign [language of Sanskrit], it is called "sutra," a term with five common meanings. Although it can be interpreted according to these five meanings, the two essential meanings are "wellspring" and "a [carpenter's] string" [that is used to draw a line] with ink. These correspond with the two meanings of *jing* [noted above]: "Dharma" and "eternal." Thus, the [Chinese term] *jing* has been substituted for [the Sanskrit word] "sutra."

Each sutra has a different name. In this case, the first section of the sutra is called "The Lion's Roar of Queen Śrīmālā," which refers to a person. The second section is called "The Correct and Extensive [Sutra Proclaiming] the Great Expedient Means of the One Vehicle," which refers to the Dharma. Together, these phrases constitute the title by referring both to the person [who expounds the Dharma] and the Dharma [that is expounded]. Therefore, [the complete title is] "The Lion's Roar of Queen Śrīmālā: The Correct and Extensive Sutra Proclaiming the Great Expedient Means of the One Vehicle."

The Three Divisions
of Buddhist Sutras

In response to the needs of the world, the Great Sage teaches the Dharma to sentient beings. When he does so, regardless of whether a sutra is of many or few volumes, or whether it illuminates a profound or shallow principle, he expounds it in three divisions. The first division is the "introductory teaching," where "introductory" refers to the stage that leads gradually [to the main teaching]. The second division is the "main teaching," where "main" refers

to the main body of the sutra. The third division is the "propagation of the   1b
teaching," which means transmitting [the teachings of the sutra] to future generations.

The Buddha needs these three divisions because sentient beings, until
the present, have been distracted by their attachment to external objects and
their spirits have become ever more dull. If they suddenly heard the profound principles, they would be unable to accept them and put them into
practice. Even worse, this could produce a slanderous mind, and so [cause
listeners] to fall into one of the three unfortunate destinies [of animals, hun-
gry ghosts, and hells]. For this reason, the Great Sage first shows extraordinary signs that cause sentient beings to desire [to listen to the teaching].
[Indeed, having witnessed] these initial signs, their minds are then ready to
listen to the profound principles. The Buddha then expounds the main body
of the teaching. Having completed the introductory and the main teachings,
all sentient beings can receive the benefit [of the sutra].

Out of compassion, moreover, the Great Sage expounded the Dharma
not only for the benefit of those living at that time but also for those to come,
so that they would be equally blessed. Thus, at the end [of the sutra], he
expounds [the last division] called the "propagation of the teaching," which
explains the means by which to promote [the sutra to future generations].

The following sections [of the sutra] correspond to these three divisions.
From the beginning of the sutra to "[Queen Śrīmālā and her attendants,] with
pure minds, praised the true merits of the Buddha," is the introductory teaching. The main teaching begins with "The Tathāgata's body, marvelous in
form, is unequaled in the world" and concludes with "You have already been
familiar with countless buddhas, and can expound the meaning." The propagation of the teaching begins, "At that time the World-honored One emitted a brilliant light that shone upon the great assembly," and ends at the
sutra's conclusion.

Part I

Commentary on the Introductory Teaching

The sutra begins with the introductory teaching, which has two sections. The first is the "general introduction" and the second is the "specific introduction." Since five elements, including "thus [I have heard]," are common to all sutras, this section is called the "general introduction." Because the passage that begins with "sending a letter and feeling the [presence of the] Buddha" is clearly meant for this sutra alone and not for another sutra, it is called the "specific introduction."

The General Introduction

The general introduction has two subsections. The first subsection shows that the teaching transmitted by Ānanda, [a cousin and key disciple of the Buddha,] was free from error, demonstrating that the person transmitting it can be trusted. The second subsection addresses the place of the teaching, the assembly that heard it, and the fundamental principles that were taught, demonstrating that the Dharma can be trusted. The trustworthiness [of the transmitter] comes first because it is people who transmit the Dharma. And because the Dharma is transmitted by people, its trustworthiness is shown afterward.

Transmission of the Teaching

[The first subsection of the general introduction includes the phrase] "like this," [which appears in "I have heard like this," often rendered, "Thus I have heard"]. This phrase addresses in general terms an entire teaching. When two things are similar, they are described as being "like" each other. But when one thing is not different [in any way from another thing], it is said to be [identical to] "this" [thing]. [The former principle of similarity is illustrated] in a comparison of the speech of the Tathāgata and Ānanda, which are clearly not identical because the former speaks with a golden mouth and eight distinct voices, while the latter speaks with just one physical voice.

They are similar, however, [because both speak with a voice that can be heard]. The text thus uses the term "like" to describe them. But while their speech differs in these ways, [the truth] expressed by each is a single thing, and so the meaning of [the words each speaks] is said to be "[identical to] this [truth]."

The phrase "I have heard" means that Ānanda has heard the teaching directly from the Buddha, and so his transmission is free from error. It also shows that the teaching is free from the errors of the non-Buddhists who claim self-enlightenment [without hearing the Tathāgata's teachings]. The phrase "at one time" means that even though the teachings of the sutras expounded by the Tathāgata are innumerable, when Ānanda attained the state of the Buddha's enlightenment, or *samādhi,* he understood all of them at once. Thus, the sutra says "at one time."

The Audience

The second subsection addresses the place of the teachings and the assembly that listened to them, demonstrating that the Dharma can be trusted.

Śrāvastī is the name of a city. In the Liang dynasty (502–557) it was called "the city of famous things." This city flourished and its name was exceptionally famous, being heard at great distances in the four directions, and so it was known as "the city of famous things." Śrāvastī was located in the country of Kośala, one of sixteen great countries. In the sutra, the name of the city is taken to represent the entire country, which is simply referred to as "Śrāvastī." The sutra also refers to the Jeta Grove and Anāthapiṇḍada Garden. Here, "grove" is associated with Prince Jeta and "garden" is associated with the elder Anāthapiṇḍada. Together, the two built a spiritual practice center, which is known by the names of both men. It is thus called "the Jeta Grove and Anāthapiṇḍada Garden."

The assembly that listened together to the Buddha's teaching has been abbreviated and so appears to be incomplete. One interpreter states that at the time the sutra was explained, the Buddha was inside the palace while the *deva*s were in the heavens above and the court maidens were with him on the earth below. Since the bodhisattvas were therefore absent, this sutra lacks proper verification. However, at the beginning of the sutra's final section—the propagation of the teaching—it states "[the Buddha] emitted a brilliant light that shone upon the great assembly," [which is a description that traditionally includes the bodhisattvas]. How then can it be said that the necessary audience was not present?

And even though this passage has the elements required to show that the Dharma can be trusted—the place of the teaching and the required audience who listened together to it—one interpreter asks why only the court maidens who appear in the royal palace at Ayodhyā are described. This is because in the [final section of the sutra], when it was entrusted to future generations, the teaching was done at this place and before this audience. It is clear, therefore, that this information was abbreviated.

The Specific Introduction

The second section [of the introductory teaching], the specific introduction, has two subsections. The first subsection begins with "At that time, King Prasenajit [and Queen Mallikā]" and ends with "[the messenger Candirā] respectfully offered [their letter] to Śrīmālā." This is called "introduction to the external conditions." The second subsection begins with "Śrīmālā accepted the letter with joy" and ends with "praising the true merits of the Buddha." This is called "introduction to the internal cause." The first subsection refers to the letter sent [by the king and queen to their daughter]. Since it explains the external conditions of the sutra, it is called "introduction to the external conditions." The second subsection refers to Śrīmālā's silent contemplation and perception of the Buddha. Since it explains the internal cause of the sutra, it is called "introduction to the internal cause."

External Conditions

The first subsection, the introduction to the external conditions, has three parts. The first part describes the king and queen's conversation in which they discuss Śrīmālā's intelligence, agreeing that it is the proper time for her to hear the profound Dharma and engage in virtuous deeds. The second part begins with "The queen said [to her husband, 'Now is the proper time']." Immediately afterward, they sent a letter to Śrīmālā so she could hear of the Buddha's merits. The third part begins with "the messenger [Candirā] presented the letter [to Śrīmālā]." This passage describes the messenger receiving the letter, taking it to Ayodhyā, and presenting it to Śrīmālā.

[The first part describes the king and queen discussing their daughter's intelligence.] In [this section of] the sutra, "time" refers to the proper time for Śrīmālā to hear the eternally abiding truth. "Their faith in the Dharma was only recent" means that the king and queen's faith in the Mahayana teachings was not of long duration. For a long time they had believed only in the Hinayana, not in the Mahayana. But one day, when the Tathāgata was beneath a tree expounding the Dharma, King Prasenajit approached him to offer praise while beating a drum. Although the Buddha knew the answer, he asked [his disciple Ānanda], "What is this sound?" Ānanda replied truthfully [and described the king's approach]. The Buddha said [to King Prasenajit], "You are a king of the world who beats the drum of birth and death. But I am the king of the Dharma who beats the drum of truth." This scene was the beginning of the Buddha's teaching of the *Dharma Drum Sutra*. It was also the time when the king and queen first developed faith in the Great Vehicle. Soon thereafter, they sent a messenger to proclaim this news to their daughter Śrīmālā. As such, one interpreter states that "time" refers to the time at which the Buddha delivered the *Dharma Drum Sutra*.

There are also varied interpretations of the passage "their faith in the Dharma was only recent." But by examining the sutra from beginning to end, one can see that only the interpretation noted above is correct. Thus, I have not listed these other interpretations. [The next passage in the sutra reads, "They spoke these words together: 'Śrīmālā, our daughter, is sharp, wise, and quick-witted, she has penetrating intelligence and quick comprehension.'"] Here, the phrase "our daughter" expresses words of praise. It suggests that no one surpasses a father and mother in looking after their child, just as no one knows a subject like a king. When speaking of one's own child, one naturally describes only his or her virtues. Since Śrīmālā, who was bright, virtuous, and capable of hearing about the path of the Great Vehicle, was their child, the king and queen naturally refer to her as "our child."

"She is sharp, wise, and quick-witted": One whose ears hear well is called "sharp," while one whose mind clearly discerns is called "wise." And one who listens closely and discerns quickly and clearly is called "quick-witted." "Penetrating intelligence and quick comprehension": One who hears the superficial but arrives at the profound is called "penetrating." This quality comes from listening closely. Having the capacity to clearly comprehend and deeply illuminate is called "intelligence." This quality comes from discerning deeply. To encounter a principle and to immediately understand it is called "quick comprehension." This quality comes from being quick-witted. The former passage points to Śrīmālā's innate abilities, while the latter describes her activities. These two passages complement each other: to receive the teaching [properly], one must listen closely. Thus, Śrīmālā's ability to listen is praised first. This demonstrates that she was capable of receiving the Dharma.

"Quickly understands the Dharma," means that having heard something just once, Śrīmālā immediately understood it and so did not need to hear the teaching again. The passage "Her mind will not doubt [the teaching]," means that her mind was open and clear and did not become mired in doubts like those who follow the Hinayana. [King Prasenajit and Queen Mallikā said,] "At the proper time, we should send a letter to arouse her mind of enlightenment." Here, "time" has two meanings: the time of year and time as an opportunity. Both meanings should be remembered since both contain the truth [that can be received by Śrīmālā].

From "the queen said [to her husband, 'Now is the proper time']" is the second part [of the introduction to the external conditions]; that is, their sending the letter [to Śrīmālā]. "Succinctly praising the innumerable merits of the Tathāgata": this passage means that because these immeasurable, holy merits could not be explained in detail, only three are described: [the Dharma body, liberation, and wisdom].

The third part describes the messenger arriving in Ayodhyā and presenting the letter to Queen Śrīmālā. See the sutra. This passage indicates that [Śrīmālā] correctly received the true [teaching]. See the sutra.

The Internal Cause

The introduction to the internal cause, the second subsection of the specific introduction, begins with "Śrīmālā accepted the letter [with joy]." This subsection can be divided into five parts.

The first part describes Śrīmālā's accepting the letter with joy. See again the sutra. This part also includes "producing a rare state of mind," which refers to hearing the eternally abiding truth. That is, because the primordially existent and eternally abiding truth is rarely heard, [Śrīmālā's state of mind] is referred to as "rare."

The second part is the first line of verse in which Śrīmālā expresses the desire to worship the Buddha. But having only seen [her parents'] letter, how can Śrīmālā say, "I have heard the voice of the Buddha"? This is because the voice transmits one's intention, and a letter transmits the voice [of its writer]. As such, having read the letter, Śrīmālā received the meaning of the Buddha's eternally abiding truth. It is in this way that she "heard" the voice of the Buddha. Moreover, whether one reads, hears, or contemplates [the Buddha's words]—in this case, in a letter—one "hears" [the voice of the Buddha]. [In the sutra, Śrīmālā then says,] "one whose [voice] has never been [heard] in the world." This passage suggests that even though [Śrīmālā's] original state [was described above as being "inconceivable," in her current embodied form] her [sense of] self may have prevented her from hearing that eternally abiding truth [before she received the letter].

[She continues, "If what I have said is] real and true." This means that because the Sage's body is perfect and is not false, it is called "true." And since it possesses unchanging, perfect merits that are not unreal, it is called "real."

[The third part] is the line of verse that describes Śrīmālā's silent contemplation and perception of the Buddha. This passage means that the Tathāgata responds to the needs of sentient beings in the world without discrimination. Even so, Śrīmālā says, "I am but an ignorant woman who is one among many in the world. I request that out of compassion you let me see you."

[The fourth part] is the line of verse explaining that the Buddha, sensing Śrīmālā's request, appeared before her in the sky. [The Buddha appeared in the sky] because his movements would have been restricted [had he appeared] in the palace. He may also have done so to show that the Tathāgata's Dharma body is formless, like space. [When expounding the Dharma,] the Tathāgata constantly emits a light from the top of his head that is about seven feet in length. Now, since he wanted Śrīmālā to expound the principles of the eternally abiding perfection of the One Vehicle, he emitted this light from his entire body.

[The fifth part] is the fourth line of verse, in which Śrīmālā worshiped the Tathāgata with the three types of activities associated with [the body, speech, and mind]. See the sutra. "[Bowed their heads and] touched his feet as a sign of respect": even though the Tathāgata was in the sky, Śrīmālā and her attendants made the customary gesture of reaching out to touch his feet as a sign of respect. It was not the case that they touched his feet directly.

2b

Part II

Commentary on the Main Teaching

The second division of the sutra, the main teaching, begins with the line of verse, "The Tathāgata's body, marvelous in form, [is unequaled in the world]." This division has fourteen chapters, which are organized into three main sections. The first section includes the sutra's first five chapters on the main teachings, which address the essence of the teachings and all types of virtuous deeds. The second section includes the eight middle chapters, which explain the realm of the teachings, taking up the conditioned and unconditioned forms of the Eight Noble Truths. The third section is the final chapter. It examines those who practice the teachings, taking up the bodhisattvas who do so by engaging in the three types of patience.

The five chapters of the first section that explain the essence of the teachings can be divided into two subsections: Chapters One through Three, and Chapters Four and Five. The first subsection explains "self-practice." Although Śrīmālā was originally an inconceivable being, she appeared in the world at the seventh stage of the bodhisattva. These first three chapters explain the practices of [bodhisattvas such as Śrīmālā at the] seventh stage, which are called "self-practice." The last two [of the first five] chapters explain "other-practice," meaning the practices of bodhisattvas at the eighth stage and above. Since these bodhisattvas have moved beyond the practices of the seventh stage [of Śrīmālā], they are called "other-practice." The three chapters addressing self-practice are: "Chapter One: Praising the True Merits of the Buddha," "Chapter Two: The Ten Main Ordination Vows," and "Chapter Three: The Three Great Vows."

Chapter One: Praising the True Merits of the Tathāgata

The central message of "Chapter One: Praising the True [Merits] of the Tathāgata" is that Śrīmālā had not heard the eternally abiding truth until she received her parents' letter. Having now heard that eternally abiding truth, she praises

13

it and vows to take refuge in it. But this form of refuge differs from the imper-manent refuge [of the Small Vehicle]. Indeed, the foundation for engaging in the virtuous behavior [of the Great Vehicle] is first taking refuge [in the Mahayana]. That is, because Śrīmālā wants to broadly illuminate the path of all virtuous practices, she naturally begins by taking refuge [in the teach-ings of the Great Vehicle]. In this regard, the *Sutra of the Upāsaka Precepts* states that if one receives the precepts without first taking refuge in the Three Treasures, then one's commitment to the precepts will not be firm, just as the color in a cloth dyed with no adhesive agent [will soon wash out].

This chapter can be divided into two parts. The first part is the five lines of verse that praise the eternally abiding truth and describe the vow to take refuge. The second part begins with the next line of verse, "have compas-sion and protect me," and concludes at the end of the chapter, where Śrīmālā requests the Buddha's protection.

1.1: Praising the Eternally Abiding Truth

The five lines of verse of the first part praising [the eternally abiding truth] can be divided into four sections. 1) The first two lines praising the Dharma body, 2) the next line praising liberation, 3) the next line praising wisdom, and 4) the final line praising all three virtues collectively. However, the buddha stage is generally said to possess myriad virtues. Why then have only these three virtues been selected for praise? This is because the Dharma body is the foundation of the myriad virtues, liberation eliminates [the men-tal afflictions], and wisdom is [the perfect] knowledge [of the Buddha]. Indeed, among the myriad virtues, these three are essential. And by taking up these three virtues, the others will naturally arise. Thus, these three alone are praised. It was noted above, moreover, that when Śrīmālā's parents discussed the innu-merable holy virtues, they could not describe in detail each one and so chose to extol these same three. Śrīmālā follows this model. While there are varied interpretations of this material, the essential meaning has been expressed above. Therefore, I have not recorded them.

2c

1.1-1: Praising the Dharma Body

The two lines of verse that praise the Dharma body [read as follows: 1) "The Tathāgata's body, marvelous in form, is unequaled in the world. Incomparable and inconceivable, we now honor you. 2) The Tathāgata's form is inexhaustible; so too his wisdom. All phenomena eternally abide, and so I take refuge in you"]. [Traditionally,] they have been divided into two subsections: A) The first one and a half lines that praise the manifestation body (*nirmāṇakāya*) of the Buddha, and B) the last half of the second line of verse that praises the true body (*dharmakāya*) of the Buddha. [These two bodies complement each other;] that is, without the true body as the source, the manifestation body would not appear, just as without the appearance of the manifestation body, the source would remain hidden. Thus, in passages of praise, both [bodies] are generally praised together.

Here [the phrase] "The Tathāgata's body, marvelous in form, is unequaled in the world" praises his peerlessness. This means that even Brahma, high in the heavens above, cannot gaze down upon the top of the Buddha's head. "Incomparable and inconceivable" offers a comparison suggesting that the minds of sentient beings cannot imagine [these qualities of the Buddha]. "The Tathāgata's form is inexhaustible" means that those who are spiritually aware can see the manifestation body of the Buddha. And while that which has form naturally comes and goes in the world, it is said that if one develops this spiritual awareness, the [Tathāgata, in the form of the] manifestation body, will always appear. These four passages praise the Tathāgata's form. Next, "so too his wisdom" praises the Buddha's mind as being incomparable and inexhaustible, just as his form was praised above. "We therefore worship you, [O World-honored One,]" concludes praise of the manifestation body.

One interpreter argues, "Since this last passage [concludes the section praising] the manifestation body, it should appear directly after the first two passages of the second verse [above—that is, 'The Tathāgata's form is inexhaustible; so too his wisdom']. But the one who recorded the sutra [selected this order because he] desired to conclude each verse with some form of praise."

"All phenomena eternally abide" is the second subsection, which praises the true body of the Buddha. While his manifestation body appears in response to the needs of sentient beings, the true body is immovable and unchanging. Here, "eternally abide" suggests that which is immovable. Since the remaining virtues all naturally arise on the path to enlightenment, only that which can "eternally abide" is praised here.

My interpretation is slightly different [than this traditional interpretation]. The first line of verse praises the manifestation body and the next line is devoted entirely to praising the true body of the Buddha. Moreover, the statement "The Tathāgata's form is inexhaustible" means that it must also be eternally abiding. This passage thus praises the formless, eternally abiding aspect of the Buddha's true body. How can this be? That is, if the Tathāgata manifests with form, how then could that form be inexhaustible? It is precisely because [the true body, the source of the manifestation body,] has already been called "inexhaustible." As such, it is also self-evidently formless and permanent. Indeed, it is said that "the Tathāgata's form is inexhaustible." And since the Buddha's inexhaustible wisdom also appears in the form [of the manifestation body], wisdom itself takes on material form. "So too is his wisdom" thus praises the true body. This suggests that [the Buddha's wisdom] is also inexhaustible and eternally abiding. Finally, "All phenomena eternally abide" is a general reference to all the phenomenal elements associated with the true body.

1.1-2: Praising Liberation

The next line of verse praises liberation. [It reads: 1) "Having eliminated the mind's affliction and the four kinds of errors of the body. 2) Having already arrived at the undaunted stage, we thus honor you, Dharma King."] Here, "[Having eliminated] the mind's afflictions" refers to the three poisons [of the mind: craving, hatred, and ignorance,] and the four distorted views[: seeing the impermanent as permanent, suffering as pleasure, the impure as the pure, and non-self as the self]. The following passage, "[having eliminated] the four kinds of errors of the body," refers to the four great elements [of earth, water, fire, and wind]. These two passages thus praise liberation from the four evil entrenchments of the three realms [of desire, form, and formlessness].

One interpreter [agrees that the phrase "mind's afflictions" refers to the three poisons but] argues that "the body" should be taken as the three evil activities of the body, [killing, stealing, and licentiousness,] and that "the four [distorted views]" refers to the four evils of speech, [lies, slander, duplicity, and flattery]. For this interpreter, these collectively constitute the ten evils, and this section explains the evil entrenchments in the three realms.

3a The following line of verse reads, "Having already arrived at the undaunted stage, [we thus honor you, Dharma King]." Here, "the undaunted stage" refers to one possessing the adamantine mind. Indeed, there are four types of evil demons: those of the heavens, afflictions, aggregates, and death. The adamantine mind cannot be defeated by heavenly demons or by non-Buddhists, and it has subdued the demon of the afflictions by purifying and exhausting the mental disturbances. At this stage, however, the adamantine mind is free from neither the activities of the demon of the aggregates nor from the arising and ceasing of the demon of death. This is called "the undaunted stage," [also rendered as "the difficult-to-subdue stage"].

One interpreter argues instead that the undaunted stage refers to the buddha stage. At the buddha stage, since one cannot be subdued by the four types of demons, one has reached the "undaunted" or "difficult-to-subdue stage." [This interpreter argues, therefore, that in contrast to the previous section, this] passage praises liberation from the evil entrenchment of ignorance outside the three realms.

Yet another interpreter argues that the two passages [describing liberation from the afflictions of the mind and the body] praise "liberation with remainder," while the passage that follows praises "liberation without remainder." Exhausting the cause of the afflictions is called "with remainder," while exhausting their fruit is called "without remainder." The previous passages praise escaping from the four entrenchments [of the three realms], and show how elimination of the cause of the afflictions leads to elimination of their fruit. The following passage praises the elimination of ignorance, showing how the destruction of the fruit of the afflictions also proves the elimination of their cause. This interpreter concludes that this teaching proves, therefore, that [the cause and the fruit of the afflictions] can be destroyed.

Dharma Master Fayun (467–529) [offers another interpretation], stating that there are two types of birth and death: "limited cyclic existence" and "inconceivable transformation." [Regarding the passage, "Having eliminated the mind's afflictions,"] he argues that "mind" refers to the fruit of inconceivable transformation, and "[having eliminated] the afflictions" refers to its cause. [In the passage, "Having eliminated the four kinds of errors of the body,"] "body" refers to the fruit of limited cyclic existence, and "[having eliminated] the four kinds [of errors]" refers to its cause.

He also argues that the previous passage [describing the elimination of the mind's afflictions] shows how cutting off entrenched ignorance leads to the destruction of the fruit of inconceivable transformation. The next [passage, describing the elimination of the body's errors,] explains the elimination of the four entrenchments, and thus the destruction of the karmic effects of limited cyclic existence. It can thus be called "subduing the afflictions."

Master Fayun continues, "'Having already arrived at the undaunted stage' refers to the two types of mental obstructions that can prevent the development of wisdom. The first obstruction prevents one from seeing the marks of phenomena, while the second prevents one from perceiving impermanence. If the adamantine mind arises, however, it cuts off and exhausts these obstructions, thereby illuminating the marks of phenomena and removing the fetters of delusion [that prevent clear perception of impermanence]. [Since this realm shows how difficult it is to eliminate these afflictions, the adamantine mind] is thus called 'difficult to subdue.'"

But Master Fayun also argues that even at this advanced stage the mind still harbors afflictions, as one has not yet escaped impermanence, and so the fruit [of inconceivable transformation] still remains. But the sutra [states that this is difficult to subdue; it] does not say it "cannot be subdued" [and so suggests that there is a way to escape impermanence]. [Indeed, that path is suggested in the word] "already," which appears in the passage, "Having already arrived at the undaunted stage." "Already" means to have "passed beyond," and so suggests one who has "passed beyond" the adamantine mind and arrived at the buddha stage. Here, having destroyed the fetters [of the mind], one is freed from the impermanence of birth and death. Master Fayun concludes that in this way, the cause and fruit [of both limited cyclic existence and inconceivable transformation] are extinguished, and one is thus liberated.

My interpretation is slightly different. In particular, I believe that that which is difficult for the adamantine mind to subdue refers only to the demons of the aggregates and death. Since the Tathāgata has already passed beyond these two realms, it is called "having arrived at the undaunted stage." As such, "We thus honor you, Dharma King" concludes this section praising liberation.

1.1-3: Praising Wisdom

The next line [of verse is the beginning of the third section that] praises wisdom. It reads: "1) Knowing all that is to be known, and by complete mastery of this body of wisdom. [2) Encompassing all phenomena, we therefore worship you."] In this passage, "that is to be known" refers to what was called "the mother of wisdom" in the Liang dynasty. "The mother of wisdom" refers, in turn, to the realm of absolute truth. That is, since emptiness is the basis from which wisdom emerges, it is called "mother." Since wisdom arises from emptiness, which is itself unconditioned, it is called "mastery." In this way, these two passages praise the wisdom of emptiness.

[The next line of verse reads,] "Encompassing all phenomena, [we therefore worship you]." Here, "Encompassing all phenomena" refers to the capacity to illuminate and understand at once the distinctions among the myriad phenomena of the world. [In contrast to the wisdom of emptiness, however,] this phrase praises the wisdom of existence, which is a form of conventional truth. Although it is a form of wisdom, it is an inferior sort that cannot properly be called "mother."

One interpreter says that the first two passages in this section praise "the wisdom of truth," while the next passage praises "expedient wisdom." [In discussing the phrase] "that is to be known," he argues that since these two types of truth can produce wisdom, they are both properly called "mother of wisdom." He also argues that the passage "by complete mastery of this body of wisdom" suggests the ability to freely use the wisdom that emerges from complete mastery of these two types of truth. [This interpreter concludes his argument by] stating that the passage "encompassing all phenomena" shows how the Buddha uses expedient means to attract and teach sentient beings so that they will engage in virtuous behavior. 3b

The section praising wisdom concludes, "We therefore worship you."

1.1-4: Praising the Dharma Body, Liberation, and Wisdom

The next line of verse praises together [the Dharma body, liberation, and wisdom]. [That line reads: "We now worship you who transcends name and measure, the one who is beyond compare. We now worship the (teacher of the) limitless Dharma, the one who exceeds all comprehension."] See the sutra.

1.2: Śrīmālā Requests the Buddha's Protection

From "Have compassion and protect me, [thereby causing the seed of Dharma to grow,]" to the end of the chapter is the second part of Chapter One. This part describes Śrīmālā's requesting the Buddha's protection. This means that when Śrīmālā praises and takes refuge in the Buddha's eternally abiding truth, if he does not respond by protecting her, then the act of taking refuge itself is unworthy of respect. Thus, Śrīmālā asks the Buddha for protection.

This part has four sections. 1) The first line of verse in which Śrīmālā directly requests the Buddha's protection. Here, "Dharma" refers to the Dharma body, the seed of which is all virtuous deeds. 2) The next line of verse describes the Tathāgata's granting protection to Śrīmālā. [Śrīmālā states, "'In this and in future lives, I ask you, O Buddha, always to accept me.' (The Buddha replies:) 'I have been teaching you for a long time in your previous lives.'"] And while Śrīmālā requests his protection only for her current and future lives, the Tathāgata also states that he had [taught and] protected her in previous lives, illustrating the depths of his protection.

3) The following one and one-half lines show that after the Buddha granted Śrīmālā protection, she makes the same request again as a sign of respect. [This section reads: "'I teach you now, and will do so in the future.' (Śrīmālā responds:) 'I have already produced merits, and will do so again in remaining lives. Because of these virtuous deeds, I hope to see and to be accepted by you in the future.'"] In this section, [Śrīmālā thinks that] because the Tathāgata had acknowledged helping her for a long time, she must have produced virtuous [deeds in previous lifetimes]. Moreover, "remaining lives" refers to the future. If the Buddha has protected Śrīmālā in the past and present, and will also do so in the future, then she will not stop performing virtuous deeds. [To confirm this,] she asks the Buddha to offer a prediction.

4) "The Buddha [offered this prediction] to the assembly." This passage describing the Buddha's prediction can be divided into six subsections. A) The Buddha acknowledges the cause [of Śrīmālā's becoming a buddha]. B) From "You will make offerings [to immeasurable buddhas]" describes the fruit [of Śrīmālā's becoming a buddha]. C) From "Your buddha land [will have no evil destinies]" describes this as an undefiled land. D) From "sentient beings of your land" describes the Buddha's prediction [that those who inhabit this buddha land will be] pure. E) From "When Queen Śrīmālā [received this prediction]" describes the desire of humans and *deva*s [to be reborn in that land]. F) Explains the Buddha's prediction that humans and *deva*s [would indeed be reborn in that land]. See the sutra.

Chapter Two:
The Ten Main Ordination Vows

The second part of "self-practice" is "Chapter Two: The Ten Main Ordination Vows." It begins with "At that time, Queen Śrīmālā, having heard this prediction, [respectfully stood up and took the ten main ordination vows]." This chapter describes Śrīmālā's praising the Buddha's truth and reveals that the foundation for taking refuge in that eternally abiding truth is practicing virtuous deeds. But the refuge taken by Śrīmālā differs from that of earlier times; here, she professes the ten great vows that are distinct from the five precepts of the Small Vehicle. Indeed, these precepts need to be renewed [to meet the needs of those living today].

This chapter has three parts. The first describes the proper means for receiving the precepts [that one vows to follow]. The second, which begins "O World-honored One, from this day [until I attain enlightenment]," describes Śrīmālā's taking the precepts. The third begins with "O Dharma King, the World-honored One" and concludes at the chapter's end. This third part describes Śrīmālā's standing before the Buddha and taking these vows, thereby eliminating the doubts [of the assembly].

Moreover, as she prepares to take these vows, Śrīmālā realizes she must do so not only in the correct form but also in a calm state of mind. That is, with the proper form and a calm mind, she prepared herself to take the vows. The second part of the chapter describes Śrīmālā's taking the precepts. However, as soon as she took them, doubts arose among some in the assembly. There were those who thought that because Śrīmālā had taken the form of a woman, her will was weak. And now, having taken these serious and far-reaching vows, they worried that she might be unable to put her words into practice. Therefore, the third part shows Śrīmālā's taking these vows and cutting off their doubts by promising to put into practice the vows she had taken.

2.1: The Proper Means for Receiving the Precepts

The first part begins with "She respectfully stood up." Even though it is customary to prostrate on the ground when taking the precepts, Śrīmālā stood up instead. She did so because the Buddha had appeared in the sky. If she had prostrated herself on the ground, it would have been difficult to hear the Buddha's words. "Receiving the ten main ordination vows"[: in this phrase, the word "receiving" has two meanings.] The first refers to the state of mind in which one is ready to receive the precepts, while the second refers to [the process of] receiving the ten precepts themselves. These are referred to as the "ten main ordination vows" because, as previously noted, they differ from the five precepts of the Small Vehicle. That is, these precepts taken by Śrīmālā are meant [to produce] the eternally abiding wisdom [of the Great Vehicle].

2.2: Śrīmālā Takes the Ten Vows

The second part of the chapter describes Śrīmālā's taking the ten vows. It can be divided into three subsections. The first subsection consists of [her vow to follow] precepts one through five. These are called "the disciplinary precepts" and are meant to prevent negative behavior. [The word "disciplinary" combines two ideas. The first,] "rule," is a type, while "deportment," the second, means "behavior." These five precepts are thus meant to promote the practice of positive types of behavior, enabling one to remain on the Buddhist path. The second subsection begins with "[I will not accept material things] for my own benefit." It includes the four vows called "the precepts benefiting sentient beings." The third subsection begins with "Embracing the true Dharma and never forgetting it." This points to the tenth vow, which describes the precept of cultivating goodness.

Those who wish to teach others must first correct themselves, and so they begin with self-cultivation[, which requires taking the disciplinary precepts]. This is the basis for the practice of the bodhisattvas who correct their own behavior so that they can teach and save sentient beings. The next step is to take [precepts six through nine,] the precepts benefiting sentient beings. Since the path of educating and saving sentient beings does not consist solely of stopping evil, practitioners must also cultivate virtuous behavior; indeed, the third subsection is called "the precept of cultivating goodness."

In this way, although the basis of the first subsection is self-cultivation, it also reveals the importance of teaching others. And while teaching others is the thrust of the second subsection, it also illuminates self-cultivation. The third subsection illuminates both self-cultivation and teaching others. As a group, these are the practices of the bodhisattva, which are described below in greater detail.

2.2-1: The Five Disciplinary Precepts

The five disciplinary precepts of the first subsection can be divided into three components. The first component includes the vow that relates to the five Hinayana precepts that were taken in earlier times; this is the vow not to develop an attitude in which one would transgress any of these earlier precepts. Since the Hinayana teachings of the precepts are meant to restrain the body and speech, but not the mind, they are understood as preliminary practices that put one on the path to ultimate purification. But the vow [of the Mahayana bodhisattva], which is taken first, does not invalidate these earlier precepts.

The second component includes [the second and third] vows, which are meant to prevent evil acts toward those who are in higher and lower [positions than oneself]. The third component includes [the fourth and fifth] vows that are meant to prevent evil acts toward self and others.

The second vow [of the second component] reads, "I will show neither pride [nor jealousy] toward the worthy elders"; this vow refers to the three types of "worthies," [rulers, parents, and teachers,] and to other "elders" in high positions. The third vow, "I will not hate sentient beings," is a general reference that includes the varied types of sentient beings.

Here, we examine three explanations for [why the Buddhist practitioner] should avoid pride and jealousy toward those above and hatred and anger toward those below. One explanation says that people normally want to be equal to their superiors, and so become jealous [of their higher position]. But they also want to do as they please [toward those below them], and so become angry [when the latter do not respond as they wish]. Since neither attitude is on the Buddhist path, one must eliminate jealousy toward those above and anger toward those below.

A second explanation argues instead that people often feel anger, not jealousy, toward those above them. This is because those above arrogantly enjoy their high positions and despise the masses below, thereby causing great anger among their subordinates. This second explanation argues, more- 4a over, that those below display little jealousy toward those above them because they naturally respect their virtue and authority. Here, those above feel much pride or even arrogance, but little anger, toward those below them. Indeed, feeling that those below are naturally beneath them, they feel great pride in themselves. And thinking that those below will do exactly as they wish, they generally do not become angry [with their subordinates]. [But these attitudes do not accord with the Buddhist path, on which] one must not exhibit even a little jealousy toward those who are above. How much more so this is true that one should not exhibit even a little pride toward those who are below. Similarly, one must not express even a little anger toward those who are below, just as one must not do so toward those who are above. These explanations address [human tendencies]—here, to [emphasize one's own benefit and] slight [that of others]—to illustrate a more fundamental point [about the Buddhist precepts].

The third explanation states that the worthy ones and the elders should be respected. Arrogance and respect are incompatible because one who is filled with the former cannot display the latter. Similarly, those in subordinate positions are worthy of kindness. Anger and kindness are incompatible: one who is filled with the former cannot display the latter.

The third component of the five disciplinary precepts includes [the fourth and fifth] vows, which are meant to prevent evil acts toward self and others. This includes refraining from being jealous [of others' physical appearance or material possessions] and stingy with one's own possessions. See the sutra.

2.2-2: The Four Precepts Benefiting Sentient Beings

The second subsection, the four vows [six through nine], represents the precepts benefiting sentient beings. These precepts can be divided into two elements. The first element, vows [six and seven], illuminates the compassionate mind that brings joy to other beings. The second element, vows [eight and nine], illuminates the sympathetic mind that removes the suffering [of other beings].

Since the first element includes two vows, it can naturally be divided into two. The sixth vow illuminates the fruit of [the compassionate mind] that brings joy to other beings. The seventh vow illuminates the cause of [the compassionate mind] that brings joy to other beings.

The sixth vow begins, "I will not accept material things for my own benefit." This passage illustrates the "good of restraint." The following section of this vow reads, "All that I receive [will be used to help sentient beings who are poor and who suffer]." It illustrates the "good of virtuous activity."

The seventh vow begins, "I will not, for my own benefit, practice the four methods [of the bodhisattva to help others: giving, loving speech, beneficial acts, and cooperation]." This passage also illustrates the good of restraint, while the next, "for the benefit of all sentient beings," illustrates the good of virtuous activity. In the conclusion to the seventh vow, "a mind that lacks worldly attachments" can be understood to be free from craving, "a mind that does not become overwhelmed" to be free from hatred, and "a mind that is unobstructed" to be free from delusion.

[But there are other interpretations of these passages.] One interpreter argues, for example, that "a mind that lacks worldly attachments" points to those whose compassion displays no hint of attachment. Indeed, if one is attached [to worldly things], then one's teaching of the Buddhist path will naturally be influenced by the afflictions. This interpreter also argues that ["a mind that does not become overwhelmed"] means that if one wearies of birth and death [because one has become overwhelmed by the needs of sentient beings], then one's ability to teach them will inevitably be compromised.

Another interpreter argues, "a mind that lacks worldly attachments" points to those distinguished simply by not being worldly, "a mind that does not become overwhelmed" indicates those not associated with the two vehicles, and "a mind that is unobstructed" refers to Mahayana bodhisattvas.

The second element of this subsection, consisting of vows eight and nine, illustrates the sympathetic mind that removes the suffering of others. It can also naturally be divided into two: the former vow illustrates the fruit of removing suffering, while the latter vow illustrates the cause of removing suffering.

The eighth vow begins, "If I see those beings who are solitary and alone, [chained in the dark, with sickness and disease, who are distressed and suffering because of calamities and hardships]." This passage illustrates the good of restraint. The following part of this vow, "I must offer them comfort," illustrates the good of virtuous activity.

[The elements of this passage can be understood as follows.] A child without a parent is "solitary," while an elderly person without a child is "alone." A prison is "dark," while a shackled prisoner is "chained." Everyday illness is called "sickness," while extreme illness is called "disease." Problems that come from within are "calamities," while those caused by another are "hardships." Self-criticism is called "distress," while external annoyances are called "suffering."

This vow continues, "Through these principles, I will offer them benefits. [Only after that will I depart.]" In this passage, "principles" refers to [behavior that accords] with the teachings [of the eternally abiding truth] and that helps alleviate the ten types of suffering. "Only after that [will I depart]" means that Śrīmālā will not leave these sentient beings who suffer until each has reached enlightenment.

4b   The ninth vow illustrates the cause of removing suffering, and includes both the good of restraint and the good of virtuous activity. The beginning of this vow, "When I see those who catch and raise [animals]," illustrates the good of restraint, while "When I gain this power" illustrates the good of virtuous activity. Here, pursuing animals in the wild is called "catching," while keeping animals [on one's property] is called "raising."

The ninth vow continues, "The evil acts that contravene the discipline." This passage refers to the sixteen restraints of evil [behavior associated with particular professions]. See the *Nirvana Sutra*. The following line, "transgressing the precepts," refers to those who have broken a vow already taken. [These passages can also be understood as follows.] "The evil acts that contravene the discipline" refers to those who intended from the beginning to commit evil acts, while "transgressing the precepts" refers to those who intended to do good but ended up committing evil.

[In taking this vow, Śrīmālā states,] "When I gain this power." Her statement refers to two kinds of power: vital power and the power of the path. She continues, "in whatever place [I see sentient beings]"; this means that if one does not act in accord with the good of virtuous activity, then the path to liberation will become obstructed and sentient beings will transmigrate among the six destinies. Thus, wherever bodhisattvas see those committing egregious acts, they will use their vital power to subdue them. Wherever they see those committing mildly bad acts, they will use the power of the path to teach them. If sentient beings refrain from evil and practice good, then the holy teaching will last for a long time. If the holy teaching lives on in the world, then good will prevail and evil will disappear. Indeed, the sutra states, "*deva*s and humans will thrive and evil paths will diminish." If those who are vessels of the path increase, then the wheel of the Buddha-Dharma will turn eternally.

2.2-3: The Precept of Cultivating Goodness

The third subsection has one vow, [the tenth,] called "the precept of cultivating goodness." This precept has three aspects. The first aspect illustrates not forgetting the embrace of the true Dharma, while the second explains why one must not forget embracing the true Dharma. The third concludes the discussion of not forgetting the embrace of the true Dharma.

The first aspect begins with "I will never forget embracing the true Dharma." It was stated above that embracing the true Dharma is the practice of bodhisattvas at the eighth stage and above, and so is called "other-practice." Since Śrīmālā has appeared at the seventh bodhisattva stage, for her not forgetting to embrace the true Dharma means not to forget the aspiration to attain the eighth and higher bodhisattva stages. That is, Śrīmālā should not forget, even for a moment, her intention to embrace the true Dharma. This does not mean, however, that she herself has already [attained the eighth stage] where one's mind does not forget, even for a moment, embracing the true Dharma.

The second aspect includes three practices and three aspirations. The former are the practices of bodhisattvas at the eighth stage and above, while the latter are the aspirations of bodhisattvas at the seventh stage and below. The three practices are: embracing the true Dharma, following the Great Vehicle, and engaging in the perfections (*pāramitā*s). But this distinction [between practice and aspiration] does not mean that those at the seventh stage and below are not part of the Great Vehicle. Rather, it suggests that the meaning of "great" has not yet been fully revealed to them. Why? It is because bodhisattvas at the seventh stage and below have only severed the afflictions and passed beyond the three realms, just like practitioners of the two vehicles. But they have yet to reach the eighth stage and above, and so are unable to [directly intervene] in the various destinies that are part of the process of transmigration. It is in this way that the complete meaning of "great" is not yet clear to them.

[We can better understand this distinction by examining the perfections, the last of the three practices.] The perfections of the bodhisattva are often referred to as "reaching the other shore." And while bodhisattvas at the seventh stage and below have crossed over to the other shore devoid of marks, they are not yet able to discern [the eternally abiding truth in a single thought like bodhisattvas at the eighth stage and above]. Thus, the complete meaning of the perfections is not yet clear to them. Although bodhisattvas at the seventh stage and below engage in all virtuous practices, here again they cannot do so in a single moment of thought. Therefore, their practice cannot be called "fully embracing the true Dharma," [the first of the three practices]. As such, it is said that the three practices of embracing the true Dharma, following the Great Vehicle, and engaging in the perfections are fully established only by bodhisattvas at the eighth stage and above.

The three aspirations of bodhisattvas at the seventh stage and below express their desire to attain a state of mental equilibrium in which they can 4c constantly engage in these three practices. And while the three practices— the activity of the singular mind of bodhisattvas at the eighth stage and above—are described with different names, each emerges [from the single principle of embracing the true Dharma]. Thus, if one forgets embracing the true Dharma, then all three practices will be forgotten completely. And if the three practices are forgotten, then the aspiration for the three practices will also be forgotten.

Even though there should be a section in the text describing the aspiration for the perfections, it has been omitted. When listing the three practices in order, embracing the true Dharma is first. But when listing the aspirations in order, the Great Vehicle is first. This order is followed only for convenience, however, and has no more significant meaning.

The tenth vow continues, "Following their desires, [they will never transcend the level of the common person]." This describes those who fall away from these practices and engage in evil acts. Indeed, the third and final aspect begins with "I have seen in this way [the incalculable errors of these people]." It concludes discussion of not forgetting the embrace of the true Dharma and suggests that forgetting the true Dharma leads to calamity, while constantly remembering it leads to blessings. Therefore, these vows must never be forgotten.

2.3: Removing the Doubts of the Assembly

From "O Dharma King, the World-honored One" is the third and final part of Chapter Two. It describes Śrīmālā's taking the vows before the Buddha and removing the doubts of the assembly. This part can be divided into four points. 1) Śrīmālā takes the vows in front of the Buddha. 2) From "At the time Śrīmālā uttered these words" describes a shower of flowers [pouring from the sky] and [divine] music ringing out as proof that Śrīmālā's words were not false. That is, this rain of flowers proved that Śrīmālā's words were truthful and that her practice will bear fruit. 3) From "Having seen these splendid flowers [and heard the divine music]" describes the elimination of the assembly's doubts and its desire [to remain with Śrīmālā in future lives]. 4) This point describes the Buddha's prediction [that this desire would be realized]. See the sutra.

Chapter Three:
The Three Great Vows

Chapter Three begins with "At that time, Śrīmālā took again [the three great vows] before the Buddha." It is the third of the three chapters on self-practice and describes taking refuge in the Great Vehicle by accepting precepts that differ from those of earlier times. This represents a superior aspiration, one that is an essential part of embracing the eternally abiding Dharma body. It differs from the tradition of earlier times, which focused on [eliminating suffering by] restraining the body and by developing wisdom that eliminates [the objects of consciousness].

This chapter has three components. The first describes Śrīmālā's taking these vows. The second component begins with "through these virtuous roots" and describes the three great vows she professes. The third component begins with "At that time, the World-honored One [offered a prediction to Śrīmālā]." It describes the Buddha's acknowledgement that Śrīmālā will fulfill her vows.

The first component includes the phrase "by the truth of these vows." It refers to Śrīmālā's taking the three great vows a second time. This act is meant to show that bodhisattvas take vows not for themselves but for the sake of other sentient beings. Indeed, in the first vow Śrīmālā states, "May I comfort [innumerable and unlimited] sentient beings." One interpreter argues, however, that "by the truth of these vows" simply means that these practices will certainly be carried out.

The second component describes Śrīmālā's directly professing the three great vows, and so naturally includes these three vows. [After "Through these virtuous roots"] the first vow adds ["may I obtain] the wisdom of the true Dharma." Here, "wisdom of the true Dharma" refers to the eternally abiding wisdom of the Buddha. The second vow reads, "[Having obtained this wisdom of the true Dharma,] I vow to explain it for the benefit of sentient beings." In the third vow, Śrīmālā says, ["Having embraced the true Dharma, I will abandon body, life, and wealth, and] will protect the [true] Dharma."

The first and the third vows deal mainly with self-cultivation but also illuminate teaching others. The middle vow explains teaching others but also addresses self-cultivation. In this way, these three great vows function similarly to the ten main ordination vows described above.

The third component of this chapter describes the Tathāgata's acknowledgment that Śrīmālā will fulfill her vows. See the sutra.

These three great vows constitute the "vows of the anterior stage" that are [taken by bodhisattvas at the seventh stage and below]. In this chapter, "embracing these vows" points only to those vows of the anterior stage, which are not included among the vows of the eighth stage and above.

Chapters Four and Five: "Other-Practice"

5a   From "At that time, Śrīmālā said to the Buddha" describes the teaching itself. This material, which includes Chapters Four and Five, marks the beginning of the second subsection of the sutra's first five chapters, addressing "other-practice." The first, "Chapter Four: Embracing the True Dharma," describes all the virtuous deeds produced when one embraces the true Dharma. Indeed, in just a single thought, bodhisattvas at the eighth stage and above can produce all the virtuous deeds performed by members of the five vehicles[: humans, *devas*, disciples (*śrāvakas*), self-enlightened ones (*pratyekabuddhas*), and bodhisattvas at the seventh stage and below]. The second is "Chapter Five: The One Vehicle." In the chapter's title, "one" means that this vehicle is all-inclusive. That is, the One Vehicle encompasses all the virtuous deeds produced by bodhisattvas at the eighth stage and above as well as those performed by members of the five vehicles.

Chapter Four:
Embracing the True Dharma

Here we examine Chapter Four, whose title, "Embracing the True Dharma," can simply refer to the mind with the capacity to embrace[, that is, to understand and then to actualize] the myriad virtuous deeds. It is, therefore, called "embracing." Since performing these virtuous deeds accords with the truth and is not evil, it is called "true." And because this practice contains a body of rules meant to guide the conduct of sentient beings, it is also called "Dharma."

But there are many other interpretations of the phrase "embracing the true Dharma." One observer [offers a broader interpretation,] arguing that the myriad virtuous deeds can be embraced in the practices of all sentient beings. That is, from the lower stages of ordinary sentient beings up to the highest stage of the sages, all are capable of embracing the true Dharma. Another interpreter argues that because the virtuous deeds of bodhisattvas at the level of the "outer ordinary" are done with a dualistic mind, those at this level have not, therefore, fully embraced the true Dharma. But those beings at the level of the "inner ordinary" and above have fully embraced the true Dharma. Yet another interpreter argues that because [those at the level of the] "inner ordinary" have not yet attained true liberation, even they have not yet fully embraced the true Dharma. This third interpretation maintains that because bodhisattvas at the "first ground" and above have attained true meditative insight, they alone have fully embraced the true Dharma.[8]

My interpretation is as follows. Bodhisattvas at the eighth stage and above can, in a single thought, embrace all virtuous deeds.[9] Indeed, this is the central meaning of "embracing." Since their practices correspond to the eternally abiding truth and are not evil, they are called "true." And since they serve as rules for the behavior of sentient beings, they are called "Dharma."

But the practices of bodhisattvas from the first to the seventh stage accord with the untainted truth, and so can also be called "true." Moreover, because their practices serve as a rule for sentient beings, they too can be called "Dharma." But [unlike bodhisattvas at the eighth stage and above, those at the seventh stage and below] are incapable of practicing the myriad virtuous deeds in a single thought since they have not completely overcome dualistic thinking. It is in this sense that one can say that they have yet to fully embrace the true Dharma. This interpretation can be confirmed by examining the content of the sutra itself. That is, if bodhisattvas at the seventh stage and below were capable of fully embracing the true Dharma, then the sutra would not state, "The bodhisattva vows, numerous as the sands of the Ganges River, are all part of the one great vow that is called 'embrace of the true Dharma.'" It is useful, therefore, to distinguish between "self[-practice" for bodhisattvas at the seventh stage and below] and "other[-practice" for bodhisattvas at the eighth stage and above].

Divisions of Chapter Four

[This chapter has traditionally] been divided into two parts: The first starts at the beginning of the chapter and ends with "having great merits and great benefits." The second part, which explains the [body of] practices associated with embracing the true Dharma, begins with "Śrīmālā said to the Buddha, 'I will now receive the spiritual power of the Buddha,'" and concludes at the end of the chapter.

My interpretation of this chapter is slightly different. That is, the central message of this chapter is that [these virtuous deeds] emerge [when one has embraced the true Dharma]. But when sentient beings hear the three vows mentioned above, they consider them extreme. Thus, the section from the beginning of the chapter to the passage ending with "having great [merits and] benefits" explains how the vows of bodhisattvas at the seventh stage and below—vows as numerous as the sands of the Ganges River—are, in fact, contained within the vow in the single thought of bodhisattvas at the eighth stage and above. And so the highest teaching is contained in these [vows]. In my interpretation, moreover, the second part of the chapter also begins with "Śrīmālā said to the Buddha, 'I will now receive the spiritual power of the Buddha.'" This part explains the emergence of [the myriad virtuous deeds after one has embraced the true Dharma]. [This view offers a more logical understanding of this material, which will become clear as we break down the chapter into more detail below.]

4.1: Śrīmālā's Vow to Embrace the True Dharma

The first part of this chapter explains Śrīmālā's vow to embrace the true Dharma. It has two branches: the first branch takes up the vow to embrace the true Dharma, while the second branch describes the Tathāgata's praise.

4.1-1: The Vow to Embrace the True Dharma

The first branch has three components: 1) describes Śrīmālā's listening to the [Buddha's] request; 2) describes the Buddha's authorizing [Śrīmālā's] words; and 3) describes the vow to embrace the true Dharma and begins with "Śrīmālā said to the Buddha."

The first component begins with ["I will now] receive the spiritual power of the Buddha [and explain the great vow that disciplines and is indistinguishable from the truth]." When an outer form is proper and reverential, it has "power"; when the inner mind is difficult to fathom, it is called "spiritual." In this passage, the word "receive" means that the Tathāgata has sanctioned Śrīmālā's explanation of the teaching. But this sort of spiritual power does not refer to the magical techniques by which trees and stones can be made to speak. In the three previous chapters [that dealt with "self-practice,"] Śrīmālā did not seek the Buddha's spiritual power. Here, however, she asks to receive it [because she is dealing with the "other-practice" of bodhisattvas at the eighth stage and above, who are more advanced than she]. This request is meant to highlight the differences between these two types of practice. In this section, "the great vow that disciplines" refers to a mind that always adheres to the principles and so can be called "disciplined." And one who does not intend to engage in unwholesome deeds reflects this great vow. "Indistinguishable from the truth" means [that the vows taken by Śrīmālā] do not differ at their core from the previous vows given by the Buddha or from his previous teachings.

[For a description of the second component in which the Buddha] authorizes Śrīmālā's words, see the sutra.

The third component takes up the vow to embrace the true Dharma, and includes, "[The bodhisattva vows,] numerous as the sands in the Ganges River, are all contained in the one great vow." "One great vow" refers to the vow that is contained within a single thought of bodhisattvas at the eighth stage and above. This statement clearly means that the vows of bodhisattvas at the seventh stage and below—vows as numerous as the sands in the Ganges River—are all contained in this vow of a single thought of bodhisattvas at the eighth stage and above. Indeed, the sutra clearly states, "all [these vows] are contained in the one great vow." The sutra continues, "that is called 'embracing the true Dharma.'" This passage describes the essence of the one great vow and the myriad practices of the true Dharma that emerge from it. It points to the wide range of activities that can be performed in just a single thought of bodhisattvas at the eighth stage and above. The sutra emphasizes this relationship, stating, "Embracing the true Dharma is truly the great vow."

4.1-2: The Tathāgata Praises Śrīmālā's Words

From "The Buddha praised Śrīmālā" is the second branch of the first part of this chapter, which describes Śrīmālā's embracing the great vow and the Tathāgata's praise. This section has five components. 1) The Buddha praises Śrīmālā's current virtues. 2) From "For a long time, you have [been cultivating virtuous roots]" praises the past causes [of Śrīmālā's current virtues]. 3) From "Your explanation [of embracing the true Dharma]" praises Śrīmālā's explanation as agreeing with the teachings propounded by the buddhas [of the past, present, and future]. 4) From "Having received supreme enlightenment, [I will always explain embracing the true Dharma]" praises Śrīmālā's words as agreeing with those of Śākyamuni. Although Śākyamuni is one of the buddhas, since he is master of the entire teaching he is addressed separately. 5) From "In this way, I will also explain [embracing the true Dharma]" praises the unlimited merits of embracing the true Dharma.

Here, "unlimited merits" means that the basic principles of embracing the true Dharma are deep, profound, and far-reaching. Since they cannot be fully explained, they are said to be "unlimited." The following passage, "the wisdom and eloquence of the Tathāgata are also unlimited," helps us to resolve the following doubt: If the unlimited merits of embracing the true Dharma [cannot be fully explained], who, then, could understand and explain them to sentient beings? This doubt can be easily resolved, however, by noting that the Buddha's wisdom, which arises from these unlimited principles, is itself
5c   unlimited. Since the Buddha's limitless wisdom—also called "universal cognition"—illuminates these very principles, what doubts could remain?

Indeed, the passage beginning with the question "Why is that?" offers an explanation of the limitlessness of the Buddha's wisdom. Even so, some still express doubt, asking, "Why is the Tathāgata's wisdom limitless?" This doubt can be resolved by noting that the principles that underlie embracing the true Dharma have great merits and benefits. Thus, it must also be true that the Buddha's wisdom that emerges from these principles is also unlimited. But there is another explanation [that helps resolve such doubts completely]. The virtuous deeds that arise from embracing the true Dharma are unlimited because the very act of embracing the true Dharma activates access to the Buddha's transcendent wisdom and the ability to teach sentient beings. In this way, these merits and benefits are said to be inexhaustible and therefore must also be unlimited.

4.2: Practices of Those Who Embrace the True Dharma

From ["Śrīmālā said to the Buddha,] 'I will now receive the spiritual power of the Buddha'" is the second part of this chapter, which explains the practices of those who have embraced the true Dharma. I say that this part explains the emergence [of the myriad virtuous deeds after one has embraced the true Dharma]. It can be divided into two branches. The first branch explains the practices of embracing the true Dharma, while the second branch begins with "At that time, the World-honored One was pleased with Śrīmālā's explanation [of the powers gained by embracing the true Dharma]." It concludes at the end of the chapter. This second branch describes again the Tathāgata's praise.

4.2-1: The Practices of Embracing the True Dharma

The first branch has three components: The first addresses the body of practices by which one embraces the true Dharma and [the kinds of virtuous fruit] that are produced by those who have done so. The second begins with "For example, like at the beginning of time." It explains the emergence [of the myriad virtuous deeds, and further illustrates these deeds through metaphorical language]. The third begins with "O World-honored One, 'embrace of the true Dharma.'" This component describes the act of embracing the true Dharma and the true Dharma that is embraced as an essential unity. This third component is meant to resolve the doubts of sentient beings.

4.2-1-1: The Body of Practices Associated with Embracing the True Dharma

The first component of the first branch has three aspects. The first aspect describes [Śrīmālā's] receiving the request [of the Buddha], while the second describes her hearing [and then considering] it. The third begins with

"Śrīmālā said to the Buddha," and addresses again the body of [practices associated with embracing the true Dharma]. See the sutra.

[This section of the sutra reads, "The meaning of the breadth of the embrace of the true Dharma is immeasurable. It encompasses all the Buddha's teachings that are expressed in the eighty-four thousand Dharma gates."] Here, "The meaning of the breadth" clearly refers to this body of practices, although one interpreter maintains that it simply refers to the previous passage [in which Śrīmālā agrees to explain the true breadth of embracing the true Dharma]. In this interpretation, moreover, the phrase "is immeasurable" explains this breadth. Since the "eighty-four thousand Dharma gates" [mentioned in this section of the sutra] have been widely discussed in other commentaries, they are not addressed here.

4.2-1-2: The Myriad Virtuous Deeds

The second component of the first branch examines [the myriad virtuous deeds] that are produced [when one embraces the true Dharma]. It does so with four metaphors that are of two types. The first type examines these deeds from the perspective of the Dharma, while the second does so from the perspective of the practitioner. They can be distinguished because the first type of metaphor begins by describing the embrace of the true Dharma but does not mention the good sons and daughters, while the second type always mentions the good sons and daughters.

The two metaphors of the first type can naturally be divided into two. The first is the metaphor of the cloud, suggesting something covered by shade. This means that bodhisattvas at the eighth stage and above who have embraced the true Dharma offer the "shade" [of protection and compassion] to all sentient beings that are destitute. The second is the metaphor of the great waters, illustrating how bodhisattvas at the eighth stage and above can wash away [the filth of the world]. That is, having embraced the true Dharma, they can wash away the impurities of sentient beings.

4.2-1-2-1: The Metaphor of the Cloud

The metaphor of the cloud has two parts: an opening metaphor and a combining metaphor.[10] The opening metaphor has four phrases. The first phrase is "For example, like at the beginning of time." It compares [the time of the world's creation] to the initial stage in which bodhisattvas at the eighth stage and above begin constructing the true body of the Buddha. The second phrase is "like a great cloud that arose." It compares [this great cloud from the time of creation that showers the world with myriad benefits] to the exposition of the teachings by the manifestation body of the Buddha. These two phrases illustrate [the virtuous deeds] produced when one embraces the true Dharma. The third phrase is "a multicolored rain pouring down," which compares [this beneficial rain] to the cause of the [myriad virtuous deeds] performed by members of the five vehicles. The fourth phrase, "many types of jewels," compares [the value of these jewels] to the fruit of the [myriad virtuous deeds] performed by members of the five vehicles. In this way, these two phrases offer metaphorical language to describe [the virtuous deeds] performed by members of the five vehicles.

The combining metaphor, the second part, has three phrases; the first phrase is "In this way, embracing the true Dharma." It is a "combining" metaphor because it joins [and explains the compatibility of two metaphors; here,] "at the beginning of time" and the "[great] cloud that arose," both of which illustrate [the kinds of virtuous fruit that can be produced by those who have embraced the true Dharma]. The combining metaphor suggests, therefore, that bodhisattvas at the eighth stage and above who have begun to construct the true body of the Buddha appear in response to the needs of the world to teach sentient beings. That is, it compares the construction of these bodies to the beginning of time when a great cloud arose, [showering down upon the world a beneficial rain and many types of jewels].

The second phrase of the combining metaphor, "brings a shower of innumerable rewards," connects these rewards to the "many types of jewels." This means that bodhisattvas at the eighth stage and above who have embraced the true Dharma help produce the fruit [of innumerable rewards] for members of the five vehicles, which are, therefore, like "a shower of many types of jewels."

The third phrase of the combining metaphor, "brings a shower of innumerable virtuous roots," connects these roots to "a multicolored rain pouring down" from the section describing the virtuous deeds performed by those who have embraced the true Dharma. This means that [embracing the true Dharma] is the cause that produces [the myriad virtuous deeds performed by members of] the five vehicles like a multicolored rain shower.

4.2-1-2-2: The Metaphor of the Great Waters

The second metaphor of the first type, the metaphor of the great waters, has three parts: an opening metaphor, a combining metaphor, and a metaphor that offers a conclusion to the first two metaphors.

The opening metaphor has four phrases. The first phrase, "at the beginning of time," offers a metaphor for the initial construction of the true body of the Buddha by bodhisattvas at the eighth stage and above. The second phrase, "the collection of great waters," is a metaphor for the explanation of the Dharma by the manifestation body. Together, the first two phrases offer examples of [the benefits] that emerge from embracing the true Dharma. The third phrase, "the many thousands of great worlds," offers a metaphor for the benefits that emerge when bodhisattvas of the Great Vehicle [embrace the true Dharma]. Finally, the fourth phrase, "forty billion varied types of continents," offers a metaphor for the benefits that emerge for the four vehicles [of humans, *deva*s, disciples, and self-enlightened ones].

The second part, the combining metaphor, has five phrases. The first phrase, "In this way, by embracing the true Dharma," combines "at the beginning of time" and the "great accumulated waters" to describe [the virtuous deeds] performed [by those who have embraced the true Dharma]. This offers a comparison—that is, when bodhisattvas at the eighth stage first begin constructing the true body of the Buddha and manifest to explain the Dharma, it is like the beginning of time [when the many worlds and continents] emerged from the collection of great waters.

The second phrase is "[By embracing the true Dharma,] the innumerable worlds of the Great Vehicle and the supernormal powers of all the bodhisattvas emerge." It is combined with "the many thousands of great worlds that emerged [from the great waters]." The third phrase, "the peace and happiness of all these worlds," is combined with the human vehicle, which corresponds to the first ten billion continents that emerged at the time of creation from among the forty billion mentioned above.

The fourth phrase, "the power to do as one wishes in all worlds," is combined with the *deva* vehicle, which corresponds to the next ten billion continents. The fifth phrase, "the peace of the supramundane worlds," is combined with the two vehicles [of the disciples and self-enlightened ones], corresponding to the third and fourth tens of billions of continents. Since practitioners of these two vehicles have been liberated from the three realms, they are discussed together.

The third part of the metaphor of the great waters compares and then summarizes the first two types of metaphors. It begins with ["The peace of the supramundane worlds] that has not yet been obtained by *deva*s and humans since the beginning of time." Here, "since the beginning of time" addresses the first part of the opening metaphor, while "that has not yet been obtained by *deva*s and humans" takes up the conclusion to the combining metaphor. This means that instead of "the peace of the supramundane worlds," the sutra employs "that which has not been obtained by *deva*s and humans" to illustrate this point. In this way, the opening metaphor takes up the beginning of the passage, [stating "when the world was created,"] and the combining metaphor takes up the end of the passage[; that is, "the peace of the supramundane worlds"]. The middle of the passage has been abbreviated simply with "and." "All these emerge from [embracing the true Dharma]": [like the opening metaphor] that describes the many thousands of great worlds and the forty billion varied types of continents that have all emerged at the beginning of time, this section describes [the innumerable worlds of the Great Vehicle], which have not yet been attained by *deva*s and humans, as emerging when one embraces the true Dharma.

These two metaphors of the cloud and great waters have three possible interpretations. The first interpretation argues that these metaphors are meant to illustrate the origin [of the Buddha's true body]. Since they both refer to "the beginning of time," they use the same language and express the same meaning. The second interpretation argues that these two metaphors are meant to illustrate the Buddha's manifestation body. Here, the former metaphor describes manifestation from a great cloud, while the latter metaphor does so from the collection of great waters. Thus, while the meanings of both address manifestation, the language used to illustrate the metaphors is distinct. According to the third interpretation, these metaphors are meant to illustrate [the virtuous deeds] produced [by those who have embraced the true Dharma]. In this interpretation, the former metaphor points to the people of the five vehicles together but segregates cause from effect, while the latter metaphor describes them separately but combines cause and effect. In this way, both their language and meaning are different. In fact, these different

6b

interpretations are insignificant, since the Great Sage's explanation of the Dharma takes up and clarifies these issues.

4.2-1-2-3: The Metaphor of the Heavy Burden

The next passage [states], "[embrace of the true Dharma is] like the great earth, [which supports four heavy burdens. What are the four? They are 1) the great ocean, 2) the mountains, 3) grasses and trees, and 4) sentient beings]." This passage represents the second type of metaphor, which describes the sorts of virtuous deeds produced by those who embrace the true Dharma. This second type includes two metaphors: the first is called the "metaphor of the heavy burden," which illustrates the burden of teaching and saving sentient beings borne by bodhisattvas at the eighth stage and above. The second is called the "metaphor of the jewel storehouse," which illustrates the stores of jewels that bodhisattvas at the eighth stage and above can use to benefit sentient beings.

The metaphor of the heavy burden has two parts: an opening metaphor and a combining metaphor. The opening metaphor has two components. 1) The first two phrases offer a metaphor meant to show how bodhisattvas at the eighth stage and above can bear the burden of teaching sentient beings. 2) From "What are these four burdens?" is a metaphor meant to illustrate the nature of the burden of this teaching that they bear. The second component has four phrases: A) "The great ocean" is a metaphor for those of the bodhisattva [vehicle], suggesting that they widely embrace sentient beings just like the great ocean embraces and receives living things without limit. B) "The mountains" is a metaphor for those of the self-enlightened vehicle, suggesting that they stand out in the world just like a collection of towering peaks. C) "Grasses and trees" is a metaphor for those of the disciple vehicle, suggesting that they are many in number, like grasses and trees. D) "Sentient beings" is a metaphor for the human and *deva* vehicles, suggesting that both groups transmigrate in cyclic existence just like the birth and death experienced by other sentient beings.

The combining metaphor of the heavy burden is divided into three components. The first combines the metaphor, the second concludes the metaphor, and the third praises the people who can carry these heavy burdens.

The first component has two halves: the first half describes those people who can carry these burdens, and the second describes the burden of the Dharma they carry. The first half addresses the phrase "surpassing the great earth." Although the earth carries only the burden of things possessing material form, bodhisattvas carry not only this burden but also that of offering the spiritual teaching. That is, bodhisattvas must transform [both the bodies and minds of sentient beings by helping them to eliminate] evil and cultivate good. They are described, therefore, as "surpassing the great earth."

The second half of the first component is a combining metaphor of the burden of teaching the Dharma, but it reverses the order of the combination. That is, sentient beings[, who appear at the end of the opening metaphor,] are taken up first here. See the sutra. [After addressing the "human and *deva* vehicles," which correspond to the metaphor of sentient beings,] "the disciple vehicle" is taken up. It corresponds with the metaphor of the grasses and trees, while "the self-enlightened vehicle" corresponds with the metaphor of the mountains. "The Mahayana" corresponds with the metaphor of the great ocean. This metaphor means that bodhisattvas at the eighth stage and above can bear the burden of teaching all sentient beings of the five vehicles, just like the great earth bears the four types of burdens.

The second component concludes the combining metaphor. See the sutra.

From "O World-honored One, [good sons and daughters who embrace the true Dharma]" is the third component of the combining metaphor praising those who can bear these heavy burdens. [The passage that follows states that these goods sons and daughters, "without being asked, express their friendship for the sake of all sentient beings."] See again the sutra. "Friendship" in this passage may seem to simply mean helping another person. But to help that person only after being requested is not true friendship. Therefore this passage states that "without being asked, they express their friendship." Indeed, the next passage compares the bodhisattva's teaching of sentient beings to that of the compassionate mother concerned for her infant, and so is described as "becoming the Dharma mother of the world."

4.2-1-2-4: The Metaphor of the Jewel Storehouse

The second metaphor of the second type, the metaphor of the jewel storehouse, begins with "It is like the great earth that has four kinds of jewel storehouses." This metaphor shows how bodhisattvas at the eighth stage "store" the jewel of the teaching for the benefit of sentient beings. This metaphor has two parts: an opening and a combining metaphor.

The opening metaphor has two components, a direct metaphor and a summarizing metaphor. The direct metaphor has two halves: the first two phrases of the first half create a metaphor describing that which can be stored. See the sutra.

The second half of the direct metaphor draws on the following four phrases to create a metaphor for the Dharma that is stored [like a precious jewel]. In this section, "priceless" is a metaphor for the bodhisattva vehicle; "high value" is a metaphor for the self-enlightened vehicle; "middle value" is a metaphor for the disciple vehicle; and "somewhat valuable" is a metaphor for the human and *deva* vehicles.

The passage "These are called the four types of jewel storehouses [of the great earth]" is the summarizing metaphor of the opening metaphor.

The second part of this metaphor [of the jewel storehouse], a combining metaphor, has three components that combine, praise, and explain the identity of the first two. Component one has two aspects: the first is a metaphor describing [the precious jewels] that are stored, and the second is a metaphor showing [the correspondence between particular jewels and types of practitioners]. The relevant sutra passage for the first aspect reads, ["In this way, good sons and daughters who embrace the true Dharma and construct the great earth] receive the most precious of these four types of jewels: that is, sentient beings." This passage can be interpreted in four ways.

The first interpretation states that the virtuous acts of the five vehicles are naturally associated with those sentient beings [who belong to each vehicle]. Since bodhisattvas at the eighth stage are constantly thinking about promoting this virtuous behavior, they are said to "receive the jewel of sentient beings." The second interpretation states that bodhisattvas at the eighth stage receive this jewel of sentient beings for teaching the four types of sentient beings[: other bodhisattvas, disciples, self-enlightened ones, and humans and *deva*s]. The third interpretation argues that by embracing the true Dharma bodhisattvas at the eighth stage receive the jewel of teaching the four types of sentient beings. The final interpretation emphasizes that the virtuous roots of the four types of sentient beings are received by bodhisattvas at the eighth stage, and so they are said to "receive the jewel of sentient beings."

The first and second interpretations differ only because the former highlights the root and the latter highlights the branch. The overall meaning is, however, the same. But the third and fourth interpretations differ based on what is received—that is, while the former points to [embracing the true Dharma], the latter addresses [the virtuous roots of sentient beings]. Thus, both the words and the meaning of the third and fourth interpretations are different. The fourth interpretation agrees with the content of the sutra, but does not fully illustrate the connection between the jewels that are stored [and the bodhisattvas who use them to teach sentient beings]. But from the following passage, [which concludes the relevant section of the sutra,] we can infer that this is an important connection. [That passage reads, "In this way, all good sons and daughters who embrace the true Dharma will receive this jewel of sentient beings and will also obtain exceedingly rare merits."] And while the third interpretation is also good, its analysis is too indirect. We should follow, therefore, the thought expressed in the first and second interpretations.

Among the four types of jewels, only those described as "priceless" can logically be considered as ultimate. How then could it be argued by some that the other three types[—that is, those of high value, middle value, and some value—]can also be described as ultimate? This is because superior 7a things are often grouped with lesser [things, and so even though lesser in relative terms they are still of high quality. They can, therefore, be considered part of a broader category of things that are] ultimate. One interpreter argues similarly that the three remaining valuable things all are of sufficiently high value to be designated collectively as "ultimate."

From "Who are the four?" is the second aspect of the first component, which takes up [the correspondence between particular jewels and types of practitioners]. From "those sentient beings who have not heard [the Dharma]" accords with "some value." From "[those who want to become] disciples" accords with "middle value." From "[those who want to become] self-enlightened ones" accords with "high value." And from "[those who want to become] Mahayana [bodhisattvas]" accords with "priceless."

From "In this way, [all the good sons and daughters who have embraced the true Dharma attain the precious jewel of sentient beings]" is the second component of the combining metaphor that praises [bodhisattvas at the eighth stage and above].

From "O World-honored One, [the great jewel storehouse is the embrace of the true Dharma]" is the third component of the combining metaphor, which explains the identity [of the first two]. That is, the metaphor of the heavy burden offers a conclusion [to embracing the true Dharma] but does not explain their identity. The metaphor of the jewel storehouse explains this identity but does not offer a conclusion [to embracing the true Dharma]. [This structure can be understood as follows.]

The metaphor of the heavy burden states that these things[—the great ocean, mountains, grasses and trees, and sentient beings—]are borne by the body. Indeed, [bearing a heavy burden like these] is a difficult endeavor, and it simply cannot be undertaken by those who have not [embraced the true Dharma]. [Since this material unmistakably describes only those who have embraced the true Dharma and can bear these burdens,] even if their identity is not explicitly stated, it is clear that [these teachings] can be trusted. Therefore, while a conclusion to the metaphor is offered, this identity is unnecessary and has been omitted.

On the other hand, because the metaphor of the jewel storehouse describes [material objects] that possess value, it is more difficult to illuminate the meaning of the identity [between these objects and those who have embraced the true Dharma]. Since it is not a heavy burden that is borne by the body, it is, in this sense, relatively easier to store these jewels. Thus, the identity of the two is explained but a conclusion is not offered, [since it is unnecessary]. Finally, the metaphor of the heavy burden describes bodhisattvas as "surpassing the great earth," while the metaphor of the jewel storehouse refers to "receiving the jewel of sentient beings." These passages have the same meaning.

4.2-1-3: Resolving the Doubts of Sentient Beings

From "O World-honored One, embracing the true Dharma and those who embrace the true Dharma" describes the third section of the first branch: the practice of embracing the true Dharma. This section explains the identity between [the act of embracing the true Dharma and those who perform this act], and is meant to eliminate the doubts of sentient beings. In the second section above [that describes the benefits and merits of practitioners, the metaphors of the cloud and the great accumulated waters] were used to explain [the myriad virtuous deeds] that emerge from embracing the true Dharma. [The metaphors of the heavy burden and the jewel storehouse] that followed explained those deeds by focusing on those [who embrace the true Dharma].

Even so, some still raise doubts, saying, "A person is clearly not the Dharma, just as the Dharma is not a person. Since they are so clearly different, the metaphors used to describe them cannot be the same." From this initial distinction between people and the Dharma, other such doubts arise. For example, some argue that the myriad practices of the true Dharma clearly differ from the act of embracing the true Dharma. Or, [they argue] that those who embrace the true Dharma are not identical to the perfections of the bodhisattva. By examining what is meant by the term "identical," however, we can resolve all such doubts.

The relevant material can be divided into two aspects. 1) From the beginning of this section to "the one who embraces the true Dharma is identical to the perfections" explains the identity of the Dharma to itself. 2) From "O World-honored One, I now accept your spiritual power and propound the great meaning [of the true Dharma]" explains the identity of people and the Dharma. Even so, the doubts noted above about [a fundamental difference between a] person and the Dharma may still exist, as such doubts cannot be dispelled with just a perfunctory explanation. Rather, the obvious identity of the Dharma to itself is explained first, so that those who have such doubts can gradually come to understand these identities. Afterward, the identity of a person to the Dharma can be explained and those doubts dispelled.

4.2-1-3-1: Identity of the Dharma to Itself

The first aspect, the identity of the Dharma to itself, has two halves. 1) The myriad practices of the true Dharma are identical to the mind that embraces it. 2) From "The perfections are not different from [the one who embraces the true Dharma]" explains that the perfections of the bodhisattva are identical to the myriad practices associated with the true Dharma. The first half [of this first aspect] has five passages. The first two passages address [the embrace of the true Dharma and the mind that embraces it]. The middle two passages illuminate how these two qualities "are not different from" each other, while the fifth passage explains their identity.

The first passage, "embracing the true Dharma," explains that which one embraces by engaging in the myriad practices of the true Dharma. The second passage, which also reads "embracing the true Dharma," refers to the mind that can embrace the true Dharma. [The third passage,] which reads, 7b

45

"not different from the true Dharma," explains that the mind that can embrace the true Dharma does not differ from all the virtuous practices of one who has embraced the true Dharma. [The fourth passage,] which reads, "not different from embracing the true Dharma," explains that all the virtuous practices of one who has embraced the true Dharma do not differ from the mind that can embrace it. [The fifth passage,] which reads, "The true Dharma is identical to one who has embraced the true Dharma," explains that all the virtuous practices of one who has embraced the true Dharma are identical to the mind that embraces it.

Although the sutra itself should follow this passage with "those who embrace the true Dharma are identical to the true Dharma," this passage has been omitted. This is likely because bodhisattvas at the eighth stage and above have already established the Dharma body. As such, all the virtuous deeds of the true Dharma have been firmly established in their minds, and so it must also be true that their minds are firmly established in all the virtuous deeds of the true Dharma. For them, mind and Dharma are unified; that is, they are not two separate entities. In this way, it becomes clear that all virtuous deeds of the true Dharma are identical to the mind, and that the mind is identical to all virtuous deeds of the true Dharma.

But bodhisattvas at the seventh stage and below have not yet established the Dharma body. They are thus incapable of practicing all virtuous deeds in a single thought since they have not yet reached the stage in which [their minds are identical to all the virtuous deeds of the true Dharma].

The second half [of the identity of the Dharma to itself] explains that the perfections are identical to all the virtuous deeds of the true Dharma. This aspect has three points. 1) Explains the identity [of the perfections with all virtuous deeds of the true Dharma]. 2) From the question "Why?" takes up the teaching of the six perfections, showing that the true Dharma is identical to these perfections. 3) From "In this way, O World-honored One" concludes the section explaining these identities.

1) "The perfections are not different": this passage means that embracing the true Dharma is not different from the perfections. "The embrace of the true Dharma is the perfections" explains their identity. But the text has omitted the following sentence, ["The perfections are the embrace of the true Dharma,"] and it is thus again deficient.

2) The second point takes up the six perfections and explains that the true Dharma is identical to these perfections. But some express doubts about their identity, stating, "How is the true Dharma identical to the perfections?" The correct explanation is that they are identical because bodhisattvas at the eighth stage and above can save sentient beings by responding to their individual capacities. As such, they are capable of practicing these six perfections in a single thought. Moreover, since the practice of these six perfections corresponds to the truth and is not evil, it is called "true." Since the teaching serves as the rule for sentient beings, it is called "Dharma." And because bodhisattvas practice these teachings without discrimination, they are called "perfections." [It is in this way that we can view the six perfections as] identical to the true Dharma. Indeed, each of the six perfections can be understood in this way. In the relevant passage, "their" refers to bodhisattvas at the eighth stage and above.

3) From "In this way, [O World-honored One]" concludes the third point, explaining these identities.

4.2-1-3-2: Identity of People and the Dharma

From "O World-honored One, I now [accept your spiritual power and propound the great meaning of the true Dharma]" explains the identity of people and the Dharma. This second aspect can be divided into three components. 1) Explains the identity of people and the Dharma. 2) From "Why? [If good sons and daughters who embrace the true Dharma must abandon the three types of things to embrace the true Dharma]"—this section further interprets the identity of people and the Dharma. 3) From "What are these three things?" reveals the meaning of the "three renunciations."

The first component begins with "Embracing the true Dharma [and those who embrace the true Dharma]." Clearly, the first part of the sentence describes the Dharma, while the second part addresses the people [who embrace it]. The next passage, "not different from embracing the true Dharma," means that people are not different from the Dharma they embrace. Likewise, this phrase can be restated as "the Dharma is not different from the people who embrace it." Together, these two phrases explain why people and the Dharma are not different.

Next, although the identity of people and the Dharma should also be restated [as "Embracing the true Dharma is identical to the good sons and daughters who embrace the true Dharma]," this passage has been omitted from the sutra. It is clear, however, that this component, the second, explains that people and the Dharma are identical because the sutra states that "the good sons and daughters embrace the true Dharma."

The second component explains the meaning of the identity of people and the Dharma. But some raise doubts, asking, "How can people be identical to the Dharma?" Such doubts can be resolved as follows. When embracing the true Dharma, bodhisattvas at the eighth stage and above renounce the three types of things[: body, life, and wealth]. In this way, the mind that renounces these things is identical to the mind that embraces the true Dharma. In other words, with the mind of renunciation, these bodhisattvas have already completed these practices. How then could it be that the mind that has completely embraced the true Dharma is different from those who have renounced these three things?

The third component takes up in detail the meaning of renouncing these three things, which were only touched upon above. This section can be divided into four points. Number 1 explains the renunciation of these three things. Number 2 begins with "O World-honored One, in this way, [those good sons and daughters]" and praises those who have renounced the three things. Number 3 begins with "O World-honored One, the good sons [and daughters]" and explains the proper time to renounce the three things. Number 4 begins with "O World-honored One, I see how embrace of the true Dharma [has great power]." It draws on the example of the Buddha as proof [of the power of embracing the true Dharma].

The first point can be divided into two halves. The first half addresses in a general way the three things and corresponds to the following sutra passage: "What are the three things? They are body, life, and wealth." The second half begins with the phrase "renouncing the body" and addresses each of the three renunciations. Naturally, the explanation of the renunciation of the body begins with the phrase "renouncing the body." So too the renunciation of life begins with "renouncing life," and the renunciation of wealth begins with "renouncing wealth."

Previous observers argue that renouncing the body means to renounce the self and so become like a slave, while renouncing life means to die for the sake of another person. Here, however, while it is true that renouncing one's life and body are both forms of death, their meaning is actually distinct. If one offers one's body to a starving tiger, this is an example of renouncing the body. Or, if a loyal retainer, seeing danger, gives his life [for his master], this is renouncing one's life. But renouncing one's wealth is different because it deals with things outside the body.

[This section of the sutra reads, "Good sons and daughters who renounce the body, in present and future lives without limit, separate from the sufferings of old age, sickness, and death. They also receive unending, innumerable, and mysterious merits, and thereby obtain the Dharma body of the Tathāgata."] Here, "future [lives] without limit" refers to the future that is without limit. This passage explains what is called "normal renunciation," [whereby one renounces the three things in both the present and the future]. Another interpretation of this passage argues that "future [lives] without limit" refers to the adamantine mind. Next, "Having separated from old age, sickness, and death" refers to the birth and death of limited cyclic existence, while "unending" refers to "inconceivable transformation." The word "obtain" refers to the merits received by sentient beings. But the merit of possessing the wealth of the Dharma is not like worldly wealth that is held [or destroyed] by the five things[: kings, pirates, evil sons, fire, and water].

In the next passage, "receive the extraordinary offerings of all sentient beings," the words are slightly out of order. The passage should read "receive the offerings of all extraordinary sentient beings." And if one interprets this passage according to the language of the sutra, it is from humans and *deva*s that these extraordinary offerings are received.

From "O World-honored One, [in this way, those good sons and daughters]" is the second of the four points, which praises those who have renounced the three things. See the sutra.

From "O World-honored One, the good sons and daughters [who have embraced the true Dharma]" is the third point that explains the [proper] time to renounce the three things. This passage describes the merits of protecting the Dharma at times when there are those who seek to destroy it. This means that those who protect the Dharma when it is under threat receive great merit. This point has two halves. The first half explains the proper time to renounce the three things: when there are those who seek to destroy the Dharma, one 8a must act with the mind firmly on the true path. The second half begins with

"Those who become friends in the Dharma." It explains that at the proper time the Buddha will offer a prediction that those who renounce the three things [will eventually become buddhas]. See the sutra.

From "O World-honored One, I see [how embrace of the true Dharma has great power]" is the fourth point of this component explaining renunciation of the three things. It draws on the example of the Buddha as proof [of the power of embracing the true Dharma], and also shows how the words of Śrīmālā are true.

4.2-2: The Tathāgata's Praise of Śrīmālā

The second branch of the chapter's second part begins with the phrase "At that time, the World-honored One [was pleased] with Śrīmālā's explanation [of the powers gained by embracing the true Dharma]." This branch describing the Tathāgata's praise has two sections: the first is his praise of Śrīmālā, while the second begins with "In this way, [embracing the true Dharma has immeasurable and unlimited merits]." This passage is the conclusion to the Buddha's praise.

The first section has two aspects: 1) direct praise of Śrīmālā, and 2) indirect praise of Śrīmālā. [The first aspect is not discussed further.] The second aspect has three components. The first offers the metaphor of a strong man, which illustrates the superiority of those [who have embraced the true Dharma] to those humans and *devas* [who have not]. The second aspect offers the metaphor of the King of the Bulls, which shows how those who have embraced the true Dharma also surpass the self-enlightened ones and the disciples. The third offers the metaphor of Mount Sumeru, which illustrates the superiority of those who [have embraced the true Dharma] to even those bodhisattvas of the Great Vehicle at the seventh stage and below. Each of these three components has an opening and a combining metaphor. See the sutra.

Here, moreover, the reference to "embracing the true Dharma" means that bodhisattvas at the eighth stage and above can engage in all [these virtuous] activities as a single practice. The following passage reads, "In this way, the mind that embraces [the true Dharma]"; it points to the mind engaged in all virtuous practices. And while bodhisattvas at the seventh stage and below can also renounce body and life, they cannot do so in a single thought like bodhisattvas at the eighth stage and above. Relative to [that of bodhisattvas at the highest levels, therefore,] this is a lesser form of renunciation.

The second section of this second branch is the conclusion to the Buddha's praise. It makes four points: 1) broad promotion [of embracing the true Dharma], 2) broad conclusion [of the merits that accrue to those who embrace the true Dharma], 3) brief promotion [of embracing the true Dharma], and 4) brief conclusion [of the merits that accrue to those who embrace the true Dharma].

The first point begins with "To elucidate these teachings for sentient beings." It refers to the human and *deva* vehicles, and offers a metaphor that corresponds to the strong man described above. "To guide sentient beings" refers to the two vehicles, and offers a metaphor that corresponds to the King of the Bulls. "To establish sentient beings in the true Dharma" refers to bodhisattvas at the seventh stage and below, and offers a metaphor that corresponds to Mount Sumeru. Each of these passages offers broad promotion of embracing the true Dharma.

The second point begins with "In this way, [embrace of the true Dharma] has great benefits." It concludes the [discussion of the benefits received by] the human and *deva* vehicles. "So too it offers great blessings" concludes the blessings that accrue to practitioners of the two vehicles. "Also great fruits" concludes the benefits that accrue to Mahayana bodhisattvas at the seventh stage and below. These passages correspond to the three metaphors noted already [of the strong man, the King of the Bulls, and Mount Sumeru]. This section is called the "broad conclusion."

From "Śrīmālā, in this way, even if I [explain the benefits of embracing the true Dharma" is the third point], the brief promotion [of embracing the true Dharma]. From "Therefore, [embracing the true Dharma offers innumerable and unlimited merits]" is the fourth point, the brief conclusion. See the sutra.

Chapter Five:
The One Vehicle

The second part of the main teaching's subsection addressing "other-practice" is "Chapter [Five]: The One Vehicle." It begins with the passage, "The Buddha said to Śrīmālā, 'Now you should further explain [embrace of the true Dharma].'" This chapter describes how all the virtues that emerge from embracing the true Dharma and from the teachings of the five vehicles all belong to the One Vehicle. The chapter can be divided into two parts: The first describes those who enter the One Vehicle, while the second explains the essential unity of the Three Treasures. The One Vehicle is the cause of the essential unity of the Three Treasures, just as the essential unity of the Three Treasures is the fruit of the One Vehicle. That is, fruit and cause form a single body. The second part of the chapter addresses this essential unity of the Three Treasures by explaining the oneness of fruit and cause.

In earlier times, the Three Treasures were seen as the steps of a ladder rather than as an essential unity, and the five vehicles were seen as distinct paths. But the Buddha put forth these views as skillful means; that is, they were not 8b true explanations of the ultimate teaching. Today, however, each of the five vehicles is seen to be part of the One Vehicle. In today's view, moreover, each vehicle possesses the cause that will enable its practitioners to realize the single fruit of the eternally abiding truth. As such, the earlier view of the Three Treasures as a stepladder was not a definitive view. Instead, only the eternally abiding, essential unity of the Three Treasures offers ultimate refuge.

[If we consider the chapter's title, "The One Vehicle,"] "one" can simply mean "not two," and "vehicle" can mean that which can serve as a transport. There are, however, other interpretations of the meaning of "one." There is, for example, the interpretation that "one" does not have any meaning beyond negating the notion [of three separate vehicles of the bodhisattvas, self-enlightened ones, and disciples]. Thus, it is called "one." A second interpretation argues that "one" means there is one, single fruit, and "vehicle" is a name given to express the cause. According to this perspective, although myriad types of virtuous deeds can emerge from this cause, each ultimately returns to this one, single fruit. It is this sense of "one"—that is, "one" fruit—that appears in the name and is meant to distinguish it from the cause. Yet a third interpretation states that both "one" and "vehicle" are names associated with the cause. Although there are many virtuous practices that emerge from this cause, their underlying meaning is the same. They can thus be called "one."

Although the first interpretation is not bad, one can raise the following sorts of doubts. In the pure lands of the ten directions, if distinctions were not made among the teachings of the three vehicles, then there would be no reason to explain the path of the One Vehicle. But it is the case that in all of these pure lands of the ten directions, the teachings of the One Vehicle are explained. As such, how then could it be that "one" is used simply to negate the three vehicles? But the second and third interpretations can both be used, although many of today's exegetes [accept the third], taking "one" to refer to the cause.

[If we consider the word "vehicle,"] we can distinguish the Great and the Small Vehicles as follows. Practitioners of the former do not seek individual salvation but are concerned first with saving other sentient beings. Since the eventual fruit for all on this path is buddhahood, it is called the "Great Vehicle." In contrast, practitioners of the latter path view saving sentient beings as troublesome. Since they pursue a form of individual salvation that seeks to eliminate the mental afflictions, their path is called the "Small Vehicle."

Even though the broader meaning of the "Great Vehicle" and the "One Vehicle" is the same, we can identify minor differences. For example, the Great Vehicle is another name for the path of the bodhisattva, which is one among the three vehicles [that also include the vehicles of the self-enlightened ones and the disciples]. Yet the One Vehicle is called neither the "three vehicles" nor the "two vehicles." Although the *Prajñāparamitā-sūtra* and the *Vimalakīrtinirdeśa* are called "teachings of the Great Vehicle," they are not referred to as "[teachings of] the One Vehicle."

Like the previous analysis of the One Vehicle, the meaning of "great" has different interpretations. For example, those exegetes who argue that "one" refers to the single fruit also argue that "great" is a name given in reference to that fruit. That is, the buddha fruit is "great." But those exegetes who argue that "one" refers to the single cause argue instead that "great" is the name for that cause. This means that rather than seeking individual salvation, bodhisattvas of this path seek instead to bring all sentient beings to [the other shore of enlightenment]. In this way, they each possess a vast mind that [can be seen as the cause that leads to the salvation of sentient beings]. The vehicle itself is thus called "great."

Next, if we turn to the main teachings of the One Vehicle, there are two types of virtuous deeds. The first is called "rewarded virtue" and the second is called "cultivated virtue." Although the former can reduce the severity of the serious afflictions, it is a stage that reaches the diamond absorption, and thus does not reach the ultimate buddha fruit. In other words, while rewarded virtue helps one progress along the path, it is not the essential teaching. Since it is limited in this way, we take up here only the key elements of the second type, cultivated virtue.

If we consider the relationship between liberation and virtuous deeds, liberation has often been understood as the root [or foundation] of the vehicle, and virtuous deeds as its branches. Here, however, [we reverse this] by taking virtuous deeds, not liberation, as the foundation. Why? Because on the Buddhist path there are "unimpeded" and "impeded" [forms of wisdom]. If liberation were viewed as the foundation of the vehicle, it would not be an "expansive" vehicle [because it would not be available to all sentient beings]. But the performance of virtuous deeds is different. That is, if one calls out just a single time "Hail [to the Buddha]," is this not a virtuous act? Since all sentient beings can perform such simple virtuous deeds, we can describe the latter type of vehicle as "expansive," and we will thus take these deeds to be the foundation of the vehicle.

8c

But the virtuous deeds practiced by a worldly person in the three realms do not constitute the foundation of the vehicle. This is because a vehicle should liberate practitioners from the cycle of birth and death, offering them the expectation of attaining the eternally abiding buddha fruit. But virtuous deeds performed by a worldly person in the three realms offer only the expectation of fruits within those realms, not the eternally abiding buddha fruit. As such, they cannot be considered the foundation of the vehicle. On the other hand, all the virtuous deeds of the three vehicles are part of the One Vehicle once their attachment to the three provisional teachings has been abandoned.

One interpreter states that although in the past and present interpretations of these virtuous deeds have varied, ultimately there is but one type of virtue. It is unnecessary, therefore, to collect [these myriad virtuous deeds within the One Vehicle, since their essence is the same]. As teachings, however, the names and [methods for establishing] meaning differ, and so from this perspective it is necessary to assemble [the teachings of these three vehicles] in the One Vehicle. He notes that the sutra states, "the continuation of the true Dharma and the extinction of the true Dharma are explained for the purpose of the Great Vehicle." [This interpreter concludes by noting that] the attachments of those of the three vehicles can be understood as explained above.

5.1: Those Who Enter the One Vehicle

The first part of this chapter, which addresses those who enter the One Vehicle, can be divided into three sections. 1) From the beginning of the chapter to the section ending with "the good actions of the supramundane world" offers a general description of how the teachings of the five vehicles enter the One Vehicle. 2) The passage beginning with "Just as the six principles are explained by the World-honored One" addresses how the cause of enlightenment of the two vehicles is part of the One Vehicle. 3) From "O World-honored One, the arhats and self-enlightened ones are fearful" addresses how the fruit of enlightenment of the two vehicles is part of the One Vehicle.

The previous chapter addressed [the virtuous deeds] that emerge from the mind that has embraced the true Dharma. But it did not take up in detail the virtuous deeds performed by members of the five vehicles, and has not, therefore, fully explained their meaning. This chapter thus exhaustively takes up both those who practice these teachings and the fruits of that practice, showing that [the activities of] each of these vehicles is part of the One Vehicle.

In the general summary of these vehicles with which we begin, we note that humans and *deva*s had yet to pursue [the Buddhist path]. Indeed, the names "Great Vehicle" and "Small Vehicle" were not known to them. It is sufficient, therefore, to simply summarize them. Conversely, bodhisattvas of the seventh stage and below have, from the beginning, pursued the path of the Buddha, and so have naturally been part of the Great Vehicle. There is thus no need to offer detailed arguments about these bodhisattvas either. Rather, we will focus on [the disciples and self-enlightened ones, practitioners] of the two vehicles who have received the respect of sentient beings but have a different understanding of the cause and fruit of enlightenment. Therefore, we carefully examine below their relationship to the One Vehicle.

As background [to this analysis], the previous chapter addressed only the meaning of embracing the true Dharma by bodhisattvas at the eighth stage and above, establishing the principles of "other-practice" [that do not include the two vehicles]. The present chapter, however, describes those who embrace the true Dharma and the product of their activities in relation to all five vehicles; since each is said to be part of the One Vehicle, some ask how the phrase "other-practice" can be used here [without contradicting this earlier material]. We can understand [this apparent contradiction] by considering closely the words [of the sutra]. When arguing from the perspective of truth, bodhisattvas from the first through the seventh stages have already established faith in the meaning of the One Vehicle. But when arguing from the perspective of the teaching, bodhisattvas at these seven stages have progressed on the path by cutting off the afflictions and contemplating the nature of phenomena, just like practitioners of the two vehicles. It is in the latter sense that they do not yet fully understand the meaning of the One Vehicle. Thus, when arguing from the perspective of those who fully understand the meaning of the One Vehicle, it is only bodhisattvas at the eighth stage and above who do so. It is from these two perspectives that this chapter on the One Vehicle refers to "other-practice."

5.1-1: General Description

This section first summarizes [how the teachings of the five vehicles are part of the One Vehicle]. It has two subsections: 1) The Buddha requests Śrīmālā to explain the teaching, and 2) Śrīmālā accepts his request and does so.

5.1-1-1: The Buddha Requests the Teaching

In "Chapter Four: Embracing the True Dharma," Śrīmālā first requested the Buddha's permission to speak before making a statement. In this chapter, however, the Buddha himself makes the request first. And in the last chapter, Śrīmālā[, having received the Buddha's permission,] expounded the profound principles of the "other-practice" [of bodhisattvas at the eighth stage and above], but did not dare proclaim them herself [because, as a bodhisattva of the seventh stage, she was not sufficiently advanced to engage in such practices]. Therefore, the Buddha first requested Śrīmālā to explain the teachings so that no one would doubt that her explanation agreed with his own.

In this chapter, the Buddha does not wait for Śrīmālā's request but instead initiates the teaching by requesting her to explain it. He tells her, "Now, you should again explain the embrace of the true Dharma that was expounded by all the buddhas." In this way, the Buddha requests Śrīmālā to expound the teaching, just like the buddhas before her, regarding the practitioners and their acts that are part of the One Vehicle.

5.1-1-2: Śrīmālā Accepts the Buddha's Request

The second subsection describes Śrīmālā, having received the Buddha's request, explaining the teaching. This subsection has two halves. The first describes the virtuous deeds performed by those who embrace the true Dharma, and the second begins with "O World-honored One, just as the [eight great rivers emerge from] Lake Anavatapta, [so too the virtuous deeds of all the disciples and self-enlightened ones, of the world and supramundane worlds, emerge from the Great Vehicle]." This half explains how [the five vehicles] are all part of the One Vehicle.

5.1-1-2-1: The Virtuous Deeds of Those Who Embrace the True Dharma

The first half has two components: the first component summarizes these deeds and the second interprets them. The first describes Śrīmālā saying to the Buddha, ["Embracing the true Dharma] is, in this way, the Mahayana." This passage explains how the mind that has embraced the true Dharma is the same as the mind of the Great Vehicle. The second component explains that which is included in the One Vehicle, having already established that the mind that embraces the true Dharma and the various teachings that emerge from it are one. Although [the language of the sutra] may seem to suggest that the focus of this section is the [virtuous deeds of the five vehicles], the central concern is the [virtuous deeds of those who have embraced the true Dharma].

5.1-1-2-2: The Five Vehicles as Part of the One Vehicle

The second half of the subsection, the results of embracing the true Dharma, also has two components. The first offers two metaphors that illustrate the unity of the teachings, while the second concludes the discussion of the Great Vehicle.

The first metaphor describes the eight rivers [that flow from Lake Anavatapta]; this metaphor has two parts: an opening and a summary. Lake Anavatapta, located near the peak of the Kunlun mountain range [in China], is called the "dragon without heat." Since a dragon lives in this lake, it is the basis of the name. The water that flows from the lake in the four directions forms eight rivers. The water of these eight rivers is thus indistinguishable from the water in Lake Anavatapta. In other words, the water of these rivers is not different from that of the lake. In a similar way, the teachings of the four vehicles, [those of humans and *deva*s, disciples, self-enlightened ones, and bodhisattvas at the seventh stage and below,] that emerge from the Great Vehicle are the Great Vehicle itself. That is, [just as the water in the eight rivers cannot be separated from that of the lake from which it emerged,] the teachings of the four vehicles cannot be separated from those of [the Great Vehicle].

This metaphor means, therefore, that the Great Vehicle itself is the origin [of the other Buddhist teachings]. For the summary, see the sutra.

The second metaphor, [the metaphor] of the seed, [also has an opening and a summary]. This metaphor illustrates how a seed relies on the earth to grow. [Dependent on the earth,] the seed is then the [source of that which grows and flourishes on the] great earth. In a similar way, the four vehicles rely on the Great Vehicle to grow, and in this sense are the Great Vehicle. One interpretation of this metaphor argues, "By relying on the earth to grow, a seed is not separate from the earth. Likewise, by relying on the Great Vehicle to grow, the five vehicles are not separate from the Great Vehicle. And while they are mutually inclusive in this way, some still ask how can they be described as the same thing. This is because the seed eventually returns to the earth." In just this way, the metaphor of the seed is meant to suggest that these vehicles all eventually return to [the Great Vehicle]. For the second part, the summary, see the sutra.

In this section of the sutra, "the world" refers to the realms of *deva*s and humans, while "the supramundane world" refers to bodhisattvas of the Great Vehicle at the seventh stage and below. The metaphor of the seed includes bodhisattvas at the seventh stage and below because [even though they have progressed further along the path than practitioners of the other vehicles] they had, in earlier times, been part of the three vehicles.

The relevant passage begins, "In this way, [all the virtuous deeds of the world and the supramundane worlds, of all the disciples and self-enlightened ones, emerge from the Great Vehicle]." This passage concludes the second component of the second half of the subsection [describing the virtuous deeds produced by embracing the true Dharma]. In this passage, the "Great Vehicle" refers to Mahayana bodhisattvas at the seventh stage and below.

5.1-2: The Cause of Enlightenment of the Two Vehicles

Section two of the first part of this chapter begins with "In this way, the World-honored One [explained the six principles]." This section shows how the cause of enlightenment of the two vehicles is part of the One Vehicle. It has five subsections. The first subsection addresses these six principles, which were studied in former times as part of the teachings of the Small Vehicle. Here, however, they are included in the One Vehicle. The six principles are

9b

[expressed as pairs]: 1) the teaching of the Buddha that flourishes and declines, 2) embracing virtuous behavior and freeing oneself from evil behavior, and 3) taking up the religious life first by leaving home and finally by taking the precepts. Together, [these three pairs] represent the six principles.

The second subsection begins with "Why? [Because the continuity of the true Dharma is taught for the benefit of the Great Vehicle]." This subsection summarizes the flourishing and eventual decline of the Buddha's teaching. The third subsection begins with "Although the *Prātimokṣa* [and the Vinaya have different names, they have the same meaning]." It summarizes the precepts that help one engage in virtuous behavior and free oneself from evil behavior. The fourth subsection begins with "leaving home [and receiving ordination]." It summarizes taking up the religious life first by leaving home and finally by taking the precepts. The fifth subsection begins with "The arhats [take refuge in the Buddha]" and compares the fruit and cause [of enlightenment].

5.1-2-1: The Six Principles

The first subsection begins with "In this way, the World-honored One taught these six principles." This passage explains the six principles that are the source of two types of wisdom: "the wisdom of exhausting [the afflictions]" and the "wisdom of non-arising." The six principles [can be understood as follows:] "The continuation of the true Dharma and the destruction of the true Dharma" takes up the flourishing and decline of the teaching. The two phrases of this sentence describe the conditions in which practitioners of the two vehicles can obtain the fruit of enlightenment. Here, "The continuation of the true Dharma" refers to the five hundred-year period after the death of the Buddha, in which the teaching was still vibrant and had not yet declined. This phrase thus explains the flourishing of the Dharma. [The second part of the sentence,] "the destruction of the true Dharma," refers to the period that follows these first five hundred years. [This second period,] known as the "semblance Dharma," describes the decline of the Dharma.

The two terms, "*Prātimokṣa*" and "Vinaya," describe the precepts by which one engages in virtuous behavior and frees oneself from evil behavior—the second [of the three] pairs [that make up the six principles]. They describe the cause that enables practitioners of the two vehicles to obtain the fruit of enlightenment. *Prātimokṣa* means to be free from the afflictions and to safeguard [one's position on the path] to liberation. This term illustrates how one becomes virtuous. *Vinaya* means "to eliminate evil," and describes the precepts that promote virtue by eradicating evil.

[The third pair begins with] "Leaving home [to take up the religious life] and receiving the precepts." The two phrases of this sentence naturally explain taking up the religious life first by leaving home and finally by taking the precepts. They describe the entire process by which a person first leaves the home of his or her parents to take refuge in the Three Treasures outside of worldly affairs, and then accepts the teaching that promotes virtuous behavior. After explaining the beginning of the religious life, the phrase "receiving the precepts" refers to the ceremony of the four announcements taken as part of the "disciplinary precepts." This section explains the culmination of the process of ordination.

These six passages[, expressed as three pairs,] explain the six principles. "For the benefit of the Great Vehicle, [the World-honored One] taught these six principles": this passage describes how [each of the six principles is part of the Great Vehicle].

5.1-2-2: The Flourishing and Decline of the Teaching

The second subsection begins with "Why? [Because the continuity of the true Dharma is taught for the benefit of the Great Vehicle.]" This subsection takes up the flourishing and eventual decline of the Buddha's teaching. That is, [after the Buddha's death] there was a period during which the Dharma continued, but that period was followed by [a period of] decline. See the sutra. The passage that follows [the question] "Why?" [with which this section begins addresses the decline of the true Dharma].

5.1-2-3: Summary of the Precepts

The third subsection begins with "Although the *Prātimokṣa* [and the Vinaya have different names, they have the same meaning]." This subsection summarizes the precepts by which one can engage in virtuous behavior and free oneself from evil behavior. It has four points: the first explains that the *Prātimokṣa* and the Vinaya form a single body. The second explains the precepts and begins with, "The Vinaya is studied by practitioners of the Great Vehicle." The third begins with the passage "Why? [Because one follows the

Buddha by leaving home and taking ordination.]" The Buddha embodies the Great Vehicle. If one follows him by leaving home and taking ordination, how then could one not also be [established on the path of] the Great Vehicle? The fourth offers a conclusion to this section on the precepts, and begins with "Therefore, [the explanation of proper behavior according to the Mahayana precepts]." See the sutra.

5.1-2-4: Leaving Home and Taking Up the Religious Life

The fourth subsection, which begins with "leaving home," summarizes taking up the religious life first by leaving home and finally by taking the precepts. This subsection has three components. The first explains [the process of entering the religious life and taking ordination in] the Great Vehicle. The second begins with "Therefore" and explains how the Great Vehicle differs from the Small Vehicle. The third begins with "Why? [Because the arhat leaves home and takes ordination by relying on the Tathāgata.]" This passage also explains how the Great Vehicle differs from the Small Vehicle. Since the Buddha embodies the Great Vehicle, if one takes refuge in his teaching by leaving home to take up the religious life, how could one then be on the path of the Small Vehicle?

Among these pairs, only the *Prātimokṣa* and the Vinaya are thought to be the same. For example, the flourishing and subsequent decline of the Dharma clearly occur at different times. When one leaves home to take up the religious life and finally takes the precepts, there is a clear beginning and end to these activities. Occurring at different times, they cannot be described as identical. But the *Prātimokṣa* and the Vinaya differ from the other pairs because they are a single body and they occur at the same time. They are thus described as being the same.

5.1-2-5: Comparing the Fruit and Cause of Enlightenment

The fifth subsection begins with "The arhats [take refuge in the Buddha]." This subsection compares [the fruit] and cause of enlightenment. It has two components. The first component describes [the arhats who take refuge in the Buddha and are afraid]. The second component begins with "Why? [Because arhats have not completed all practices.]" It explains why [arhats take refuge in the Buddha and yet are afraid].

The first component begins, "The arhats take refuge in the Buddha," which means that arhats have not yet completed all the virtuous practices. The next passage, "the arhats are afraid," means that they have not yet completely eliminated evil acts.

The second component has two halves. The first half describes the reasons why arhats have not yet completely eliminated evil behavior. The sutra states, "[Because arhats] have not completed all practices," which means that [although arhats perform virtuous deeds in the three realms described above,] they are not on the path on which they can engage in such practices outside of those realms. The sutra states that they thus "live in fear." That is, since arhats have not yet escaped from the realm of inconceivable transformation, their hearts are filled with fear. Indeed, the following section of the sutra offers a metaphor illustrating this fear, stating, "it is as if a person with a sword meant to injure him." The sutra adds, "Therefore, arhats have not yet experienced ultimate joy." This passage, which concludes the first half of the second component, suggests that because they have not yet escaped inconceivable transformation, arhats cannot experience ultimate joy.

The second half of this component begins with the question, "Why?" This section describes the virtuous practices that have not yet been completed [by the arhats]. [The sutra distinguishes them from the Buddha, stating that] "Since the Buddha is a refuge, he need not then seek another refuge." This passage explains that because the Buddha possesses self-reliant virtue, he does not need to seek refuge elsewhere. The next section of the sutra offers another metaphor that illustrates this point. See the sutra. The passage that begins with "In this way, [the arhats are afraid]" combines this material. For that summary, also see the sutra.

5.1-3: The Fruit of Enlightenment of the Two Vehicles

The third section of part one, which addresses those who enter the One Vehicle, begins with "O World-honored One, the arhats [and self-enlightened ones are afraid]." This section explains how the fruit of enlightenment of the two vehicles is part of the One Vehicle. This section has six subsections. 1) From the beginning of the section to the passage ending with "[In this way, the arhats] are far from the state of nirvana" criticizes the four types of wisdom of the arhats and describes the fruit of nirvana attained by them as being provisional. 2) From "Why? [Because it is only the Tathāgata, the Worthy, Perfectly Enlightened One who attains final nirvana and possesses all merits.]" This passage explains the basis for this criticism. 3) From "Why? There are two types of [birth and] death": this passage describes the two types of birth and death, and elaborates on the material discussed in the previous section.

4) From "Why? Because there are afflictions that [cannot be eliminated by the arhats and self-enlightened ones]": this section addresses the two types of mental afflictions and elaborates on the meaning of [the two types of birth and death] discussed in the previous section. 5) From "O World-honored One, the arhats, self-enlightened ones, and bodhisattvas in their final body" offers concluding remarks on each of the first four sections. 6) From "O World-honored One, those who first attained this stage" concludes discussion of the two vehicles being part of the One Vehicle.

5.1-3-1: Criticism of the Four Types of Wisdom of the Arhats

The first of these six subsections criticizes the four types of wisdom of the arhats and describes the fruit of nirvana attained by them as provisional. These four types of wisdom are 1) the wisdom of the cessation of the self, 2) the wisdom of those firmly established in the pure practices, 3) the wisdom of accomplishing that which had to be done, and 4) the wisdom that one will not be reborn. Practitioners of the two vehicles believe that having attained these four types of wisdom, they have also [realized] the fruit of final nirvana. But Queen Śrīmālā criticizes this path as incomplete[, arguing that it is a provisional path, not the ultimate path expounded in the sutra]. And if these four types of wisdom are provisional, then the path of those who realize it must also be lacking, as it produces what is called "the fruit of conditioned activity." So, too, if the nirvana experienced by those on this path is provisional, then the realization of the truth of the cessation of suffering is also incomplete. As such, they have not yet produced what is known as "the fruit of unconditioned activity," and so this path must be criticized as being both incomplete and provisional. Since their path is limited in these ways, arhats should immediately turn toward the ultimate path of the Buddha.

The sutra states in this regard, "Since phenomenal elements of life remain [for the arhats and self-enlightened ones]." This passage means that for living

10a

things in the phenomenal world the afflictions are inevitable, and so they are called "the phenomenal elements of life." Those who understand the realm in which the afflictions have been exhausted possess "the wisdom that has exhausted [the afflictions]." Since the afflictions remain for practitioners of the two vehicles, however, their form of wisdom is provisional.

The sutra continues, "There is birth [in cyclic existence]." And while this passage would seem to criticize the "wisdom of non-arising" [of the arhats], it simply argues that for those on this path, birth itself has not been exhausted because the afflictions have not yet been exhausted. But this passage does criticize [the arhats] for believing that the wisdom [they have realized is sufficient] for exhausting [the cycle of rebirth. In other words, this is the first type of wisdom noted above, the "wisdom of the cessation of self"].

The following passage states, "They have not completed all the pure practices and so remain impure." This means that although practitioners of the two vehicles have overcome the afflictions of the three realms, they have not eliminated all the afflictions and so are still impure. Since the realm of wisdom experienced by the arhats is impure, how could it be said that they have attained ultimate wisdom? This passage thus criticizes [the second type of wisdom,] "the wisdom of those firmly established in the pure practices."

The sutra continues, "Since their activities are provisional, they still have actions to be done." This passage means that although practitioners of the two vehicles have already completed the necessary practices [in the three realms], they still have practices to complete outside those realms in order to overcome all the afflictions. And so this passage states, "they still have actions to be done." Having actions yet to perform, how could the wisdom [they have developed] by contemplating the objects [of the world] be complete? This passage thus criticizes [the third type of wisdom,] "the wisdom of accomplishing that which had to be done."

The sutra adds, "Since they have not yet crossed over [to the other shore], they still have [mental afflictions] that must be cut off." This passage criticizes [the fourth type of wisdom,] "the wisdom that one will not be reborn." The passage that says "Since they have not yet crossed over" means that they have not yet transcended the realm of inconceivable transformation; while "they still have [mental afflictions] that must be cut off" means that they still possess entrenched ignorance that must be eliminated. Since they must therefore be reborn, birth has not yet been exhausted. How then could this sort of wisdom be taken to be ultimate?

The next passage reads, "Since the [afflictions] have not been cut off, they are far from the realm of nirvana"; this passage criticizes the fruit of nirvana [attained by practitioners of the two vehicles] as being provisional. Here, "Since the [afflictions] have not been cut off" means that entrenched ignorance has not yet been eliminated. Since all mental disturbances have not yet been cut off, they are still subject to inconceivable transformation. How then could they be said to have attained final nirvana?

5.1-3-2: Praise and Criticism of the Enlightenment of the Two Vehicles

The second subsection begins with "Why? [Because it is only the Tathāgata, the Worthy, Perfectly Enlightened One who attains final nirvana and possesses all the merits.]" This explains the reasons for the praise [offered by the Buddha] and the criticism offered by Śrīmālā. In earlier times, the Tathāgata had said that [the enlightened state reached by practitioners of the two vehicles] was ultimate. But here, because Śrīmālā criticizes that view, there appear to be conflicting views, one praising and the other criticizing [the earlier teachings]. [This apparent conflict] must be explained to resolve the following doubt. "In earlier days, why did the Tathāgata state that [the teachings of the two vehicles] were ultimate, but Śrīmālā now criticizes this view?" It is because when the Tathāgata praised the earlier teachings, he was using skillful means. That is, it was not intended as an explanation of ultimate truth. Indeed, Śrīmālā now criticizes those teachings, stating that ultimate truth exists in the Tathāgata alone, not in the two vehicles.

We can also address these doubts by considering five items found in the passage above that begins, "Why? [Because it is only the Tathāgata, the Worthy, Perfectly Enlightened One who attains final nirvana and possesses all the merits.]" [In this section of the sutra, the merits of the Tathāgata are described as] "all[-encompassing]," "immeasurable," "incomprehensible," "pure," and "revered," although their order has no special meaning. [In the passage describing the Tathāgata's merits that are revered by sentient beings, the sutra adds, "the arhats and self-enlightened ones meditate on liberation, have the four types of wisdom, and ultimately reach the nirvana of the annihilation of body and mind."] Here, "meditate" refers to the functioning of wisdom, while "liberation" refers to eliminating the afflictions. Likewise, the "four types of wisdom" explain the essence of wisdom, while the "nirvana of the annihilation of body and mind" explains liberation. This material thus describes those possessing an unconditioned and immovable [mind], those who have attained the [liberation and] nirvana [of the two vehicles].

5.1-3-3: The Two Types of Birth and Death

10b   The third subsection begins with "Why? There are two types of birth and death." This subsection naturally describes the two types of birth and death. It also elaborates on the two activities of praising and criticizing addressed in the last subsection, where it was noted that although the Buddha praised [at one time the teachings of the two vehicles as being ultimately true], that was no more than his skillful means. Indeed, Śrīmālā now criticizes these previous teachings, stating that ultimate truth exists in the Buddha alone, not in the two vehicles.

In taking up these two types of birth and death, we consider the reasons why the Buddha used his skillful means to praise the two vehicles [as ultimate], and why Śrīmālā now criticizes them as provisional teachings. Indeed, some express doubts regarding this last point, asking, "Why did [the Buddha] praise these teachings in the past [as the ultimate truth], but now they are said to be no more than skillful means? And why does ultimate truth exist in the Tathāgata alone, not in the two vehicles?" To answer these questions, we examine the two types of birth and death that are described in the sutra: limited cyclic existence and inconceivable transformation. In the past, the Buddha stated that the elimination of limited cyclic existence by practitioners of the two vehicles was the ultimate truth. But it is clear now that his praise for those who had done so was no more than skillful means [since attaining ultimate truth] also requires transcending inconceivable transformation. Because practitioners of the two vehicles have not yet done so, the ultimate truth resides in the Tathāgata alone, not in the two vehicles.

[This third subsection] has four components. The first describes in a general way the two types of [birth and] death. The second component begins with "[the birth and] death of limited cyclic existence [that refers to sentient beings who live in delusion]." It details the two types of [birth and] death. The third begins with "In these two types of [birth and] death[, it is through limited cyclic existence]." This component explains how the Buddha's past praise of the two vehicles was skillful means. The fourth begins "Having yet to exhaust [all the afflictions or future births]." It explains why the teachings of the two vehicles are provisional.

5.1-3-3-1

(This component is not mentioned.)

5.1-3-3-2: Analysis of the Two Types of Birth and Death

Although sages can be found in the three realms, they are far outnumbered by those examined here, who are called "sentient beings who live in delusion." [Arhats and self-enlightened ones have generally been seen to be] at the seventh bodhisattva stage and below, and so have not yet attained the birth and death of inconceivable transformation. Here, however, those at the eighth [bodhisattva] stage and above are called "arhats" and "self-enlightened ones," which simply reflects the names they were given in earlier times. The sutra then states, "Until they reach ultimate, supreme enlightenment," which refers to the diamondlike mind that is the cause for attaining the ultimate fruit of enlightenment.

We can distinguish four types of birth and death based on the following qualities. 1) Tainted karma is the cause and the afflictions associated with the four entrenchments are the conditions for the fruit. One's physical appearance may be beautiful or ugly, and one's life span may be long or short. This is called "limited cyclic existence." 2) Untainted karma is the cause and the afflictions associated with entrenched ignorance are the conditions for the fruit. Here, one's body is formless and one's life span is limitless. One possesses the light of awakening that illuminates the darkness of delusion, and with each thought, one freely transforms oneself. This state is called "inconceivable transformation."

3) Tainted karma with superior virtue is the cause and the remaining habitual tendencies associated with the three realms are the conditions for the fruit. Here one has a physical form and one's life span is limited. Although similar to limited cyclic existence, it also exhibits the arising and cessation of phenomena in each thought, like the birth and death of inconceivable transformation. It is thus called "birth and death of the mid-space of the two realms." 4) The last type emerges from the earliest moment of transmigration. It lies

outside the three realms and lacks even untainted karma. Here, one undergoes birth and death because of the transmission of fundamental delusion. This is called "birth and death from the earliest moment of transmigration."

In the forms of birth and death experienced by bodhisattvas at the sixth stage and below, down to those living in the three unfortunate destinies, phenomena arise and cease in each thought. For this group, the form and substance of the body are distinct and life spans are limited. So too, each of the realms in which they are born has its own limit. Thus, all of these groups experience limited cyclic existence. And while bodhisattvas at the eighth stage and above also have a limited life span, it is much longer than that of these other groups. For these bodhisattvas, moreover, the previous thought is the cause of the next thought's fruit, which means that their minds move unimpeded and immediately from thought to thought. They thus experience the birth and death of inconceivable transformation.

Although bodhisattvas at the seventh stage have physical form, they are not troubled by the afflictions and so cannot be said to experience limited cyclic existence. And while they perceive the arising and cessation of phenomena in each thought, since they have physical form, they cannot be said to experience the birth and death of inconceivable transformation. Their condition is thus like one who stands between two pillars, and so is called the "birth and death of the mid-space of the two realms."

Next, since at the earliest moment of transmigration there was no untainted karma, this condition cannot be viewed to be the same as inconceivable transformation. That is, those who experience it have not yet entered the three realms and become deluded [by the things of these realms]. And so their process of birth and death cannot properly be considered limited cyclic existence. Since they experience the continuation of consciousness that possesses the afflictions, they can, with each thought, fall into [the three realms]. As such, this state must be viewed as a separate type of birth and death.

Among the three types of birth and death that include limited cyclic existence, inconceivable transformation, and the mid-space of the two realms, we can identify twelve truths[, four of each type. But the fourth type of birth and death] is associated only with the two truths of suffering and origination. Together, we can thus identify fourteen distinct truths [associated with these four types of birth and death].

One interpreter argues, however, that at the earliest moment of transmigration, someone fortuitously met the Buddha, practiced his path, and realized enlightenment. As such, this list should also include the truths of cessation and the path, making a total of sixteen truths. But this interpretation is incorrect. This is because at the earliest moment of transmigration, [one is outside the three realms]. If one were to enter the three realms, one would naturally become attracted to worldly things, and so would become aware of suffering and enjoyment. One would thus seek to eliminate suffering by following the eightfold path. [Since one does not enter these three realms in this fourth type of birth and death, however, there is no such attraction.] Thus, there is no need for the last two truths, and so they have not been included [with the other fourteen].

In [the birth and death] in the mid-space of the two realms, the conditions [for transmigration are the remaining habitual tendencies of the three realms], not the active afflictions. In the birth and death associated with the earliest moment of transmigration, it is unclear whether these active afflictions have been eliminated. Therefore, [both the third and fourth types of birth and death] are insufficient for demonstrating that the Buddha possesses the ultimate truth. If they had to be classified, however, birth and death in the mid-space of the two realms would be associated with that of limited cyclic existence, and the earliest moment of transmigration would be associated with the birth and death of inconceivable transformation. The important point of this discussion, however, is the nature of limited cyclic existence and inconceivable transformation. Therefore, Śrīmālā [limits her discussion to these two types of birth and death], arguing that limited cyclic existence is provisional and inconceivable transformation is ultimate.

5.1-3-3-3: The Buddha's Praise of the Two Vehicles as Skillful Means

The third component begins with "In these two types of [birth and] death [it is through limited cyclic existence]." It explains how the Buddha's past praise [of the two vehicles] was skillful means. At that time it was [taught] that by eliminating the four types of wisdom, one had attained ultimate truth.

5.1-3-3-4: The Two Vehicles Lack Ultimate Truth

The fourth component begins with "Having yet to exhaust all the afflictions [or rebirths]." This section states that the ultimate teaching is not to be found in the two vehicles. This can be understood as follows. Since practitioners of the two vehicles have not eliminated all the afflictions, their paths cannot be described as being ultimately true. And while the language of the sutra clearly states that the two vehicles are not the ultimate truth, by reading between the lines we can understand that the Buddha's earlier praise of them as ultimately true was simply skillful means. It is thus the case that the ultimate does, in fact, reside in the Tathāgata alone. This reading naturally accords with the principles of the sutra.

The model text understands this material as follows. "The passage that begins 'In these two types of [birth and] death' is the conclusion to the [third subsection], in which the Buddha praises [the two vehicles]. [The passage beginning with] 'Having yet to exhaust all delusions' summarizes the criticisms made by Śrīmālā."

5.1-3-4: The Two Types of Afflictions

The fourth subsection takes up the two types of afflictions. It begins with "Why? [Because there are mental afflictions that cannot be eliminated by the arhats and self-enlightened ones.]" This section explains in general terms the fruit [of enlightenment realized by practitioners] of the two vehicles. It also elaborates on the two types of birth and death from the previous section, illustrating the conditions in which one can and cannot escape them. This subsection has two halves: the first takes up the two types of afflictions in a general way, and the second begins with the phrase "There are two types of delusion." It takes up the essence and characteristics of the afflictions in greater detail.

11a

5.1-3-4-1: General Description of the Two Types of Afflictions

The first half begins with the doubts of some who ask, "Why can the Tathāgata escape these two types of death but practitioners of the two vehicles cannot?" We can resolve these doubts as follows. There are two types of afflictions: the four entrenchments and entrenched ignorance. Since the Tathāgata has already eliminated these two types of afflictions, he has also escaped from the two types of birth and death. Since practitioners of the two vehicles have eliminated only the four entrenchments, they have escaped only from limited cyclic existence.

5.1-3-4-2: Detailed Explanation of the Two Types of Afflictions

The second half addresses the essence and characteristics of the afflictions. It has four components. 1) Addresses the essence and characteristics of the two types of afflictions. 2) Begins with "[O World-honored One,] the power of these four entrenchments [is the foundation] for all the active afflictions." This section compares the relative power of these two types of afflictions. 3) Begins with "[O World-honored One,] conditioned in this way [by tainted karma from birth in the three realms]." It explains the differences among karma-producing activities. 4) Begins with "In this way, O World-honored One, there is the entrenchment that desires existence itself." It explains the process by which the afflictions are eliminated.

5.1-3-4-2-1: The Essence and Characteristics of the Two Types of Afflictions

The first component, which addresses the essence and characteristics of the two types of afflictions, has two halves. The first interprets the four entrenchments[, the first type of affliction]. The second begins with "O World-honored One, the mind is not related to [beginningless, entrenched ignorance in this way]." It interprets the second type of mental affliction, that associated with entrenched ignorance.

The first half begins with "[O World-honored One, among the afflictions that arise, the association of] the mind [with its mental functions] is momentary." [The phrase "the mind with its mental functions"] refers to consciousness, while "the association of" refers to [the three other mental aggregates:] sensation, conception, and volition. In the second half, "The mind is not related to" refers to the fundamental afflictions that are not associated with these four states of mind. Indeed, "beginningless" points to the time before [the emergence of the afflictions associated with entrenched ignorance].

5.1-3-4-2-2: The Relative Power of the Two Types of Afflictions

The second component of this section addressing the essence and characteristics [of the afflictions] begins with "[O World-honored One,] the power of these four entrenchments [is the foundation for all the active afflictions]." This component compares the relative power [of these two types of afflictions: the four entrenchments and entrenched ignorance].

This component has five points. The first explains the weakness of the four entrenchments relative to entrenched ignorance. The second begins with "O World-honored One, [the power] of entrenched ignorance [is even greater]." This section describes the far greater power of entrenched ignorance relative to the four entrenchments. The third begins with "For example, [the power of entrenched ignorance] is like that of Māra, [the Evil One]." This section offers a comparison showing that the power of entrenched ignorance is far greater than that of the four entrenchments. The fourth begins with "as numerous as the sands of the Ganges River." It too illustrates the superior power of entrenched ignorance. The fifth begins with "In this way, O World-honored One, [entrenched ignorance is supremely powerful]." This section concludes the discussion of the superior power of entrenched ignorance.

The first point begins with "All the active afflictions." This phrase refers to the active afflictions that are as numerous as the sands of the Ganges River. They emerge from entrenched ignorance and prevent sentient beings from practicing virtuous behavior. They are thus called the "active afflictions." The terms "ground" and "seeds" [appear in the passage, "the power of these four entrenchments is the ground in which the seeds of the active afflictions grow]." This means that the basis for the individual afflictions lies in a set of common characteristics, called the "ground." Since the individual characteristics of the afflictions grow out of these common characteristics, they are called "seeds." Indeed, those who have interpreted entrenched ignorance and the four entrenchments argue that the former is the "ground" of the active afflictions, and the four entrenchments are the "seeds" that grow out of the fundamental characteristics. The next passage takes up the weakness of the four entrenchments relative to entrenched ignorance.

The second point begins "O World-honored One, [the power of entrenched ignorance is even greater]." This section describes the far greater power of entrenched ignorance [relative to the four entrenchments], and so repeats some of the material described in the last section. In this section of the sutra it states, "Among these four types of entrenchments, the desire for existence itself." In this passage, "the desire for existence itself" refers to the afflictions associated with the formless realm. The term "types" refers to [the other three types of entrenchments:] attachment to form, attachment to desire, and the unenlightened view that sees all phenomena springing from a single ground. Together, these are the four entrenchments.

The third point offers an opening and a combining metaphor that illustrates the power [of entrenched ignorance is far greater than that of the four entrenchments]. See the sutra.

The fourth point begins, "as numerous as the sands of the Ganges River." This section also illustrates the superior [power of entrenched ignorance]. The passage that follows, "[causes the active afflictions] to abide for a long time," means that from the distant past entrenched ignorance has been the foundation [for the afflictions associated with the four entrenchments]. [Since it supports these afflictions] it is thus described as "superior." The sutra states, "The [wisdom attained by members of the] two vehicles cannot eliminate [the four entrenchments]. It is only the enlightened wisdom of the Buddha that can eliminate them." This passage addresses the difficulties associated with eliminating the superior [power of entrenched ignorance]. In that passage, "the enlightened wisdom [of the Buddha]" refers to his understanding of emptiness. Although the means by which he eliminates them has not been explained in detail, the term is meant to suggest the power of entrenched ignorance. One interpreter states, "When the diamondlike mind has cut off and exhausted the mental disturbances, one reaches the stage called 'studying the [wisdom of the] Buddha.' Therefore, this stage is also called, 'the Tathāgata's enlightened wisdom that cuts off [the afflictions].'"

The fifth point begins, "In this way, [O World-honored One, entrenched ignorance is supremely powerful]." This concludes the discussion of the superior power of entrenched ignorance. See the sutra.

5.1-3-4-2-3: Differences among Karma-producing Activities

The third component of this subsection addressing the essence and characteristics of the afflictions begins with "[O World-honored One,] conditioned in this way [by tainted karma from birth in the three realms]." It explains the differences among karma-producing activities, and has four aspects.

The first aspect explains that the afflictions associated with the four entrenchments have been "enriched" with tainted acts that lead to birth in the three realms. [In the passage that introduces this component,] "conditioned" refers to the afflictions associated with the four entrenchments, which can help to create karma that will eventually bear fruit. In other words, the four entrenchments serve as a condition for the production of that fruit. Here, "tainted karma that is the cause [of rebirth in the three realms]" is a general reference that leads into a discussion of both good and bad acts.

The second aspect begins, "In this way[, the three forms of mind-made bodies of the arhats, self-enlightened ones, and powerful bodhisattvas are conditioned by entrenched ignorance and caused by untainted karma]." This passage explains how the mental disturbances associated with entrenched ignorance, when "enriched" with untainted acts, lead to rebirth in the realm of inconceivable transformation.

The third aspect begins, "At these three stages[, the three types—the mind-made, the body-made, and birth from untainted action—are based on entrenched ignorance]." This passage explains how entrenched ignorance "enriches" all actions that lead to rebirth in the various realms. In this passage, "At these three stages" refers to the three realms [of desire, form, and formlessness], while "the three types" refers to the three vehicles. Here, "mind-made" refers to the birth of inconceivable transformation, while "body-made" refers to birth in limited cyclic existence. "Birth from untainted action" naturally refers to birth arising from untainted actions.

One interpreter states, "In a previous section, 'mind-made' referred [not to the cause but] to the fruit of birth in inconceivable transformation, and so is also called 'untainted actions that are the cause of birth.' And while the previous section of the sutra mentions the 'three stages,' it does not distinguish clearly between [two of those stages:] form and formlessness. By distinguishing clearly [the mind-made and the body-made], however, we can clarify [this ambiguity]."

The passage that includes "based on entrenched ignorance" explains how entrenched ignorance "enriches" all actions [that lead to rebirth in the various realms]. Sentient beings believe that entrenched ignorance creates the conditions for the birth and death of inconceivable transformation, but not for limited cyclic existence. The sutra states in this regard, "[phenomena] are conditioned; that is, they are not unconditioned."

The fourth aspect begins, "In this way[, the three types of mind-made bodies and birth from untainted actions are conditioned by entrenched ignorance]." This section concludes the discussion of how entrenched ignorance "enriches" these untainted acts that lead to birth in the realm of inconceivable transformation.

5.1-3-4-2-4: The Process of Eliminating the Afflictions

The fourth component of this subsection addressing the essence and characteristics of the afflictions begins, "In this way, O World-honored One, [there is the entrenchment that desires existence itself]." This passage explains the process by which the afflictions are eliminated, and it can be divided into three parts.

The first part explains why the functioning of activities associated with the two types of entrenchments are not the same. See the sutra.

The second part explains removing the afflictions [of entrenched ignorance]. [The sutra reads, "Entrenched ignorance and the four entrenchments are different because the former is] eliminated by the buddha stage." This passage means that the buddha stage possesses all merits. The passage "[Entrenched ignorance is also] eliminated by the Buddha's enlightened wisdom" addresses eliminating the afflictions [associated with entrenched ignorance] through emptiness wisdom.

The third part explains why [the Buddha's emptiness wisdom eliminates these afflictions]. Some express doubts, asking "Why is it only at the buddha stage that [entrenched ignorance] can be eliminated? Why cannot practitioners of the two vehicles also do so?" This is because practitioners of the two vehicles, having eliminated only the four entrenchments, have not yet exhausted untainted karma. Indeed, the sutra states precisely that "They have not yet exhausted untainted karma," which means that they have not realized the state in which all the afflictions have been eliminated.

The sutra also states, ["Arhats and self-enlightened ones] have not yet obtained autonomous, unimpeded power." This statement means that since these two groups have not yet realized the highest stage of untainted action, they do not possess such autonomous, unimpeded power. 11c

Since they have realized neither [the stage of untainted action] nor complete self-mastery, they have not cut off entrenched ignorance. The sutra adds, ["The arhats and self-enlightened ones] have not yet realized [enlightenment]. 'Not realized the stage of untainted karma' refers to entrenched ignorance." This passage means that since the arhats and self-enlightened ones have not yet eliminated entrenched ignorance, they have not realized what should be realized, where the phrase, "should be realized," means the elimination of [all the afflictions].

One interpreter states, "'They have not yet exhausted untainted karma' means that afflictions still remain, and this is a reference to entrenched ignorance itself. Indeed, directly below that passage, the sutra states, 'they have not yet realized the stage of untainted karma' refers to entrenched ignorance." When reading these passages in the sutra, doubts may arise about why the Buddha alone can eliminate the entrenchment of ignorance. But these doubts are resolved later in the text where it explains the reasons that the two vehicles are unable to eliminate this type of ignorance, although simply stating [that the Buddha alone can do so] would have been sufficient.

5.1-3-5: Summary of Subsections 1–4

The fifth subsection begins, "O World-honored One, the arhats, self-enlightened ones, [and bodhisattvas in their final body]." It describes the fruit of enlightenment realized by the two vehicles, and offers an analysis of each of the first four subsections, which were explained above in only a cursory fashion. Before taking each of the four up in detail, however, [I offer the following background].

The first analysis starts at the beginning of the section and ends with "facing the realm of nirvana." It summarizes the four types of wisdom criticized in the first subsection and the incomplete nirvana [experienced by the two vehicles]. The second analysis begins with "If one knows all forms of suffering." It summarizes the second subsection, which explains that ultimate wisdom exists in the Buddha alone, not in the two vehicles. The third analysis begins, "O World-honored One, among the active afflictions." It summarizes subsection four, which looks back at subsection three to address the two types of afflictions and the two types of birth and death that can and cannot be eliminated. The fourth analysis begins with "O World-honored One, there are two types of wisdom that do not lead to rebirth." This analysis addresses the two types of birth and death from subsection three, but also offers a conclusion to subsection two, which describes [the wisdom of the Buddha] as ultimate and [that of the two vehicles] as provisional.

The model text divides this material differently, arguing instead, "From this [point in the sutra] forward is the conclusion to the second subsection stating that only the Tathāgata realizes ultimate enlightenment and, therefore, the enlightenment of the two vehicles is provisional. This analysis has four components: the first offers an initial conclusion to the subsection describing [the enlightenment of] the two vehicles as provisional. The second begins with 'If one knows all forms of suffering.' This component offers a [second] conclusion to the subsection describing the [enlightenment of the] Tathāgata as ultimate. The third begins with 'O World-honored One, if entrenched ignorance is not eliminated.' It offers an interpretation of the subsection describing the [enlightenment of the] two vehicles as provisional. The fourth begins with 'O World-honored One, among the active afflictions.' It offers an interpretation of the subsection describing the [enlightenment of the] Tathāgata as ultimate."

If we divide the sutra as the model text suggests, however, the third and fourth components are interpreting material that has already been concluded in components one and two. This approach seems slightly inappropriate because it could lead to endless interpretation. I have not, therefore, used it.

5.1-3-5-1: The Four Types of Wisdom, Incomplete Nirvana, and the Seven Virtues

The first analysis offers a conclusion to the discussion of the four types of wisdom and the nirvana [of the two vehicles]. Since both are described as being incomplete, the seven virtues associated with them must also be incomplete. The seven virtues that practitioners of the two vehicles have not completed are: 1) wisdom; 2) elimination of the afflictions (see the passage that begins "since they [have not perfected] wisdom and spiritual insight"); 3) liberation (see the passage that begins "since they have not eliminated these afflictions); 4) purity (see the passage that begins "that is called 'purity with remainder'"); 5) merit (see the passage that begins "achieve ['merits with remainder,' which is not complete merit]"); and 6) wisdom based on complete observation of phenomena (see the passage that begins "achieve '[merits] with remainder'"). These six passages criticize the four types of wisdom [of the two vehicles]. 7) Nirvana (see the passage that begins "this is called '[achieving limited nirvana])."' This passage concludes the criticism of the fruit of nirvana [experienced by practitioners of the two vehicles].

12a

Among these seven virtues, number six[, wisdom based on complete observation of phenomena,] addresses as a group numbers three, four, and five[, that is, liberation, purity, and merit]. It does so because number two had already addressed number one. And while number three addresses number two, number four does not address number three, nor does number five address number four. For this reason, number six takes up numbers three, four, and five as a group.

5.1-3-5-2: Ultimate Wisdom Exists in the Buddha Alone

The second analysis offers a conclusion to subsection two, and begins with "If one knows all forms of suffering." It states that ultimate wisdom exists in the Buddha alone, not in the two vehicles. This analysis has two halves: the first concludes the description of the Buddha as the ultimate, and the second begins with "O World-honored One, if entrenched ignorance [is not completely eliminated]." It concludes the description of the two vehicles as being provisional.

5.1-3-5-2-1: The Buddha as the Ultimate

Since it is stated above that ultimate wisdom exists in the Buddha alone, we can conclude that unlike members of the two vehicles, he has fulfilled the seven virtues. He is thus called "ultimate." This first half of the second analysis can be divided into eight points. The first point includes the first four phrases noted below, each of which includes the word "all," suggesting that the Buddha's wisdom based on observation is complete. That is, the sutra reads, ["If one knows all suffering, eliminates all sources of suffering, realizes the destruction of all suffering, and practices the all-inclusive path, one will attain permanently abiding nirvana in a world that is impermanent and broken, impermanent and afflicted]." This passage describing [the Buddha's] wisdom based on the observation of phenomena contrasts to number six [of the seven virtues], which describes the incomplete wisdom based on observation [of the two vehicles].

The second point takes up the two types of impermanence [in a world that is described as "impermanent and broken, impermanent and afflicted"]. This passage suggests that the Buddha experiences complete nirvana, and so offers a contrast to number seven, which describes the limited nirvana of the two vehicles. Here, "In [a world that is] impermanent and broken" refers to limited cyclic existence in which bodies are broken down and life spans are diminished. Likewise, "in [a world that is] impermanent and afflicted" refers to inconceivable transformation in which bodies are not broken down and life spans are not limited. But even here, the mind is pensive about the impermanence of each passing moment and so can also be described as "afflicted."

The third point includes the passage, "In an unprotected [world, a world] without a refuge[, there is both a protector and a refuge]." This passage explains that the Buddha has completed the virtue of serving as a refuge for sentient beings, which does not correspond to any of the seven virtues described above. Earlier in the sutra, that which lacks a covering is naturally called "uncovered," just as those who do not have someone of strength nearby are called "unprotected." In the passage quoted above, moreover, "without a refuge" refers to those beings that experience the birth and death of inconceivable transformation. They suffer from milder afflictions than those who are "unprotected," [since the latter group experiences the birth and death of limited cyclic existence].

The fourth point takes up the Dharma body and related issues, explaining why the Buddha has attained complete nirvana. It begins by taking up the Dharma body, which also does not correspond directly to the seven virtues. The [fifth] point takes up wisdom, which corresponds to number one above: the incomplete wisdom of the two vehicles. [The sixth] point takes up liberation, which corresponds to number three above: incomplete liberation. [The seventh] point takes up purity, which corresponds to number four above: incomplete purity. The eighth point takes up three qualities as a group[: the one flavor of wisdom, the same flavor of the Dharma body, and the flavor of enlightened liberation], which explain the Buddha's completion of the seven virtues.

[After describing a world that lacks both a protector and a refuge, the sutra states,] "Why? [Because there is the realization of nirvana where there is no distinction between superior and inferior phenomena.]" This passage introduces the three virtues [of wisdom, liberation, and purity]. "Where there is no distinction between superior and inferior phenomena." The model text interprets this passage as follows: "The Dharma bodies of the buddhas are [all equal,] possessing neither superior nor inferior qualities. Since [the sutra uses] 'equal' also to describe wisdom, liberation, and purity, they too do not possess such distinctions."

Here, however, we will interpret this passage as follows: The section describing superior and inferior phenomena corresponds to the three errors found in the Small Vehicle's view of nirvana. That is, in earlier times, the Small Vehicle described nirvana as being "with remainder" and "without remainder." This view has three errors: 1) nonconcurrence, 2) incompleteness, and 3) inequality. In this view, since the three virtues are seen to be superior or inferior relative to the other two, they are unequal. Since they are viewed as three distinct qualities, they are nonconcurrent. And since these three virtues are provisional, they are incomplete and so can be called "partial."

But the nirvana discussed in this sutra is free from these three errors since it possesses one equal flavor. It is thus called "the realm of eternally abiding nirvana." The sutra reads, "Therefore, nirvana has one equal flavor. This is called the 'flavor of liberation.'" In this passage, "one flavor" refers to wisdom, and "equal flavor" refers to the Dharma body. As such, this type of nirvana can be called "[nirvana] of the three virtues."

But those who discuss the word "nirvana" in its original language say that it has multiple meanings. It can also be interpreted as follows: Although the nirvana of earlier times was not the same as these three eternally abiding virtues, [the nirvana] described in this sutra is the same as them. It is, therefore, the nirvana of one equal taste.

In the section above arguing that practitioners of the two vehicles have not completed the seven virtues, taking refuge and the Dharma body were not discussed. In concluding the discussion of the Tathāgata as the ultimate, [the failure of the two vehicles] to eliminate [the afflictions] and praise of the virtues were not addressed since they complement each other[, and thus became clear in the course of the interpretation].

5.1-3-5-2-2: Conclusion to the Provisional Nature of the Two Vehicles

The second half of the second analysis begins with "O World-honored One, [if entrenched ignorance is not completely eliminated]." It concludes the argument that the two vehicles do not possess ultimate truth, and has four elements. The first element explains that practitioners of the two vehicles have not yet eliminated entrenched ignorance, and so have not attained the "three flavors"[: the single flavor, the equal flavor, and the flavor of liberation]. As such, their path is provisional. Element two begins with "Why? [If entrenched ignorance is not eliminated completely.]" It explains how by failing to eliminate entrenched ignorance one does not attain the "single flavor." Element three begins with "Therefore, entrenched ignorance." It explains that entrenched ignorance is the foundation for the various mental disturbances. Element four begins with, "In this way, [the active afflictions,] more numerous than the grains of sand in the Ganges River, [are eliminated by the Tathāgata's enlightened wisdom]." It concludes the discussion of entrenched ignorance serving as the foundation for the myriad mental disturbances.

For the first element, see the sutra.

The second element has two aspects. The first explains that the [mental disturbances] that should be eliminated have not yet been eliminated, and the second explains that [the single flavor] that should be obtained has not yet been obtained. [The sutra states, "Phenomena more numerous than the sands of the Ganges River that should be eliminated have not been eliminated. Therefore, phenomena more numerous than the sands of the Ganges River that should be attained have not been attained, and those that should be realized have not been realized."] The phrase "should be eliminated" refers to elimination of the distinctive characteristics of ignorance. "Should be attained" refers to seeing with wisdom the distinctive characteristics of conditioned phenomena. "Should be realized" refers to eliminating ignorance.

[The third element] begins with "Therefore, [entrenched ignorance]." It explains that entrenched ignorance is the foundation for the myriad mental disturbances. This section abbreviates [these myriad mental disturbances] by taking up twelve distinctive characteristics. The relevant passage reads, "The accumulation [of ignorance] that produces the afflictions, which are eliminated by practicing the entire path of cultivation": when practicing the path, the afflictions that must be eliminated all arise from entrenched ignorance. This passage offers a general summary, while the next eleven passages explain how the active defilements, which appear in the various realms to block progress along this path, arise from entrenched ignorance. "That [gives rise to the active defilements of the mind]." Here, the word "that," with which this passage begins, refers to entrenched ignorance, which produces the active defilements of the mind. One interpreter argues that "that" refers instead to the mind itself.

[The fourth element] begins with "In this way, [the active afflictions,] more numerous than the sands of the Ganges River, [are eliminated by the Tathāgata's enlightened wisdom]." It concludes the discussion of entrenched ignorance serving as the foundation for the myriad mental disturbances. The sutra states, "[All the active afflictions that arise] are caused [and conditioned] by entrenched ignorance." This passage means that the active afflictions, more numerous than the sands of the Ganges River, are originally nonexistent. These afflictions are caused by entrenched ignorance. Indeed, the sutra states precisely that "All [the active afflictions] are caused by [entrenched ignorance]." But these active afflictions, more numerous than the sands of the Ganges River, also arise indirectly from entrenched ignorance. The sutra states, therefore, that "all [the active defilements] are conditioned [by entrenched ignorance]."

5.1-3-5-3: Conclusion to the Two Types of Afflictions and the Two Types of Birth and Death

The third analysis begins with "O World-honored One, among the active afflictions." It offers a conclusion to the discussion of the two types of mental afflictions taken up in subsection four above, but also explains the two types of birth and death that can and cannot be eliminated, which were addressed in subsection three. The conclusion offered here follows the pattern of the previous section, which offered a conclusion to the discussion of the provisional nature of the two vehicles. That is, subsection four addressed entrenched ignorance and the four entrenchments as well as the two types of birth and death that can and cannot be eliminated. This third analysis has four subsections that address each of the four components from above.

The first component took up the essence and characteristics of the afflictions, while the second compared the relative power of their functioning. The third component explained the differences among karma-producing activities, while the fourth explained the process by which the afflictions are eliminated. Here, however, discussion of the third component explaining the differences among karma-producing activities will be abbreviated by omitting its conclusion. But each of the three remaining components includes a conclusion.

The relevant sutra passages for these conclusions are as follows. From the beginning of the section to the passage ending with "entrenched ignorance without beginning" concludes the first component, which takes up the essence and characteristics of the afflictions. The passage beginning with "O World-honored One, if [phenomena, more numerous than the sands of the Ganges River, that should be eliminated by the Tathāgata's enlightened wisdom]" concludes the second component comparing the relative power of the functioning of the two types of afflictions. And from "In this way, if all [the

12c

afflictions and active afflictions are eliminated]" concludes the fourth component, which explains the process by which [the afflictions] are eliminated.

5.1-3-5-3-1: Conclusion to the Essence and Characteristics of the Afflictions

The conclusion to the first component begins with "[O World-honored One,] among the afflictions that arise, the association of the mind with its mental functions is momentary": this passage addresses the four entrenchments. The following section of the sutra, which begins with "O World-honored One, the mind dissociated from the stage of entrenched ignorance without beginning," naturally addresses entrenched ignorance.

5.1-3-5-3-2: Conclusion to the Relative Power of the Functions of the Afflictions

The second component compares the relative power of the functioning of the afflictions. This conclusion has two halves: the first describes the power of the four entrenchments as weaker than [that of entrenched ignorance], just as the second describes the power of entrenched ignorance as greater than [that of the four entrenchments]. Here, however, only a conclusion about the greater power of entrenched ignorance is offered, since the weaker power of the four entrenchments becomes obvious through the discussion of entrenched ignorance. And just as [the material described] above included a Dharma teaching and a metaphor, this conclusion also offers a Dharma teaching and a metaphor. See the sutra. This conclusion to the second component describes the ways in which the myriad afflictions coalesce and disintegrate based on the foundation of entrenched ignorance whose greater power was described above.

5.1-3-5-3-3

(This conclusion has been omitted.)

5.1-3-5-3-4: Conclusion to Eliminating the Afflictions

From "In this way, if all [the afflictions and active afflictions are eliminated]" concludes the fourth component, which explains the process by which the afflictions are eliminated. Indeed, since it is stated above that entrenched ignorance "is also eliminated by the buddha stage and by the Buddha's enlightened wisdom," it is clear that the Tathāgata has completed the cause and fruit of enlightenment. He has, therefore, eliminated completely the afflictions.

This conclusion [to the fourth component] has three parts. The first explains the Buddha's completion of the cause of enlightenment so that he can eliminate the afflictions. The second begins with "[attaining all the merits of] the Dharma King, the Dharma Lord." This means that the Buddha, having completed the fruit of enlightenment, can eliminate the afflictions. The third begins with "For this reason, [O World-honored One]" and offers the conclusion to this section. See the sutra.

In the passage ["In this way, if all the afflictions and the active afflictions are eliminated]," "all the afflictions" refers to the common characteristics shared by the fundamental afflictions, while "the active afflictions" refers to the secondary and distinctive characteristics of the afflictions. The following passage of the sutra describes those who have eliminated the afflictions as those who are "established in the pure practices, have accomplished actions, [and do not accept rebirth]." These qualities have generally referred to the stage that precedes the development of the diamondlike mind, [which is the final stage before buddhahood]. Here, however, the Dharma body that is the fruit of enlightenment is described as "the wisdom of those established in the pure practices" and "[the wisdom] of those whose actions have been completed." [Although this is language generally used to describe enlightenment in the Hinayana,] here it represents common language [used for both the Small and Great Vehicles].

5.1-3-5-4: The Ultimate and the Provisional

The fourth analysis begins with "O World-honored One, [there are two types of wisdom] that do not lead to rebirth." This analysis addresses the two types of birth and death from subsection three but also offers a conclusion to subsection two, which describes the Buddha's wisdom as ultimate and the two vehicles' wisdom as provisional.

It was stated above that the Tathāgata has escaped from both types of [birth and] death, while practitioners of the two vehicles have only escaped from one[, that of limited cyclic existence]. This can be summarized simply here: since the Tathāgata has already subdued the four demons, he has escaped both types of [birth and] death. Since practitioners of the two vehicles have

13a

not subdued these four demons, they have escaped only one. The model text states, "From this analysis down is the conclusion of the discussion [of the two vehicles] being part of the One Vehicle."

[A more detailed breakdown of this fourth analysis] reveals two halves: the first sums up the Tathāgata's escaping the two types of [birth and] death. The second begins with "O World-honored One, [there is also the wisdom of] the arhats [and self-enlightened ones]." It explains why practitioners of the two vehicles escape only one type of [birth and] death.

5.1-3-5-4-1: The Tathāgata Escapes the Two Types of Birth and Death

The first half, which sums up the Tathāgata's escaping the two types of [birth and] death, has two elements: the first describes the Tathāgata's subjugation of the four demons and his escaping both types of [birth and] death. The second begins with "Having attained the inconceivable [Dharma body]." It takes up the myriad virtues of the Tathāgata and verifies that he has escaped from these two types of [birth and] death.

The first element begins with "[O World-honored One,] there are two types of wisdom that do not lead to rebirth." This passage offers a summary of those who can and cannot escape the two types of birth and death, and describes the wisdom that does not lead to rebirth. In this selection from the sutra, the phrase "two types" refers to the wisdom of the Tathāgata that prevents both forms of rebirth, as well as to the wisdom of the two vehicles that prevents rebirth only in limited cyclic existence.

The sutra states, ["Through the supreme control of the Tathāgata's wisdom,] he subdues the four demons." Here, the demon of the heavens represents evil conditions, while the demon of the afflictions represents evil causes. The demon of the aggregates and the demon of death together represent evil fruit. Since the Tathāgata has subdued these four demons, he has escaped the two types of [birth and] death. [Mention of the four demons is followed by the phrase,] "appears in all worlds." It refers to the two worlds of limited cyclic existence and inconceivable transformation. This passage concludes, "and is worshiped by all sentient beings." This phrase means that the Tathāgata, having subdued the four demons and transcended these two realms of [birth and] death, is worshiped by all sentient beings. It is clear, therefore, that the Tathāgata has escaped both types of [birth and] death.

The second element begins with "Having attained the inconceivable [Dharma body]." It takes up the myriad virtues of the Tathāgata and verifies that he has escaped from the two types of [birth and] death. Already possessing these exalted virtues, how could anyone think the Tathāgata incapable of escaping the two types of [birth and] death?

5.1-3-5-4-2: The Two Vehicles Escape Only One Type of Birth and Death

The second half begins with "O World-honored One, [there is also the wisdom of] the arhats [and self-enlightened ones]." This half explains why practitioners of the two vehicles escape only from one type of [birth and] death. This half also has two elements: the first element explains that even though the two vehicles have eliminated only the cause of [birth and] death in limited cyclic existence, they still believe they have passed completely beyond birth and death. The second element begins with "O World-honored One, [when the arhats and self-enlightened ones meditate]." This passage explains that [these two groups believe that] by eliminating the cause that leads to rebirth in limited cyclic existence, they have also attained the singular fruit of enlightenment. For the reasons noted above, however, they have eliminated only one type of [birth and] death.

[The first element of the second half begins with] "Crossing over the fear of birth and death." This passage refers to the arhats and self-enlightened ones overcoming their fear of limited cyclic existence. The following phrase reads, "they gradually obtain the joy of liberation [with this thought in mind]." It explains the gradual elimination of the mental disturbances of the three realms. That is, free from mental disturbances, one is naturally joyful and so can experience the joy of liberation. "With this thought [in mind]" refers to [the arhats and self-enlightened ones], who, believing themselves to be free from the fear of birth and death, think that they will not again experience the suffering of cyclic existence. But this view points only to the second type of wisdom that does not receive rebirth, meaning that practitioners of the two vehicles escape only one [type of birth and death—that is, limited cyclic existence].

The second element begins with "O World-honored One, [when arhats and self-enlightened ones meditate]." This element explains that these two groups believe that [having eliminated] the cause [of birth and death in limited cyclic existence], they have attained supreme enlightenment. The phrase "when [arhats and self-enlightened ones] meditate" refers to the time of illumination of the Four Noble Truths. One interpreter states, "'Illumination of the Four Noble Truths' means to think that one can, by individually pursuing the principles [of the Dharma], worshiping, and meditating, obtain the supreme [fruit of nirvana]."

5.1-3-6: Entering the One Vehicle

The sixth subsection begins with "O World-honored One, those who first 13b attained this stage." It explains how the fruit of enlightenment realized by practitioners of the two vehicles is part of the One Vehicle. The model text argues instead, "This passage is meant to explain the Buddha's previous appearance, it does not refer to the One Vehicle subsuming the three vehicles."

This subsection has four components: the first notes that practitioners of the two vehicles [eventually] realize during their practice that they have not yet reached the ultimate. The second begins with "Why? [Because the disciple and self-enlightened vehicles are part of the Great Vehicle.]" This component explains why practitioners of the two vehicles know [they have not yet reached the ultimate]. The third begins with "For this reason, [the three vehicles are the One Vehicle]." It explains why these other vehicles are actually part of the One Vehicle. The fourth begins with "Those who attain the One Vehicle." It explains the meaning of the fruit of enlightenment attained by practitioners of the One Vehicle.

The first component begins with the phrase "Those [who first attained this stage]." In this passage, "those" refers to members of the two vehicles and "first" refers to the preliminary practices of the "five types of skillful means." These practices are also referred to as the "three fruits" and the "four causes." The sutra continues, "and they are not deluded about the Dharma," pointing to [those practitioners] who are not confused by the principles of the eternally abiding [truth]. This sentence concludes, "nor are they dependent on others," which means that they do not rely on someone else's teachings.

The second component explains why practitioners of the two vehicles know [they have not reached the ultimate]. It is simply because, from the perspective of ultimate truth, there are no distinctions among the three vehicles. The third component begins, "For this reason, the three vehicles are the

One Vehicle." It explains why these other vehicles are actually part of the One Vehicle. The fourth component explains the meaning of the fruit [of enlightenment attained by practitioners of the One Vehicle]. As was explained above, [the teachings of the One Vehicle] that are the cause [of ultimate enlightenment] form an essential unity. Next, the special characteristics of the fruit of [that enlightenment] realized [by practitioners of the One Vehicle] is explained. This component can be divided into two halves.

The first half explains the fruit of enlightenment obtained [by practitioners of the One Vehicle], while the second half takes up and explains the essential unity of the three virtues: enlightenment, nirvana, and the Dharma body. We focus on their essential unity, [the second half,] because when sentient beings hear about enlightenment they think that the One Vehicle is concerned solely with the path to attaining it, not with attaining the two other virtues. [To highlight the importance of the virtues of nirvana and the Dharma body,] we illustrate their essential unity [with enlightenment by considering the following sutra passages].

The sutra states, "To obtain the ultimate Dharma body is to obtain the ultimate One Vehicle." This passage means that [the teachings of the One Vehicle] are the ultimate cause that leads to obtaining [the Dharma body—the ultimate fruit]. The Dharma body is [the eternally abiding] teaching, and the Tathāgata is its [ultimate] practitioner. Although [this language might seem] to suggest that the meanings of [the Dharma body and the Tathāgata] are distinct, by comparing their characteristics we can see that they form an essential unity. [That essential unity] can be understood by examining again the fruit, [that is, the Dharma body] and the cause, [that is, the One Vehicle]. That is, the Dharma body is the essence of the myriad virtues, while the One Vehicle is the direct cause of the Dharma body. And so by taking up the Dharma body in this way, we can explain how [the One Vehicle], as cause, is the ultimate.

5.2: The Essential Unity of the Three Treasures

The second main part of this chapter begins with "O World-honored One, the Tathāgata, who is not limited by time." This part takes up the essential unity of the Three Treasures, which also leads to discussion of the One Vehicle that is their single cause. Since the Three Treasures as the fruit of the teachings of the One Vehicle possess an essential unity, the cause itself must also be of such a single substance. This part has two sections. The first starts at the beginning of this section and ends with "these are limited refuges." Here, the sutra explains the essential unity of the Three Treasures that represents the ultimate teaching of the One Vehicle. That teaching is contrasted to the provisional view that takes the Three Treasures to be separate. The second section begins with "If there are sentient beings." It explains that the essential unity of the Three Treasures is the highest teaching.

5.2-1: The Provisional View of the Three Treasures

The first section begins by taking up the provisional view that considers the Three Treasures separately. It has two subsections. 1) From the beginning of the section to the passage ending with "there exists an inexhaustible refuge." This passage praises the Buddha first as one of the three separate treasures. It does so because even though this view is not ultimately true, as is the view of their essential unity, the Buddha treasure of the provisional view is identical to [the Buddha treasure of the ultimate view]. That is, the buddha of the former view cannot logically be inferior to that of the latter.

As such, when viewed as three separate bodies, the Buddha treasure is   13c
taken up first and praised as the foundation of refuge.

2) Begins with the passage "an eternally abiding refuge." This subsection explains why, among the three separate treasures, the Dharma and the Sangha are provisional. That is, the view from earlier days that took the Three Treasures as separate bodies was simply the skillful means of the Buddha. The separate bodies of the Three Treasures discussed here are true in this sense only. Even so, these distinctions of their relative truth and falsity do not compare to the ultimate teaching of the essential unity of the Three Treasures. [Since the view of these treasures as separate bodies makes such distinctions,] they are, therefore, called "provisional."

5.2-1-1: Praising the Separate Body of the Buddha Treasure

The first subsection, which praises the separate body of the Buddha, has five points: the first explains the eternally abiding refuge, the second explains great compassion, and the third encourages expounding great compassion. The fourth point encourages expounding the eternally abiding refuge, while the fifth offers a conclusion. See the sutra.

The next part of the sutra states, "At a future time," which refers to [a time very far in the future] when all sentient beings have become buddhas.

Since all sentient beings will not become buddhas, however, clearly the Tathāgata must eternally abide [to continually teach them].

5.2-1-2: The Provisional Dharma and Sangha

The second subsection explains the provisional nature of the two treasures of the separate Dharma and Sangha. This subsection has four components: the first lists [the Buddha, Dharma, and Sangha]. The second begins with "These two refuges" and explains that when [the Dharma and Sangha are viewed as separate bodies,] they are provisional refuges. The third begins with "Why? [Because the path described in the teaching of the One Vehicle leads to the ultimate Dharma body.]" It further explains why these two refuges are provisional. The fourth begins with "Therefore, [these two refuges are limited, not ultimate refuges,]" offering a conclusion to this subsection describing the provisional nature of these two refuges.

The model text states, "The passage from the beginning [of this subsection describing the essential unity of the Three Treasures] to 'the Tathāgata, Worthy, Perfectly Enlightened One' explains that the essential unity of the [Three Treasures] is the foundation for refuge." This interpretation will not be used here, however.

[As noted above, in earlier days] the Three Treasures were understood as the steps of a ladder. At that time, moreover, the teachings of the sutras were not distinguished according to those of the Great or Small Vehicles; all were part of the same "Dharma treasure." Similarly, whether those who studied the teachings were referred to as members of the Great or Small Vehicles, all were part of the same "Sangha treasure."

In this sutra, however, the superior teachings of the One Vehicle are discussed alongside those of the lesser teachings of the three vehicles. This is meant to hold up for praise only the One Vehicle with the purpose of teaching the people of the three vehicles. In earlier times, while the teachings of the Great Vehicle were already known, those of the One Vehicle had yet to be expounded. Indeed, it is only in this sutra that the One Vehicle is understood to be the Dharma treasure. Here, this teaching of the path of the One Vehicle leads to attaining the Dharma body. For those who have attained the Dharma body, there is no higher teaching of the One Vehicle. Therefore, the ultimate Dharma treasure lies only in the Dharma body. It is stated, therefore, that the One Vehicle is not the ultimate Dharma treasure.

To better understand the provisional nature of the Sangha [treasure in this view of the Three Treasures as separate bodies], see the sutra. The fourth component offers a conclusion [to this material]. Refer also to the sutra.

5.2-2: The Essential Unity of the Three Treasures as the Ultimate Teaching

Section two begins with "If there are sentient beings [who follow the discipline of the Tathāgata]." This section states that the essential unity of the Three Treasures is the highest teaching. This section has five subsections: the first explains how taking refuge in the Dharma and Sangha is the same as taking refuge in the Tathāgata. The second subsection begins with "Why? [Because the Tathāgata is not different from these two refuges.]" This passage further explains how taking refuge in the Dharma and the Sangha is the same as taking refuge in the Tathāgata. The third begins with "Why? [Because of the teaching of the path of the One Vehicle.]" This section explains why [the Buddha, Dharma, and Sangha] form a single body. The fourth validates the Buddha's teachings by quoting his sermons. And the fifth begins with the passage, "When the Tathāgata, according to the capacities [of sentient beings, teaches with skillful means]." It explains why the principles of the One Vehicle were not taught by the Buddha in earlier times.

The first subsection begins with "These two refuges," which refers to the essential unity of the Dharma and Sangha refuges. The next phrase, "are not two refuges," means that the view of these two refuges as separate bodies cannot be compared [to the view that recognizes their essential unity]. Indeed, these two passages are followed by "because they are the refuge of 14a the Tathāgata." This means that the Dharma and Sangha, as a single body, are the Tathāgata.

One interpreter argues, "When one engages in the disciplines [expounded by the Tathāgata] and arouses the mind [of enlightenment], one takes refuge in the Dharma and Sangha. This is a reference to taking refuge in the Dharma and Sangha as separate bodies. [But the passage in the sutra that states,] 'These are not two refuges' offers a negation of the Dharma and Sangha refuges as separate bodies. Indeed, the view that takes the Dharma and Sangha as separate bodies was already rejected above as a provisional teaching. Here, however, the negation of these [two refuges as separate bodies] is taken up again to offer a comparison that affirms [their essential unity]. Therefore, 'these two refuges' refers to the two refuges as an essential unity. And the passage 'taking refuge in the Tathāgata' explains this refuge from the perspective of this essential unity."

Indeed, we know that this material explains the essential unity of the Dharma and Sangha because the separate bodies [of the Three Treasures] were concluded above. The sutra continues, "To take refuge in the supreme truth [is to take refuge] in the Tathāgata." In this passage, "supreme truth" refers to the three virtues [of enlightenment, nirvana, and the Dharma body] and the four qualities [of permanence, joy, self, and purity].

The model text states, "These two phrases [that mention supreme truth and the Tathāgata] mean the Buddha treasure is supreme among [the Three Treasures] when seen as an essential unity." If this is the case, then the Buddha treasure, when viewed as a separate body, would also be supreme. But we must then ask how the Buddha treasure could be seen as supreme [among the Three Treasures] when viewed as a single body. Indeed, the sutra states in this regard, "The supreme truth of these two refuges is the ultimate refuge of the Tathāgata." This passage means that to take refuge in the essential unity of the Dharma and Sangha treasures, as well as in the three virtues and four qualities, is [to take refuge] in the ultimate refuge of the Tathāgata. The model text adds, "From 'these two refuges' concludes the discussion of the essential unity of the three refuges that are the ultimate truth."

The second subsection further explains how by taking refuge in the Dharma and Sangha, one also takes refuge in the Tathāgata; it is because these three refuges form a single body. The model text argues, "Because each of the [three refuges] represents the same ultimate truth, they are a single body." The third subsection explains how [the Buddha, Dharma, and Sangha] form a single body. They do so because each is attained through the teachings of the One Vehicle.

The fourth subsection describes the source of these arguments. That is, it quotes the Buddha's sermons as evidence for the essential unity of the Three Treasures. Naturally, each of the Three Treasures, when viewed as separate bodies, has a different substance and name, and so, logically, they can be thought of separately. This is clearly not the case, however, when they are viewed as a single body. This distinction can be understood as follows: the eternally abiding Dharma body is the Buddha treasure itself. Serving as the law for sentient beings, the Dharma body is also naturally the Dharma treasure. The Dharma body can also harmonize the principles, and so is also the Sangha treasure. Indeed, the purpose of taking refuge is to free oneself from the fetters of the world and to destroy the mental afflictions. To do so, one may first take refuge in the separate bodies of the Three Treasures. But to unerringly take refuge, one must do so through the Three Treasures as a single body. Since Śrīmālā desires only to take refuge in the fundamental [and ultimate] teachings, she rejects the view of earlier days in which the Three Treasures were seen as rungs of a ladder, seeing them instead as a single body possessing an essential unity.

The fifth subsection explains why the principles of the One Vehicle were not taught by the Buddha in earlier times. Some ask why, if these principles are as they have been explained in the sutra, the Tathāgata expounded only the teachings of the three vehicles in earlier days. It was because the Tathāgata, in accord with the capacities of sentient beings, taught these principles as skillful means. From the perspective of the true teaching, however, there is only one vehicle, not two. The model text expresses this sentiment, stating, "From 'When the Tathāgata, [according to the capacities of sentient beings, teaches with skillful means]' explains the essential unity of the Three Treasures. It also offers a conclusion to [the discussion of the three vehicles] entering the One Vehicle." Other sutras simply state that the teaching of the One Vehicle is "supreme truth," whereas the teachings of the three vehicles are "conventional truth."

Part Two of the Sutra's Main Teaching

The second part of the sutra's main teaching begins with "O World-honored One, the disciples and self-enlightened ones [first observed the Four Noble Truths with their single type of wisdom that eliminates the entrenchments]." This part includes eight chapters that explain the realm of the vehicle, addressing how the virtuous [deeds of the One Vehicle] do not arise spontaneously; rather, they arise through [understanding and putting into practice the teachings of the One Vehicle that constitute this] realm. This part also includes the key distinction between two sets of Noble Truths: the conditioned and the unconditioned. And while this is the broad meaning of these eight chapters,

14b

when we look closely at the language of the sutra itself, we see a pattern similar to the one described in the last chapter regarding the status [of the Tathāgata] as the ultimate and [the two vehicles] as provisional. In keeping to that pattern here, we will take up the realm of the One Vehicle and examine why it represents the ultimate truth. We will see also how these two types of Noble Truths serve as the basis for the cultivation of virtue, and that while the Tathāgata has mastered both types, practitioners of the two vehicles observe only one, meaning that their path is provisional.

This part has two subsections. The first four chapters offer a general explanation of this realm, while the next four offer a specific explanation of it. The general explanation takes up the conditioned and unconditioned forms of the Noble Truths, neither abbreviating nor omitting [any of the eight truths from its analysis], and describes how each is part of the realm of the One Vehicle. It is thus called the "general explanation." [But the final four chapters of this section] omit three of the truths[, of suffering, accumulation, and the path,] taking up only the unconditioned truth of the cessation of suffering as the ultimate teaching. It is thus called the "specific explanation." The general explanation of this realm includes four chapters: "Chapter [Six]: The Unlimited Noble Truths," "Chapter [Seven]: The *Tathāgatagarbha*," "Chapter [Eight]: The Dharma Body," and "Chapter [Nine]: The Concealed Truth: The Meaning of Emptiness."

The General Explanation

Chapter Six:
The Unlimited Noble Truths

"Chapter [Six]: The Unlimited Noble Truths" has five parts. The first describes the Four Conditioned Noble Truths that are realized by practitioners of the two vehicles. The second part begins with "[O World-honored One], they do not possess supramundane [wisdom]." It explains why the two vehicles do not possess supramundane wisdom. The third part begins with "O World-honored One, [supreme wisdom] is like a diamond." It discusses why the two vehicles do not possess supreme wisdom. The fourth part begins with "O World-honored One, the meaning of the term 'noble' [does not refer to all the disciples and self-enlightened ones]." It explains that practitioners of the two vehicles do not understand the noble meaning [of the Buddha's ultimate teaching]. The fifth part begins with "The Noble Truths [are not the truths understood by the disciples and self-enlightened ones]." It explains why the two vehicles do not understand these truths.

6.1: The Four Conditioned Noble Truths

The first part of this chapter reads, "[The disciples and self-enlightened ones] first observed the Noble Truths [with their singular wisdom that eliminates the entrenchments]." In this passage describing their initial observation of the Four Conditioned Noble Truths, the phrase "with their singular wisdom" refers to wisdom associated with this first set of conditioned Noble Truths, while "that eliminates the entrenchments" refers to eliminating the four entrenchments. [Indeed, the sutra refers directly to this process, stating that this is] "the wisdom that eliminates the four [entrenchments]." Since the mental disturbances can be eliminated by one possessing this wisdom, it is called the "wisdom that eliminates." Similarly, since this type of wisdom eliminates the entrenchments associated with the Four [Conditioned] Noble Truths, it is also known as the "wisdom of the four types of elimination." The sutra continues, "[Practicing] virtue and realizing [the cessation of suffering]"; this passage refers to the "unconditioned virtues." The final passage of this part reads, "[The disciples and self-enlightened ones] clearly understood the Four [Noble] Truths," which refers to the partial insight realized by these two groups into the meaning of the Four Noble Truths[, since they understand their conditioned form but not their unconditioned form].

6.2: Supramundane Wisdom

The second part of this chapter begins with "O World-honored One, [they do not possess supramundane wisdom,]" and explains why the two vehicles do not possess the highest wisdom. Indeed, the passage "They do not possess supramundane, supreme wisdom" is meant to criticize the previous belief that the diamondlike mind of the arhat was the ultimate form of wisdom, and was thus described as "supramundane," [literally, "above the world"]. Based on that belief, the fruit of the arhat's mind was called "supreme." As has been argued above, however, because the wisdom of the two vehicles is incomplete, the fruit of its practices cannot be considered the highest attainment. Here, the sutra states, "they gradually attain the four types of wisdom," suggesting that their wisdom cannot be the highest since it has

14c   not yet attained ultimate truth. The sutra adds, "they gradually attain the Four Conditioned [Noble Truths]," which means that this set of truths is not the highest because [members of the two vehicles] must still attain the Four Unconditioned Noble Truths. Since their wisdom based on the observation of phenomena is incomplete, how could it be said that they have attained supreme wisdom? The sutra continues, "The Dharma that has not been attained gradually is supramundane, supreme wisdom." This is a reference to the ultimate truth of the Buddha that explains why the two vehicles[, lacking that truth,] are not supreme. The Buddha's wisdom is the realm of absolute perfection above which there is no more advanced stage; it is thus called "the ultimate [wisdom] with nowhere left to advance."

6.3: Supreme Wisdom

The third part begins with "O World-honored One, [supreme wisdom is like a diamond.]" It explains why the supreme wisdom of the Buddha is not possessed by the two vehicles. This part has six passages that can be combined into three pairs. The first pair uses the words "is" and "is not" to describe supreme wisdom, which "is" the realm of the Buddha and "is not" the realm of the two vehicles. The second pair begins with "O World-honored One, since they lack the wisdom of the two sets of Noble Truths." It also uses "is" and "is not," but here first to explain [that supreme wisdom] "is not" [the realm of the two vehicles], and then to explain that it "is" [the realm of the Buddha]. The third pair begins with "O World-honored One, if all [these stores of afflictions] have been destroyed [by this ultimate wisdom]." This passage offers a conclusion to this analysis of the supreme wisdom that "is" [the realm of the Buddha] and "is not" [the realm of the two vehicles]. See the sutra. In this part, moreover, "diamond" is a metaphor for the Buddha's wisdom, while "they have eliminated the various entrenchments" refers to the four entrenchments.

6.4: The Meaning of "Noble"

[The fourth part,] which has two halves, begins with "O World-honored One, the meaning of [the term] 'noble.'" It explains that "noble" does not refer to [the disciples and self-enlightened ones]. The first half explains why "noble" does not refer to the two vehicles, and the second takes up the limited and partial [merits of the disciples and self-enlightened ones]. See the sutra.

6.5: The Two Vehicles Do Not Understand These Noble Truths

The fifth part, which also has two halves, begins with "The Noble Truths [are not the truths understood by the disciples and self-enlightened ones]." It explains that the two vehicles do not understand these truths. The first half explains why the two vehicles do not understand these truths, and the second explains why the Tathāgata does. The first half includes the passage beginning with "is not true," meaning their understanding of the truths of suffering and its origin is not the supreme truth. Likewise, the reference to "is not virtuous" is also meant to suggest that their understanding of the truths of cessation and the path is not the supreme truth.

The second half explains the supreme truth of the Tathāgata. See the sutra. The word "truth" means to be able to clearly discern the true meaning, and so refers to the realm of the Buddha, not to that of the two vehicles. As such, the unconditioned truths are the realm of the Buddha alone. But why is it said that even the Four Conditioned Noble Truths are not understood by [followers of] the two vehicles? It is because their understanding of these truths is not equal to the deep realization of the Tathāgata. Furthermore, even though practitioners of the two vehicles have examined the Four Conditioned Noble Truths and have eliminated the mental disturbances of the three realms, this is the skillful teaching of the Buddha. When viewed from the perspective of ultimate truth, moreover, it is only [the Buddha] and bodhisattvas above the seventh stage—that is, those who have eliminated the mental disturbances of the three realms—who fully understand the Four Conditioned Noble Truths.

Chapter Seven:
The *Tathāgatagarbha*

"Chapter [Seven]: The *Tathāgatagarbha*" is the second of the eight chapters that constitute the realm of the teaching. It begins with "The Noble Truths [offer profound meaning]," and praises the profundity of the Eight Noble Truths. Although the previous chapter described the two types of Noble Truths that are understood by the Tathāgata alone, not by practitioners of the two vehicles, the profundity of these truths was not explained. This chapter does so by examining the *tathāgatagarbha* and praising the two types of Noble Truths, which help explain the *tathāgatagarbha*. Conversely, since the *tathāgatagarbha* has already been described as profound, the Eight Noble Truths themselves must also be profound. This [relationship] also means that the two types of Noble Truths are solely of the realm of the Tathāgata, not of the two vehicles.

This chapter has five parts. The first takes up the *tathāgatagarbha* and praises the profundity of the Eight Noble Truths. The second begins with "If [one does not doubt the *tathāgatagarbha* that is hidden by] the innumerable stores [of afflictions]." It takes up the *tathāgatagarbha* and the Dharma body as means to encourage faith in the Eight Noble Truths. The third part begins with "In this way, it is difficult to know and understand [the meaning of these two types of Noble Truths]." This passage offers a general explanation of what are called the "essence" and "characteristics" of the Eight Noble Truths. The fourth begins with "In this way, the Four Unconditioned Noble Truths." This passage concludes discussion of the Four Unconditioned Noble Truths being only of the realm of the Buddha. The fifth begins with "O World-honored One, the extinction of the things [of the phenomenal world] is not the same as the elimination of suffering." This passage analyzes the [conditioned and unconditioned] forms of the Noble Truth of the cessation of suffering.

7.1: Praising the Profound Eight Noble Truths

Part One, which takes up the *tathāgatagarbha* and praises the profundity of the Eight Noble Truths, can be divided into three components. The first offers direct praise for the profundity of the Eight Noble Truths. The second component explains the reasons for this praise, and begins with "Why? [Because these truths explain the profound *tathāgatagarbha*.]" The third begins with "the realm of the *tathāgatagarbha*" and concludes the praise of these truths.

[The first component is not discussed further. The second component includes the passage,] "explain the profound *tathāgatagarbha*." And while this passage suggests that the Eight Noble Truths explain the *tathāgatagarbha*, the sutra adds, "[The *tathāgatagarbha*] explains the meaning of the Noble Truths." The latter clearly means that the Eight Noble Truths can also be explained through the lens of *tathāgatagarbha*. [The third component] includes, "Since the realm of the *tathāgatagarbha* is profound, teaching these Noble Truths is also profound." This passage describes the unconditioned truth of the cessation of suffering as the *tathāgatagarbha,* meaning that this truth must also be profound. We will see below that both types of the truth of suffering and the truth of accumulation can conceal the *tathāgatagarbha,* while [the conditioned truth of] cessation and the two types of [the truth of the] path can reveal it. Since it is difficult to explain the reasons that [the profound *tathāgatagarbha*] can be both hidden and manifest, [the Eight Noble Truths, which help to explain the *tathāgatagarbha,*] must also be profound.

7.2: Promoting Faith in the Eight Noble Truths

Part Two begins with "If [one does not doubt the *tathāgatagarbha* that is hidden by] the innumerable stores [of afflictions]." It takes up the *tathāgatagarbha* and the Dharma body as a means to encourage faith in the Eight Noble Truths. When sentient beings hear that these Noble Truths are profound and are only of the buddha realm, they immediately think the following. "If that is so, then who, besides the Tathāgata, could have faith in them? For whom did he teach these truths?"

To allay such concerns, the sutra teaches the *tathāgatagarbha* and the Dharma body as a means to encourage faith in the Eight Noble Truths. It also teaches that the unconditioned truth of the cessation of suffering is the *tathāgatagarbha,* which, when manifest, is the Dharma body. So if one can have faith in the *tathāgatagarbha* and the Dharma body, then one can also have faith in these Eight Noble Truths. In this way, the sutra promotes faith in these teachings.

When sentient beings hear that the profound teaching of the *tathāgatagarbha* is difficult to fathom, they imagine its original condition to be free from the fetters of mental disturbances—purity itself. As such, it is of a realm beyond their comprehension. To allay such concerns, the sutra offers the following explanation. When the *tathāgatagarbha* is hidden among the afflictions, then it is not free from the fetters of the mental disturbances. But if one does not doubt the principle that the *tathāgatagarbha* is hidden in this way, then one will not doubt that the *tathāgatagarbha* also manifests as the Dharma body. And if one can have faith in the principle that the *tathāgatagarbha* can be both hidden and manifest, then one can also have faith in the Eight Noble Truths. In earlier times, it was not taught that the *tathāgatagarbha* could be hidden among the mental disturbances. At that time, only the [Four] Conditioned Noble Truths were taught. But this was no more than skillful means.

In sum, this part has two halves: the first explains that to have faith in the *tathāgatagarbha* is to have faith in the Dharma body. The second begins with "To explain the *tathāgatagarbha*, [one also explains the Dharma body of the Tathāgata, the inconceivable buddha realms, and skillful means]." This means that if one can have faith in both the *tathāgatagarbha* and the Dharma body, then one will also have faith in the Eight Noble Truths. When the *tathāgatagarbha* is hidden among the afflictions, it is naturally difficult for sentient beings to have faith in it. Therefore, [the sutra] encourages developing faith in its manifest form of the Dharma body.

7.3: The Essence and Characteristics of the Eight Noble Truths

15b Part Three begins with "In this way, it is difficult to know [and understand the meaning of these two types of Noble Truths]." This passage takes up the essence and characteristics of the Eight Noble Truths. Although the two types of Noble Truths were noted above, neither the basis for their names nor their essence and characteristics were discussed in detail. We do so in the following.

This part can be divided into eight components. The first explains in general terms the two types of Noble Truths. The second begins with "What is [the meaning] of the two types of Noble Truths?" It lists the names of the two types of Noble Truths. The third explains why the conditioned and limited Noble Truths are considered together. This part corresponds to the sutra passage that states, "The Conditioned Noble Truths are the 'limited' Four Noble Truths." The fourth begins with "Why? [Because those who rely on others cannot understand all suffering.]" This passage explains why these Noble Truths are called "conditioned" and "limited."

The fifth begins with "Therefore, O World-honored One, [there is conditioned and unconditioned birth and death]." This passage addresses the two types of birth and death as well as the two types of nirvana. It also explains why there are two types of Noble Truths. The sixth, which begins with "They explain the unconditioned Noble Truths," addresses the unconditioned and unlimited types of the Noble Truths. The seventh begins with "Why? [With self-power one can know all suffering.]" It explains further why the second set of Noble Truths can be called "unconditioned" and "unlimited." The eighth begins with "In this way, [these are the Eight Noble Truths.]" It offers a general conclusion to the two types of Noble Truths.

7.3-1, 7.3-2 and 7.3-3

For a detailed [explanation] of the first three components, see the sutra.

7.3-4: The Conditioned and Limited Four Noble Truths

The fourth component explains the names of these conditioned truths in response to the question, "Why are [these truths] called 'conditioned' and 'limited'?" [The answer] can be explained [as follows]. In the sutra passage, "Those who rely on others cannot understand all suffering," the phrase "rely on others" is a reference to the two vehicles and bodhisattvas at the seventh stage. This passage means that those who rely on others cannot fully understand the Noble Truths of suffering, origination, cessation, and the path—whether inside or outside the three realms. And just as those who rely on others are called "conditioned" and "limited," so also are the truths they understand.

7.3-5: The Two Types of Birth and Death and Two Types of Nirvana

The fifth component addresses the two types of birth and death as well as the two types of nirvana. It also explains [why there are two types of Noble Truths]. This component begins with "Therefore, O World-honored One, there is conditioned and unconditioned birth and death." This passage means that because objects can be classified according to [the level of understanding of] those who observe them, they can be either "conditioned" or "unconditioned." [In just this way,] the cycle of birth and death can also be classified as "conditioned" or "unconditioned." Indeed, practitioners of the two vehicles and bodhisattvas at the seventh stage are called "conditioned people," since they understand only limited cyclic existence. On the other hand, bodhisattvas at the eighth stage and above are referred to as "unconditioned people" because they also understand the birth and death of inconceivable transformation. And so it is said that there are these two forms of birth and death: the "conditioned" and the "unconditioned."

Moreover, conditioned birth and death corresponds to the limited form of the origination of suffering and its cause, while unconditioned birth and death corresponds to the unlimited form of the origination of suffering and its cause. Bodhisattvas at the eighth stage and above understand completely the birth and death of limited cyclic existence, while those at the seventh stage and below do not yet completely understand the birth and death of inconceivable transformation. [Because of these different levels of understanding, the conditioned and unconditioned forms of birth and death] are distinguished [in the sutra].

The following passage in the sutra states, "Nirvana is also [described as 'conditioned' and 'unconditioned'—the former being nirvana] 'with remainder' and [the latter being nirvana] 'without remainder.'" Indeed, just as the objects of observation and the cycle of birth and death are named based on those [who follow the teachings], the sutra's description of nirvana follows this model; that is, it distinguishes those who experience nirvana "with remainder" and nirvana "without remainder." Practitioners of the two vehicles and bodhisattvas at the seventh stage are called "people with remainder," since they have realized nirvana with remainder. But the Tathāgata is called "the person without remainder" because he has realized nirvana without remainder. Nirvana with remainder also corresponds to the limited forms of the cessation of suffering and the path, while nirvana without remainder corresponds to the unlimited forms of the cessation of suffering and the path.

15c

7.3-6 and 7.3-7: The Unconditioned and Unlimited Four Noble Truths

The sixth component includes the passage, "The meaning of the Four Unconditioned Noble Truths is the same as that of the Four Unlimited Noble Truths." It explains the unconditioned and unlimited truths.

The seventh component begins with "Why?" It explains why the second set of Noble Truths is called "unconditioned" and "unlimited," in response to those who ask why these terms are used to refer to these truths. The answer is found in the sutra, which states, "With self-power, one can know all [suffering]." This means that bodhisattvas at the eighth stage and above who have entered the flow of the Dharma can, with each successive thought, completely understand these truths. Since [bodhisattvas at the eighth stage and above are called "unconditioned people,"] these Noble Truths are named following this pattern; that is, they are called "unconditioned" and "unlimited." And in response to those who ask how it is possible to understand completely the unconditioned truth of the cessation of suffering, it is said to be only through reverent faith in the Buddha, not through direct knowledge of the phenomenal world.

7.3-8: Conclusion to the Two Types of Four Noble Truths

The eighth component begins with "In this way, [these are the Eight Noble Truths]." It offers a general conclusion [to the two types of Noble Truths]. The sutra states, "These are the Eight Noble Truths. The Tathāgata taught the Four [Conditioned Noble] Truths." This passage means that in earlier days, the Tathāgata had taught the Four Conditioned Noble Truths for the benefit of practitioners of the two vehicles and bodhisattvas at the seventh stage. One interpreter states, "Although the Tathāgata taught these eight truths for those inside and outside the three realms, he simply combined them into [a single set of] four truths."

These two types of Noble Truths are described with ten different names. The Noble Truths inside the three realms are "created," "limited," "bounded," "conditioned," and "with remainder," while those outside the three realms are "uncreated," "unlimited," "unbounded," "unconditioned," and "without remainder." And while these ten names are meant to describe the fundamental nature of these truths, they can also be applied to the practitioners being discussed in the sutra. That is, members of the two vehicles and bodhisattvas at the seventh stage are said to experience the "five conditioned" qualities [that are created, limited, bounded, conditioned, and with remainder], while bodhisattvas at the eighth stage and above are said to experience the "five unconditioned" qualities [that are uncreated, unlimited, unbounded, unconditioned, and without remainder].

The former groups are said to experience the five conditioned qualities because they have not yet exhausted all causes, and so still have actions to perform outside the three realms. But bodhisattvas of the eighth stage and above are said to experience the five unconditioned qualities because they have exhausted all such causes through their practice, and so have no actions left to perform. One can also understand these descriptions in this way. Although bodhisattvas of the eighth stage and above fully understand phenomena inside the three realms, bodhisattvas at the seventh stage do not fully understand phenomena outside the three realms. [Indeed, these different levels of understanding] are the basis for distinguishing [the two groups according to the five conditioned and unconditioned qualities].

These [two sets of Noble Truths] can also be understood as follows. In the former set, the two truths of origination and the path are causes in the three realms: [that is, origination is the cause] of suffering and [the path is the cause] for eliminating suffering. Likewise, we can also say that the two truths of suffering and its elimination arise [based on the cause of the two truths of origination and the path]. Therefore, [the former set of Noble Truths is called] "conditioned." Since this set is not the ultimate source of enlightenment, moreover, it is referred to as being "with remainder," "bounded," and "limited." And because the nature of this set's three truths of suffering, origination, and the path is to naturally arise and cease, each of these truths can also be called "conditioned." But the truth of eliminating suffering is a cause for such conditioned activities, and so is called "that which causes conditioned [phenomena]."

Although the two truths of origination and the path outside the three realms are also conditioned, their functioning is fainter and so is unlike those inside the three realms. For this reason, they can be called "unconditioned." This distinction can also be explained as follows. [Outside the three realms,] because a previous thought becomes the cause for the succeeding thought, which is its fruit, each successive thought is new and changing. It is, therefore, difficult to identify the conditioned marks within this process. Since the two truths of suffering and its elimination arise from the unconditioned causes [of the two truths of origination and the path], they can also be called "unconditioned."

16a The model text states instead, "Because the two truths of suffering and its cessation themselves are incapable of creating fruit, they are called 'unconditioned.'" If that is the case, however, the two truths of suffering and its cessation inside the three realms should also be unconditioned. I have thus not used the model text's interpretation.

Since the principles of these four [unconditioned] truths are exhaustive and are the ultimate source, they are described as being "unlimited," "without remainder," and "unbounded." But it is only the one truth of cessation that is not subject to rising and ceasing. For this reason, it is called "unconditioned." The three other truths are thus called "unconditioned" based only on their relation to this truth of the cessation of suffering.

7.4: The Eight Noble Truths as the Ultimate

Part Four begins with "In this way, the Four Unconditioned Noble Truths." This passage concludes discussion of the Eight Noble Truths as the ultimate, since they are understood by the Buddha alone. As the name and essence of the Eight Noble Truths have already been explained, we take up now the Tathāgata as the one who has mastered these ultimate principles.

This section has four aspects. The first states that the Buddha alone has mastered these ultimate principles. The second begins with "[The activities] of the arhats [and self-enlightened ones are not ultimate]," and naturally means that the activities of the two vehicles are provisional. The third begins with "Why? [Since the elements of existence are not ultimately of inferior, middling, or superior quality, nirvana is attained.]" This passage further details why the activities of the two vehicles are provisional. The fourth begins with "Why? [Because the Tathāgata.]" This passage explains why the activities of the Buddha alone are ultimate.

[The first and second aspects are not discussed further. The third aspect] includes the passage, "not of inferior, middling, or superior quality." In this passage, "inferior" refers to the disciples, "middling" to the self-enlightened ones, and "superior" to bodhisattvas at the seventh stage. This passage explains that these three types of practitioners have not yet attained ultimate nirvana. One interpreter argues that "superior" refers instead to the Buddha, but agrees that none of these three types of practitioners has attained ultimate nirvana and states that the Buddha alone has done so.

Some ask why the Buddha alone possesses ultimate wisdom. [The fourth aspect answers this question by addressing the sutra, which states that the Tathāgata] "knows all future suffering [and has eliminated all the afflictions and the active afflictions]." Although the Buddha knows the future suffering of all sentient beings and has passed beyond suffering, practitioners of the two vehicles, who do not yet know future suffering, have not. Therefore, they do not possess ultimate wisdom. In the phrase quoted above, "has eliminated all the afflictions" refers to the fundamental afflictions, while "[eliminated] the active afflictions" refers to the secondary afflictions.

The word "accumulation" refers to the afflictions one experiences from past karma, and so is called "receiving the accumulation" of [karmic seeds from both the fundamental and secondary afflictions]. "Destroying all the elemental aggregates of the mind-made bodies, [the Tathāgata] has realized the elimination of all suffering": this passage refers to the truth of the cessation of suffering, which exists inside and outside the three realms. The passage uses the word "all" [to refer both to the elemental aggregates that constitute the phenomenal world and the suffering one experiences in that world], although it does not explain the path [to eliminate that suffering].

One interpreter argues [that in the phrase, "receiving the accumulation"], "'receiving' refers to untainted karma associated with the afflictions, while 'accumulation' refers to the collection of all one's previous karmic afflictions. 'Destroying all the elemental aggregates of the mind-made bodies' refers to the truth of the cessation of suffering, while '[the Tathāgata] has realized the elimination of all suffering' likely refers to the truth of the path." Another observer argues that "accumulation" refers to the four entrenchments.

7.5: The Two Types of Cessation of Suffering

The chapter's fifth part begins, "O World-honored One, [the extinction of the things of the phenomenal world is not the same as the elimination of suffering]." It analyzes the two types of the cessation of suffering. While each of the other six truths differs based on characteristics that are either deep or shallow, all six are related to the elements of existence. Therefore, these six truths can, in principle, be distinguished from each other [based on whether they are conditioned or unconditioned]. It is difficult to do so, however, with the two forms of the truth of the cessation of suffering. We do so here, however, by noting that in earlier days the cessation of suffering was simply a negation, while today it is taken to be absolute reality itself. Therefore, although both truths are referred to with the term "cessation," they are distinct.

This part has two components. The first explains why the Buddha's teaching of the cessation of suffering in earlier times was not ultimate truth. The second component begins with "The elimination of suffering." This passage explains why the [unconditioned truth] of the cessation of suffering is absolute reality.

16b The first component begins with the phrase, "the extinction of the things [of the phenomenal world] is not," which refers to cutting off the afflictions. It means that the elimination of the afflictions as understood in earlier times is not the true cessation of suffering.

The second component begins with "The elimination of suffering described here is beginningless, uncreated, and non-arising," explaining that which is uncreated. Indeed, the following passage reads, "it is also limitless,

inexhaustible, and eternally abiding," which explains that which is indestructible and so is not of the three times. The final passage reads, "Intrinsically pure and distinct from all the stores of afflictions": rather than the inten-
tional destruction of the afflictions, this passage means that practitioners are
naturally freed from them. Finally, the word "beginningless" can be interpreted in two ways. The first interpretation states that the truth of the cessation of suffering is primordially existent, and so is said to be "beginningless."
The second argues from the perspective of the fruit of the cessation of suffering. Since that fruit is not of the three times, it is called "beginningless."

Chapter Eight:
The Dharma Body

"Chapter Eight: The Dharma Body" is the third of the eight chapters that
constitute the realm of the teaching. It begins with "O World-honored One,
greater than the sands of the Ganges River." The central message of this
chapter is that sentient beings, having heard the teachings on the *tathāgatagarbha* described in Chapter [Seven], are encouraged to have faith in the
Eight Noble Truths.[11]

It was stated above that if sentient beings developed faith in the *tathāgatagarbha,* then they would also develop faith in the Dharma body. And
by developing faith in both they could then develop faith in the Eight Noble
Truths. So even though the *tathāgatagarbha* and the Dharma body are seem-
ingly distinct, the sutra states that with faith in the *tathāgatagarbha* one can
have faith in the Dharma body. But if they are a single body, then why are
they taken up separately? This question can be answered here by distinguishing between the conditions in which the truth is concealed by the afflictions as the *tathāgatagarbha* from the conditions in which it is manifest as
the Dharma body. And while the conditions of being hidden and manifest
may appear to be distinct, the sutra argues that they are, in fact, an essential unity.

This chapter has three parts: the first explains that the *tathāgatagarbha*
and the Dharma body form just such an essential unity. The second addresses
the wisdom by which one proves this essential unity. And the third explains
that the *tathāgatagarbha* is not of the realm of the two vehicles.

8.1: The Essential Unity of the *Tathāgatagarbha* and the Dharma Body

Part One includes the sutra passage, ["O World-honored One,] the Dharma body of the Tathāgata is not separate from, free from, nor different from the inconceivable teachings of the Buddha that are more numerous than the sands of the Ganges River." This passage explains why the *tathāgatagarbha* is the Dharma body. Here, the phrase "more numerous than the sands of the Ganges River" means that the afflictions experienced by sentient beings surpass the number of grains of sand in the Ganges River. The following passage states, ["O World-honored One,] in this way, the Dharma body of the Tathāgata is called '*tathāgatagarbha*' when it is not separate from the stores of afflictions." These passages address the essential unity of the Dharma body and the *tathāgatagarbha*.

8.2: The Wisdom of the *Tathāgatagarbha*

Part Two includes, "[O World-honored One,] the wisdom of the *tathāgatagarbha* is the Tathāgata's emptiness wisdom." This passage takes up the wisdom by which one proves the essential unity of the *tathāgatagarbha* and the Dharma body. This part demonstrates why, even though there is but one essential form of wisdom, it is active in two realms. That is, the *tathāgatagarbha* is not empty since it is not free from the afflictions, while the Dharma body is empty since it is already free from them. Therefore, wisdom associated with the *tathāgatagarbha* is "the wisdom of the *tathāgatagarbha*," while that associated with the Dharma body is the "Tathāgata's emptiness wisdom." But both types of wisdom are, ultimately, a single body of wisdom. That is, wisdom is one. If that is the case, how then could the *tathāgatagarbha* and Dharma body that are illuminated by this singular wisdom be essentially different?

8.3: The *Tathāgatagarbha* Is Not of the Realm of the Two Vehicles

Part Three explains that the realm of the *tathāgatagarbha* is not of the realm of the two vehicles. This is because the principles of the *tathāgatagarbha* are deep, mysterious, and subtle, surpassing the discriminating knowledge of the two vehicles. Since these principles were not taught in earlier times, practitioners of the two vehicles neither saw them nor mastered them.

The model text states, "The chapters on the *tathāgatagarbha* and the Dharma body should not be separated [as has been the tradition]. That is, [the latter chapter] should be viewed as a supplement [to the former], not as a separate [chapter]." Another interpreter states, "[The passage beginning with] 'more numerous than the sands of the Ganges River' is the beginning of 'Chapter Nine: The Concealed Truth: The Meaning of Emptiness.' It is here that the realm of ultimate truth is explained. In earlier times, however, the meaning of emptiness was concealed and so [the *tathāgatagarbha*] had not yet appeared." 16c

Chapter Nine: The Concealed Truth: The Meaning of Emptiness

"Chapter [Nine]: The Concealed Truth: The Meaning of Emptiness" is the fourth of the eight chapters [that constitute the realm of the teaching]. It begins "O World-honored One, there are two types of emptiness wisdom associated with the *tathāgatagarbha*." The central teaching of this chapter should be understood in the context of the last chapter, which stated that when the truth is concealed by the afflictions it is known as the *tathāgatagarbha,* but when manifest it is the Dharma body. Even so, they are a single body, as is the wisdom that illuminates the truth. But when sentient beings hear this, they become dubious, asking why, if these principles have always been true, the Buddha did not explain them in earlier times. And if no one had attained this wisdom in those times, why is it that it has only now become possible for beings to master it? It is because while this wisdom that illuminates ultimate truth has existed primordially, it was not the proper time to teach it before. Rather, at that time the teachings focused on suffering, emptiness, impermanence, and so forth, and so these teachings regarding ultimate truth remained concealed.

This chapter has two parts: the first explains why this form of wisdom [regarding ultimate truth] is primordially existent. The second begins with "[O World-honored One,] these two types of wisdom regarding emptiness." This part explains why it had not been the proper time to teach these principles in earlier days.

9.1: The Two Types of Emptiness Wisdom

The first part, which explains that this wisdom is primordially existent, has three components: the first describes the existence of this wisdom, while the second addresses the three phrases that begin with "when"[; that is, "when it is separate, when it is free, and when it is different"]. This passage explains the existence of wisdom in relation to the realm of emptiness. The third component takes up the four types of non-emptiness, which explain the existence of the wisdom of the realm of non-emptiness.

The first component begins with the declaration noted above: ["O World-honored One,] there are two types of emptiness wisdom associated with the *tathāgatagarbha.*" In this passage, ["two types of emptiness wisdom"] refers to the wisdom of the *tathāgatagarbha* and wisdom of the Dharma body, even though it would have been sufficient to simply state that there are two types of wisdom regarding the *tathāgatagarbha* without mentioning emptiness wisdom. Here, the sutra refers to "emptiness wisdom" because this realm has both an empty aspect[, as the Dharma body,] and a non-empty aspect[, as the *tathāgatagarbha,*] but the wisdom itself is of a single type: that is, emptiness wisdom. Therefore, it is called "emptiness wisdom that addresses existence."

9.2: The Improper Time to Teach These Truths

The second part begins with "[O World-honored One,] these two types of wisdom regarding emptiness." It explains that the Buddha did not teach these principles in earlier times because it was not the proper time. This part has three points. The first criticizes [followers of] the two vehicles for ignorantly believing that in earlier days it was the proper time to expound the teachings of the *tathāgatagarbha.* Since they were incapable of understanding its principles[, it was not the proper time]. The second point further explains why it was not the proper time for the Buddha to do so. The third begins with "the extinction of all suffering," and explains that the Buddha alone realizes [emptiness wisdom].

[The first point] begins with ["O World-honored One,] the many great disciples can have faith in the Tathāgata in relation to these two types of emptiness wisdom." This passage notes that even when these two types of wisdom are taken as a provisional teaching, the ignorance of [those of] the two vehicles prevents them from being able to hear [and comprehend] them. One observer says, "'The many great disciples' refers to bodhisattvas in the 'pure stages'[; that is, the first through the seventh stages]." This point includes the passage, ["All arhats and self-enlightened ones] also move within the realm of the four distorted views." This passage can be interpreted according to the traditional interpretation.

The second point begins with "Therefore, [all the arhats and self-enlightened ones do not originally see nor attain the elimination of all suffering]." For the reasons stated above, the Buddha did not expound [the two types of emptiness wisdom] before this time. Therefore, in earlier days, practitioners of the two vehicles neither saw nor heard of them.

The third point begins with "The extinction of all suffering [is realized only by the Buddha]." This point explains why only the Buddha realizes [the two types of emptiness wisdom], although the meaning of this language in the sutra is difficult to understand. Even so, it likely means that the Tathāgata does not have the four distorted views. The sutra adds, "By practicing the path, he eliminates all suffering," which means the Buddha, having mastered the path, no longer needs to practice.

The Specific Explanation

The next four chapters of the main teaching represent the second subsection, which offers a specific explanation of the [Eight Noble Truths that constitute the] realm of the vehicle. This subsection begins with "O World-honored One, among these Four Noble Truths [three are impermanent and one is permanent]." And while each of the last four chapters addressed the realm of the One Vehicle, they simply stated that it was not part of the two vehicles. They did not explain that it is the ultimate refuge. The next four chapters show that the ultimate refuge lies in the one truth of the cessation of suffering, one of the Four Unconditioned Noble Truths, not in the other seven truths. This subsection is thus called a "separate explanation" of this realm. The four chapters that make up this subsection are "Chapter [Ten]: The One Noble Truth," "Chapter [Eleven]: The One Refuge," "Chapter [Twelve]: The Distorted Truths,"[12] and "Chapter [Thirteen]: Original Purity."

17a

Chapter Ten:
The One Noble Truth

"[Chapter Ten:] The One Noble Truth" describes the ultimate refuge by separating the cessation of suffering from the three other conditioned and unconditioned Noble Truths, suggesting that only the cessation of suffering is the ultimate refuge. This chapter has three parts. The first explains why, among the Eight Noble Truths, the cessation of suffering alone is ultimate. The second begins with "The Noble Truth of the cessation of suffering [is inconceivable,] surpassing [the conditions of the conscious minds] of all sentient beings." It praises the profundity of the unconditioned Noble Truth of the cessation of suffering. The third begins with "If there are sentient beings [who have faith in the Buddha's words]." It promotes faith in the One Noble Truth of the cessation of suffering.

10.1: The Truth of the Cessation of Suffering Alone Is Ultimate

The first part analyzes [the Eight Noble Truths] and has two halves. The first establishes two principles [of impermanence and permanence].

The first half begins with ["O World-honored One, among the Four Noble Truths,] three are impermanent and one is permanent." In this passage, "three are impermanent" refers to [the conditioned and unconditioned forms] of suffering, origination, and the path. "One is permanent" refers to the unconditioned Noble Truth of the cessation of suffering. Since the conditioned Noble Truth of the cessation of suffering is described as transcending [the constant flux of the phenomenal world], it cannot be automatically eliminated [as being a permanent refuge]. But it refers simply to the elimination of conditioned suffering, and so functions as the negation [of a previous condition]. It is not, therefore, used [to explain the ultimate refuge], nor is it considered to be [permanent like the unconditioned cessation of suffering].

The conditioned and unconditioned types of nirvana were explained in the last chapter, where it was stated that practitioners of the two vehicles and bodhisattvas at the seventh stage are called "people with remainder." Thus, the enlightenment experienced by this group is called "nirvana with remainder," which is associated with the limited forms of the cessation of suffering and the path. In contrast, the Tathāgata is called "the person without remainder." The enlightenment experienced by him is thus called "nirvana without remainder," which is associated with the unlimited forms of the cessation of suffering and the path. In this chapter, however, the truth of the path is excluded from discussion and only the truth of cessation is addressed. Why are these truths treated differently in these two chapters? It is because there are two paths: the path of the cause and the path of the fruit. The path of the fruit was taken up in the last chapter, where it was stated that nirvana without remainder refers to the unlimited forms of the cessation of suffering and the path. Since this chapter is meant to explain the path of the cause, however, the truth of the path is excluded from the discussion and the truth of the cessation of suffering alone is taken up as ultimate truth.

The second half of this first part begins with "Why? [Because three of the Four Noble Truths are conditioned.]" It explains the two principles of impermanence and permanence. The explanation of impermanence has two sections: an interpretation and a conclusion. Likewise, the explanation of permanence has an interpretation and a conclusion. That conclusion begins with "Therefore, [the truths of suffering, origination, and the path are not supreme truth because they are neither permanent nor a refuge]." See the sutra.

10.2: Praising the Profound Truth of Cessation

The second part of this chapter begins with "The [Noble] Truth of the cessation of suffering [is inconceivable, surpassing the conditions of the conscious minds of all sentient beings]." It praises the profundity of the unconditioned Noble Truth of the cessation of suffering. This part has three components: The first explains why ordinary people and practitioners of the two vehicles do not pursue [the truth of the cessation of suffering]. The second component begins with "the consciousness of the ordinary person." It explains that while both groups do not see [the unconditioned truth of the cessation of suffering], the reasons for their inability to do so differ. The third begins with "extreme views," and interprets broadly the two commonly held views of ordinary people and the purity of the two vehicles' [wisdom].

The first component begins by describing those who are born blind and   17b
cannot see the many colors and forms of the world. This is a metaphor for ordinary people [who cannot see ultimate truth]. A seven-day-old baby can see myriad things [in her immediate environment] but cannot see the great sun [that is the source of light]. This is a metaphor for the two vehicles [that also cannot see ultimate truth].

The second component [explains the different reasons that ordinary people and practitioners of the two vehicles do not see the unconditioned truth of the cessation of suffering]. See the sutra.

The third component broadly interprets [the commonly held views of ordinary people and the wisdom of the two vehicles]. It has two halves. The first takes up the consciousness of ordinary people, while the second explains the wisdom of practitioners of the two vehicles.

The consciousness of ordinary people also has two halves: the first interprets the two distorted views, while the second explains the basis for their cognitive distortion. The first half, the interpretation of these two distorted views, has five points. The first point addresses the two views and begins with "The delusion of the existence of a substantial self [held by ordinary people]." This phrase points to the two false conceptions of a self: the first takes the self to be the mind and body, while the second takes the self to be separate from the mind and body. The former produces the view of annihilation while the latter produces the view of permanence. Indeed, the second point states that these two views "are referred to as 'nihilism' and 'eternalism.'" The third point begins with "Viewing conditioned phenomena as impermanent [is the incorrect view called 'nihilism']": this passage describes these two views in relation to cyclic existence and nirvana. That is, [the former view of nihilism] sees death within cyclic existence to be the complete extinction of the spirit, while [the latter view of eternalism] believes that there is an [eternal and unchanging] nirvana.

The fourth point begins with "In the sense faculties of the body": this passage explains these two views in relation to the material and mental. The former refers to the destruction of the physical body and leads to nihilism, while the latter sees the mind itself to be unceasing and leads to eternalism. The fifth point begins with "The deluded views [regarding these principles are mistaken and inadequate]" and explains that both views are contrary to the middle path. "These principles" refers to the middle path, while "mistaken" and "inadequate" describe the commonalities between the two distorted views. From "Sentient beings [who hold] these distorted views" further explains these distorted views. See the sutra.

The second half of the third component begins with "All the arhats [and self-enlightened ones]." It interprets the wisdom of the two vehicles. See again the sutra.

10.3: Promoting Faith in the Truth of the Cessation of Suffering
The chapter's third part begins with "If there are sentient beings [who have faith in the Buddha's words]." This section promotes faith in the One Noble

Truth of the cessation of suffering. It has three components. The first explains that following the words of the Buddha is the correct view. The second component begins with "Why? [The Tathāgata's Dharma body is the perfection of permanence.]" This passage explains why the four views [of permanence, joy, self, and purity] are the correct view. The third component begins with "[Those who view] the Buddha's Dharma body [in this way]." It concludes the promotion [of faith in the One Noble Truth of the cessation of suffering].

[The first component is not discussed. The second component] takes up perfection as both cause and fruit, although this section of the sutra focuses on the fruit of enlightenment. The relevant sutra passage [for the second and third components] reads, ["Those with the correct view are the true children of the Buddha. They emerge from the Buddha's words, from the true Dharma, and from teaching the Dharma. They attain the remaining Dharma riches.]" Indeed, the third component begins with "emerge [from the Buddha's] words," and refers to that which arises from the Buddha's teaching. "[Emerge] from the true Dharma" refers to that which arises from the principles of the true Dharma. "[Emerge] from teaching the Dharma" refers to relying on the principles of the teaching to lead ordinary people [and practitioners of the two vehicles] to sagehood. "[They attain] the remaining [Dharma] riches" refers to the seven Dharma riches [of faith, morality, shame, humility, mindfulness, renunciation, and wisdom]. And while the Buddha has already attained these riches, ordinary people and members of the two vehicles will attain them in the future if they follow his teachings. They are thus called the "remaining [Dharma] riches."

Chapter Eleven:
The One Refuge

The second of the four chapters that offer a separate explanation of this realm is "Chapter [Eleven]: The One Refuge." It begins with "O World-honored One, pure wisdom [is the perfection of wisdom attained by all the arhats and self-enlightened ones]." It explains that the one truth of the cessation of suffering is the ultimate refuge for sentient beings.

This chapter has four parts. Part One explains why the truth of the cessation of suffering alone is the ultimate refuge and states clearly that the wisdom of the two vehicles is not of this realm. Part Two elaborates on part

One, while Part Three begins with "[The World-honored One taught these four kinds of reliance] for them." It explains that the four kinds of reliance as taught in earlier days did not represent ultimate truth. Part Four begins with "O World-honored One, this one refuge [is the highest refuge,]" and explains why the one refuge described in this chapter is the ultimate refuge.

11.1: The Wisdom of the Four Kinds of Reliance

17c   Part One begins with "Even so, the wisdom of the four kinds of reliance." This passage refers to the wisdom that arises from engaging in the five preparatory practices that rely on the Four [Conditioned] Noble Truths. One interpreter states, "This means that to those whom [the Buddha] taught the five preparatory practices, he also taught the path of the four kinds of reliance. It is thus called 'the wisdom of the four kinds of reliance.'"

11.2: The Provisional Nature of the Wisdom of the Two Vehicles

Part Two elaborates Part One, explaining why [the wisdom of the two vehicles is not of the realm of the unconditioned truth of the cessation of suffering]. It does so to answer doubts [about why the two vehicles are excluded in this way]. Practitioners of the three vehicles do not understand this truth simply because they are at an earlier stage of practice. And while the goal of this practice is to understand the unconditioned truth of the cessation of suffering, they have not yet reached this goal.

One interpreter expresses [and then answers such doubts as follows]: "Does this not [contradict the material discussed] above in 'Chapter [Five]: The One Vehicle'? It was stated there that at the early stage [of practice] the three vehicles were not deluded about the Dharma[, while here it describes them to be incapable of understanding the realm of the unconditioned truth of the cessation of suffering]. But this passage stating that they were 'not deluded about the Dharma' means that they still must realize [ultimate enlightenment]. It clearly does not mean that they had already done so."

11.3: Criticizing the Refuge of Earlier Times

Part Three explains that the Four Noble Truths taught by the Buddha in earlier times differ from the ultimate refuge described here. The sutra states, "The World-honored One taught these four kinds of reliance for them," meaning that in the past the Buddha had explained the Four Conditioned Noble

Truths for the two vehicles. But the passage reading ["O World-honored One,] these four kinds of reliance are the Dharma of the world" means they are not ultimate.

11.4: The Refuge of the One Vehicle Is Ultimate

Part Four explains that the one refuge of the unconditioned cessation of suffering is the ultimate refuge. Indeed, the sutra states, ["O World-honored One, this one refuge] is the highest refuge." This offers a clear statement that the cessation of suffering is the highest of the Eight Noble Truths found inside and outside the three realms. The following passage states, ["The cessation of suffering] is the supramundane, supreme [refuge]": this means that among the Four Unconditioned Noble Truths, the cessation of suffering alone is ultimate truth. Indeed, the following line reads, "[The one refuge is] the supreme refuge found in the truth of the cessation of suffering," reinforcing the chapter's central message [that this truth alone is ultimate]. One interpreter argues, however, "'[The one refuge] is the highest refuge' means that the unconditioned truth of the cessation of suffering is the highest only in relation to the Four Conditioned Noble Truths."

Chapter Twelve:
The Distorted Truths

The third of the four chapters that offers a separate explanation of this realm is "Chapter [Twelve]: The Distorted Truths." It begins with "O World-honored One, birth and death." This chapter elaborates the teachings of the previous chapter on the one refuge, which argued that the unconditioned truth of the cessation of suffering is supramundane, supreme truth; that is, it is the highest, ultimate refuge. In that chapter it was noted that when sentient beings hear this teaching, they think [that the unconditioned truth of the cessation of suffering] serves as a refuge only for those who have escaped the mental disturbances, but not for those, like themselves, who still experience those disturbances. This is not the case, however, because the unconditioned truth of the cessation of suffering is the *tathāgatagarbha*. As such, the spiritual nature of those experiencing cyclic existence is not extinguished through birth and death; rather, it continues in dependence on the *tathāgatagarbha*. Therefore, it can serve as a refuge not only for those free from mental disturbances but also for those who still experience them.

This chapter has eight parts. The first explains how the cycle of birth and death depends on the *tathāgatagarbha*. The second part describes the principle of the *tathāgatagarbha* taught in the sutra to be "well expounded." The third addresses the passage stating, "In the cycle of birth and death— the birth and death [of sentient beings—there is the extinction of the senses]." This means that both birth and death are part of the *tathāgatagarbha*. The fourth takes up from "The conventional expression [for these phenomena is birth and death]." This passage describes the difference between cyclic existence and the *tathāgatagarbha,* while the fifth part explains why the cycle of birth and death depends on the *tathāgatagarbha,* addressing the passage that begins with, "In this way, [the *tathāgatagarbha* is the foundation, basis, and ground]."

The sixth part begins with "O World-honored One, [the *tathāgatagarbha*] is not separate from, [cut off from,] liberated from, [or different from the inconceivable Buddha-Dharma]." This passage explains that the existence of sentient beings depends on the *tathāgatagarbha*. Indeed, if there were no principle of the *tathāgatagarbha,* sentient beings would not tire of suffering and so would not seek liberation. The seventh begins with "O World-honored One, the *tathāgatagarbha* [has no past time]"; it explains why the *tathāgatagarbha* is not the Dharma of the three times. The eighth part begins with "[O World-honored One,] the *tathāgatagarbha* [is not a self, a sentient being, destiny, nor a person]." It explains how the *tathāgatagarbha* differs from sentient beings' mistaken conceptions about it.

12.1: Birth and Death Depend on the *Tathāgatagarbha*

Part One begins with "O World-honored One, birth and death depend on the *tathāgatagarbha* [because the *tathāgatagarbha* is the unknowable original reality]." [The first part of this passage] highlights mistaken views about birth and death, while [the second] means that the *tathāgatagarbha* is ultimate truth; that is, all sentient beings possess its true nature. If they did not, then the teachings of the Tathāgata would die out in just a single generation, since sentient beings would be no different from the grasses and trees[, incapable of receiving these teachings]. Since they possess this nature, however, the teachings are not cut off, and these beings will eventually attain great illumination. It is said, therefore, that "birth and death depend on the *tathāgatagarbha*."

If the *tathāgatagarbha* described here is the [ultimate] principle that is the direct cause [of enlightenment], then the principle itself is the *tathāgatagarbha*. And if it is the direct cause [that leads sentient beings] to become enlightened to their true nature, then the fruit they realize is also the *tathāgatagarbha*. Here, the sutra states, "the original condition cannot be known," which does not mean that the cycle of birth and death has neither beginning nor end; it simply means, rather, that the original condition of the *tathāgatagarbha* itself is unknowable. This is because the principle of the *tathāgatagarbha* is not of the three times, serving instead as the basis of the cycle of birth and death. Therefore, the time of its origin cannot be determined. A similar interpretation states, "Indeed, it is not the case that birth and death have neither beginning nor end. Rather, ['the original condition cannot be known'] simply means that determining the beginning and end is difficult. Moreover, 'the original condition' refers directly to the source of [cyclic existence for] sentient beings."

12.2: The Principle of the *Tathāgatagarbha* That Is "Well Expounded"

Part Two describes the principle [of the *tathāgatagarbha* taught in the sutra] to be "well expounded." See the sutra.

12.3: Birth and Death Are Part of the *Tathāgatagarbha*

Part Three begins with "In the cycle of birth and death—the birth and death [of sentient beings—there is the extinction of the senses]." This section explains how both birth and death are part of the *tathāgatagarbha*. This part has two halves: the first half interprets the meaning of birth and death, and the second explains how both birth and death are part of the *tathāgatagarbha*.

The first half addresses the phrase "birth and death," which appears twice in the passage noted above. It is repeated in order to explain the meaning of birth and death separately; that is, the former pair refers to birth, while the latter refers to death. One interpreter states, "[The former pair] refers to a previous [reference in the sutra to birth and death], while the latter refers to a subsequent reference." In the passage describing "the extinction of the senses," "extinction" refers to the loss of the sense faculties' abilities to perceive their corresponding objects[—for example, the tongue and its experience of taste]. This passage ends with "and subsequently the sense faculties do not arise," which refers to the loss of the use of [the six] sense organs relative to their corresponding objects.

The second half of this part explains how the *tathāgatagarbha* is concealed [by cyclic existence]. Even so, the *tathāgatagarbha* itself has no desire to be concealed; rather, it simply becomes hidden through the cycle of birth and death.

12.4: Comparing Birth and Death to the *Tathāgatagarbha*

Part Four begins, "The conventional expression [for these phenomena is birth and death]." This passage describes the difference between cyclic existence and the *tathāgatagarbha.* That is, when the *tathāgatagarbha* is hidden within the cycle of birth and death, then it [cannot be distinguished from cyclic existence] because they form a unified body. Therefore, to show the difference between cyclic existence and the *tathāgatagarbha,* the meaning of birth and death was explained first, and the meaning of the *tathāgatagarbha* was explained next.

12.5: Birth and Death Depend on the *Tathāgatagarbha*

Part Five of this chapter begins with "In this way[, the *tathāgatagarbha* is the foundation, basis, and ground]." This passage offers a conclusion to why the cycle of birth and death depends on the *tathāgatagarbha.*

12.6: The *Tathāgatagarbha* as the Foundation for Sentient Beings

Part Six begins, "[O World-honored One, the *tathāgatagarbha* that is not empty] is not separate from, cut off from[, liberated from, nor different from the inconceivable Buddha-Dharma]." This part explains that sentient beings depend on the *tathāgatagarbha* as the foundation [for seeking enlightenment]. Indeed, if there were no *tathāgatagarbha,* sentient beings would not tire of suffering and so would not seek liberation.

This part has three points. The first explains how sentient beings, who depend on the *tathāgatagarbha,* become established on the path to liberation. The second begins with ["O World-honored One,] if there were no [*tathāgatagarbha*]." It explains that without the *tathāgatagarbha,* sentient beings would have no foundation for the path to liberation. The third begins with "Why? [Because the six forms of consciousness and the wisdom associated with mental phenomena.]" It explains why sentient beings, with no such foundation, fail to become established on this path to liberation. Indeed, the

18b

four negations noted above mean that sentient beings have not yet been freed from the mental disturbances. One interpreter says, "The body of the *tathā-gatagarbha* is truth itself, and so [too is the subject that is described as being] not separate from, cut off from[, and so forth]. That is, [the *tathāgatagarbha*] is truth itself."

12.7: The *Tathāgatagarbha* Is Not the Dharma of the Three Times

The seventh part of this chapter begins with "O World-honored One, the *tathāgatagarbha* [has no past time]." It explains why the *tathāgatagarbha* is not the Dharma of the three times. "[The *tathāgatagarbha* has] no past time" actually points to the future, while "[the *tathāgatagarbha*] is non-arising" refers to the present. Finally, "[the *tathāgatagarbha*] is inextinguishable" refers to the past.

12.8: The *Tathāgatagarbha* Is Different from Sentient Beings' Mistaken Conceptions

The eighth part begins with "[O World-honored One,] the *tathāgatagarbha* [is not a self, a sentient being, destiny, nor a person]." It explains how the *tathāgatagarbha* differs from sentient beings' mistaken conceptions about it.

Chapter Thirteen:
The Intrinsically Pure

The fourth of the four chapters that offer a separate explanation of this realm is "Chapter [Thirteen]: The Intrinsically Pure." It begins with "O World-honored One, the *tathāgatagarbha* is the storehouse of all phenomena." This chapter addresses sentient beings who have heard the teachings described in the last chapter on the distorted truths about the *tathāgatagarbha*.[13] In that chapter it was stated that the *tathāgatagarbha* serves as the foundation for sentient beings who are living in delusion; it does not say that the *tathāgatagarbha* serves as a foundation only after they have freed themselves from those delusions.

When sentient beings hear this, however, they raise the following doubts. "If the *tathāgatagarbha* is inevitably stained by birth and death, how can it serve as a venerated refuge? On the other hand, if it is said to be unstained, then it would seem to be unconnected to [birth and death]. How then can the *tathāgatagarbha* serve as a foundation [for sentient beings]?" In response to these questions, this chapter shows how the *tathāgatagarbha* is intrinsically pure, and even when it appears amid the mental disturbances it remains unstained by birth and death. Rather, it is simply concealed. This chapter has two parts. In the first, Śrīmālā explains the teaching, and in the second the Tathāgata elaborates [that which was taught by Śrīmālā].

13.1: Śrīmālā Explains the Teaching

The first part, in which Śrīmālā explains the teaching, has four components. 1) To clarify whether [the *tathāgatagarbha*] is stained or unstained [by birth and death], this component describes the five types of storehouses as a single body. 2) From "[The *tathāgatagarbha*] that is intrinsically pure" explains why it is difficult to determine whether [the *tathāgatagarbha*] is stained or unstained [by the afflictions]. 3) "Why? [In each moment, the virtuous mind is not stained by the afflictions.]" This section offers familiar examples from the world that are difficult to understand in order to illustrate the profound principle [of the *tathāgatagarbha*]. 4) From "Only the Buddha, the World-honored One[, possesses true vision and true wisdom]." This section states that it is the Buddha [alone who can determine whether the *tathāgatagarbha* is stained or unstained by the afflictions].

13.1-1: The Five Types of Storehouses

The first component describes the five types of storehouses as a single body. [These five storehouses are:] 1) The *tathāgatagarbha*—since it exists amid an accumulation of mental disturbances, it is called "storehouse." Since the *tathāgatagarbha* also includes the fruits of future enlightenment, it can also be called a "storehouse." 2) "The storehouse of all phenomena": this means that the fruit of the Buddha's enlightenment is included within and illuminates completely the phenomenal world. The storehouse of all phenomena is also referred to as the "permanently abiding Dharma-nature." 3) "The storehouse of the Dharma body": this [phrase] describes the Dharma body that encompasses the myriad virtues, and so is called "storehouse." 4) "The highest supramundane storehouse" and 5) "The intrinsically pure storehouse."

The first and last [of the five storehouses] refer to the times when the *tathāgatagarbha* is concealed [by the afflictions], while the middle three refer to the times when it is revealed. Even though the *tathāgatagarbha* can be both concealed and revealed, these five storehouses form a single body.

13.1-2: The Defiled and Undefiled

The second component begins with "[The *tathāgatagarbha*] that is intrinsically pure." It explains why it is difficult to determine whether [the *tathāgatagarbha*] is stained or unstained [by the afflictions]. In the next passage, "the external afflictions" refers to the four entrenchments, while "the active afflictions" naturally refers to the active afflictions, more numerous than the sands in the Ganges River. This material explains why it is difficult to determine whether [the *tathāgatagarbha*] is stained or unstained by these [two types of afflictions]. That is, it is difficult to understand how that which is intrinsically pure could become defiled, or how that which exists among the mental disturbances does not itself become defiled. As such, the sutra calls this the "inconceivable realm of the Tathāgata."

18c

13.1-3: The Profound *Tathāgatagarbha*

The third component begins with "Why? [In each moment, the virtuous mind is not stained by the afflictions.]" It offers familiar examples from the world that are difficult to understand in order to illustrate the profound principle [of the *tathāgatagarbha*]. This section has two halves: the first describes [the *tathāgatagarbha*] from the perspective of the path of truly existent phenomena. From this perspective, the *tathāgatagarbha* is undefiled. The second does so from the perspective of the path of phenomenal reality in constant flux. From this perspective, the *tathāgatagarbha* is defiled.

But some raise doubts, asking, "Why is it difficult to distinguish between [the defiled and undefiled]?" The sutra answers this question, stating, "The virtuous mind is momentary and so is not defiled by the afflictions." This means that the virtuous mind, from the perspective of the path of truly existent phenomena, is momentary; this also means that the afflictions arise only after a previous thought has dissipated[, thereby leaving the virtuous mind itself undefiled]. The virtuous mind is not, therefore, inextricably linked to the afflictions. It is thus illogical to argue that the virtuous mind can become defiled by the afflictions.

Similarly, the sutra states, "the unwholesome mind is momentary and is also unstained by the afflictions." This means the relationship between the unwholesome mind and the afflictions behaves in the manner described above: that is, [just as the momentary nature of the virtuous mind prevents its being stained by the afflictions,] so too the evil mind [remains free from defilement]. The sutra continues, "The afflictions do not touch the mind, nor does the mind touch the afflictions." Here, the word "touch" suggests that which "extends to" [and thereby comes into contact with] something else. Therefore, when the afflictions themselves are extinguished, they do not extend to the mind that arises subsequently, just as the mind does not touch the afflictions. How then could the mind be stained by the afflictions?

The second half of this component addresses the [*tathāgatagarbha* from the perspective of the] path of phenomenal reality, which is in constant flux. From this perspective it is defiled. The sutra states, ["O World-honored One,] there are the afflictions and there are minds that appear to be defiled by those afflictions." From the perspective of the path of phenomenal reality in constant flux, however, this is a provisional description [and so is not ultimately true. That is, the statement that there are minds that appear to be defiled by the afflictions is the skillful means of the Buddha]. In other words, the virtuous mind of one moment is not extinguished but is simply transformed as an evil mind arises in the next moment. In this way, the evil mind that arises subsequently is said to defile the virtuous mind. This material addressing the familiar phenomenal world is meant to illustrate the difficulties associated with determining whether or not the mind is defiled by the afflictions. How much more so is this true of the profound principle of the buddha-nature.

13.1-4: The Buddha Alone Discerns the Defiled and Undefiled

The fourth component begins with "intrinsically pure." It explains that it is the Buddha alone who can determine [whether the *tathāgatagarbha* is stained or unstained by the afflictions]. See the sutra.

13.2: The Tathāgata Confirms Śrīmālā's Words

The chapter's second part begins with "After Queen Śrīmālā [explained that it is difficult to understand how the inherently pure mind could be defiled]." It describes the Tathāgata's confirmation [that Śrīmālā's words are true]. This part has two components: the first describes the Buddha's acknowledging that it is difficult to understand what Śrīmālā had explained.

The second begins with "In this way, these two teachings [can be understood directly by you and the great bodhisattvas, while the disciples can do so only through faith in the Buddha's words]." This section describes those who, through faith, understand these principles that are difficult to discern.

13.2-1: The Defiled and Undefiled Aspects of the Intrinsically Pure Mind

The first component [addresses the sutra passage in which the Buddha praises Śrīmālā's words, stating,] "It is difficult to understand how an intrinsically pure mind could become defiled." This passage clearly means that it is difficult to understand how the *tathāgatagarbha* can be stained by the afflictions. The Buddha adds, "Indeed, there are two teachings that are difficult to understand completely." "Two teachings" refers to the principle of the pure *tathāgatagarbha,* and to [its being stained by the afflictions that arise in the course of] worldly affairs. Indeed, in the passage above, the Buddha states, "It is difficult to understand how an intrinsically pure mind could become defiled [by the afflictions]," suggesting that it is difficult to understand whether the principle of the *tathāgatagarbha* is defiled or undefiled.

[The following passage that focuses on the afflictions states,] "This [inherently pure] mind that has been defiled by the afflictions is [the second teaching that] is difficult to understand completely." It means that it is difficult to understand whether [the afflictions that arise in the course of] worldly affairs are defiled or undefiled. Since Śrīmālā herself finds these teachings difficult to explain, she leaves it to the Buddha to elaborate on them. Indeed, in the next passage, he restates Śrīmālā's words. He does so to clarify that although the *tathāgatagarbha* appears to be defiled from the perspective of worldly things, it is undefiled from the perspective of the [abstract] principle [of the *tathāgatagarbha*].

13.2-2: The Principles That Are Difficult to Comprehend

The second component begins with "In this way, these two teachings [can be understood directly by you and the great bodhisattvas, while the disciples can do so only through faith in the Buddha's words]." This passage describes those who can understand [these principles, which are difficult to discern, through faith in the Buddha's words]. In the previous section, Śrīmālā and the Tathāgata spoke about the difficulty of understanding the *tathāgatagarbha,* raising the issue of how one can develop faith in this teaching. This section of the sutra describes how the disciples can do so, and is thus meant to eliminate any doubts.

[The second component] has three points. The first offers a general explanation that contrasts those who can have faith in the profound teachings from ordinary people who cannot [have such faith] without difficulty. The second point begins "If my disciples [follow their faith in the teachings, then that faith will eventually be unsurpassed]." This point addresses those who can have faith: bodhisattvas who practice the patience of faith [in the Buddha] and those who practice the patience of following the teachings. The third point begins with "Once these five types of expedient observation [have been completed]": this passage concludes discussion of those who can have faith.

13.2-2-1: The Two Types of Faith

The second point can be divided into two halves. The first explains the two types of patience practiced by these bodhisattvas. The second half of the second point begins with "In accord with the wisdom of the Dharma": this passage takes up only the patience of following the teachings.

The first half of the second point begins with the passage in the sutra noted above, which reads, "If my disciples follow their faith [in the teachings], then that faith will eventually be unsurpassed." The first reference to "faith" points to the patience of faith in the Buddha, while the second, "their faith will eventually be unsurpassed," refers to the advanced stages of faith—that is, the very pinnacle of bodhisattva faith.

The next passage reads, "By following the wisdom of the Dharma that depends on the illumination of faith, they will realize ultimate [truth]." This passage further explains the patience of following the teachings. Some raise doubts, asking why this passage takes up the patience of following the teachings[, when it should logically first address the patience of faith. As noted above, the Buddha clearly states in this regard, "If my disciples] follow their faith [in the teachings], that faith will eventually be unsurpassed." This means that the patience of faith in the Buddha is a preliminary practice [to the patience of following the teachings, thereby implying that the former stage had already been reached. It was not necessary, therefore, to describe it first].

13.2-2-2: The Patience of Following the Teaching

The second half of the second point explains only the patience of following the teachings, which it does [in relation to the five observations]. The first observation is "to investigate and designate the realms of the senses [and conceptual understanding]." In this passage, "senses" refers to the conventional designation of the five senses [associated with the eyes, ears, nose, tongue, and body], while "conceptual understanding" points to the six forms of consciousness [associated with the eyes, ears, nose, tongue, body, and mind]. "Realms" refers to the six objects [of form, sound, smell, taste, touch, and concepts] that [together with the six sense faculties and the six forms of consciousness] constitute the eighteen realms of observation.[14]

The second is "the observation of karmic retribution," which refers to the observation of cause and effect. The third is the "observation of the 'latent tendencies of the arhat,'" which refers to investigating the mental disturbances associated with entrenched ignorance. The fourth is "the observation of the joy of the unimpeded mind and the joy of meditation," which refers to the observation of wisdom and meditation. Indeed, wisdom associated with the unimpeded mind is joyful because it can freely illuminate the many phenomenal realms. The fifth is the "observation of the supernormal powers of the three vehicles."

13.2-2-3: Those Who Can Develop Faith

The third point begins with "Once these five types of expedient observation [have been completed]." This section concludes discussion of those who can have faith. The sutra reads, ["The 'ultimate'] is the cause for entering the path of the Great Vehicle": this passage explains that the path of the Great Vehicle is the cause leading to the fruit of the Buddha's enlightenment. One interpreter states, "Bodhisattvas at the eighth stage and higher are the path of the Great Vehicle itself, and the two types of patience—faith [in the Buddha] and following [the teachings]—are the cause of the Great Vehicle." The following passage reads, "Faith in the Tathāgata offers great benefits. Do not slander the profound meaning [of these teachings]": this passage refers to those who first developed faith in the Buddha's words and then attained the benefits of the five observations. Indeed, it is based on the power of the five observations that these practitioners are able to have faith in the *tathāgatagarbha* principle that is difficult to understand.

Chapter Fourteen:
The True Children of the Tathāgata

The third section of the main teaching is "Chapter [Fourteen]: The True Children of the Tathāgata." It begins with "At that time, Śrīmālā [said to the Buddha]" and it describes those who practice the teachings of the One Vehicle. In other words, having examined the main teachings and the realm of the vehicle, this chapter takes up the true children of the Tathāgata. It explains how bodhisattvas who engage in the three types of patience[—faith in the Buddha, following the teachings, and non-arising—]uphold and practice the One Vehicle.

The model text states, "This chapter on the 'True Children [of the Tathāgata]' begins with the passage, 'If my disciples [follow their faith in the teachings, then that faith will eventually be unsurpassed].' This chapter takes two perspectives. The first begins with the Tathāgata's addressing only the patience of faith in the Buddha and the patience of following the teachings. Since [he takes up only two of the three types of patience,] this is an abbreviated explanation of the true children of the Tathāgata. [From the end of the Buddha's explanation, however,] Śrīmālā takes up in detail all three types of patience, thereby offering a broad explanation of the true children of the Tathāgata. Because the Tathāgata desired to extend much of the merit of teaching the sutra to Śrīmālā, he abbreviated his words and chose to explain only the patience of faith in the Buddha and the patience of following the teachings[, enabling Śrīmālā to gain merit by offering much of the teaching on this subject]. As such, these two perspectives together constitute 'Chapter [Fourteen]: Śrīmālā's [Teaching] of the True Children [of the Tathāgata].'" Use the model text's interpretation as one sees fit.

This chapter has three subsections: 1) Śrīmālā requests permission from the Buddha to explain the teaching. 2) The Tathāgata requests Śrīmālā to explain the teaching. 3) Śrīmālā describes [the true children of the Tathāgata,] beginning with, "[Śrīmālā] said [to the Buddha, 'the three kinds of good sons and daughters].'"

14.1: Śrīmālā Requests Permission

The first subsection begins with "There are other great benefits that remain." [As noted in the introduction to this chapter,] the material discussed

19b

above covered the main teachings and the realm of the vehicle but not those who actually practice these teachings. [To indicate that they have not yet been discussed, the sutra] states, therefore, "there are other great benefits that remain." But these benefits can be understood in other ways. For example, as was noted above, [the Tathāgata states it is difficult to understand whether the *tathāgatagarbha*] is or is not defiled by the afflictions and those who have faith in this teaching will receive benefits from that faith. [The other benefits described in this passage are thus meant to suggest] those benefits also accrue to those who put into practice the teachings of the sutra.

14.2.

(Not included with this commentary.)

14.3: The Good Sons and Daughters

The third subsection of this chapter has five points. The first offers general praise of the three types [of good sons and daughters]. The second point, which describes these three types, begins with "What are the three types?" The three types can be distinguished by the appearance in the sutra of the word "if." [That is, each of the descriptions of these groups starts with the word "if."] The third point begins with "These people alone are the good sons [and daughters of the Tathāgata]." This section describes the subjugation of evil people, noting that Śrīmālā herself can do so by drawing on power like that possessed by kings, *deva*s, and *nāga*s (dragon spirits).

The fourth point begins with "At that time, Śrīmālā [and her retinue]": this passage concludes Śrīmālā's teaching and describes the show of respect [she and her retinue offered the Buddha]. The fifth point describes the Buddha's praise of Śrīmālā's words. It has two halves: the first praises Śrīmālā's teaching regarding the subjugation of evil people. The second half begins with the Buddha telling Śrīmālā, "You have already been closely connected to [myriad buddhas]." This passage praises Śrīmālā's explanation of the teaching as one that accords with those of the buddhas from the past. He continues, ["You have explained] the complete meaning [of this teaching]": this passage means that Śrīmālā has covered the main teaching, the realm of the vehicle, and the practitioners of the vehicle.

Part III

The Propagation
of the Teaching

The sutra's third main division, the propagation of the teaching, begins with "At that time, the World-honored One emitted a brilliant light [that shone upon the great assembly]." This last division can be divided into three sections. The first describes the Tathāgata's return to Śrāvastī and his desire for the sutra to be widely propagated in the future. The second section begins with "At that time, the World-honored One entered the Jeta Grove." It explains the propagation of the teaching. The third begins with "At that time, Lord Indra spoke to the Buddha, saying"; this passage lists the sixteen names that describe the sutra.

Propagation of the Teaching 1:
The Buddha Returns to Śrāvastī

Section one describes the Buddha's return to Śrāvastī and has two subsections. The first describes his return to the city, while the second describes Śrīmālā and her retinue worshiping and then sending off the Buddha. The second subsection begins with "[At that time,] Śrīmālā [and her retinue faced the Buddha with palms joined as a sign of respect]." One [interpretation of this passage is that Śrīmālā herself] went outside the palace to send off the Buddha. Another argues that she sent him off with her heart. So too the passage "[The Buddha returned to Śrāvastī] and reentered the city" has two possible interpretations that are not discussed here.

Propagation of the Teaching 2:
Transmitting the Sutra

Section two explains the propagation of the sutra. It has four subsections. 1) Explains the Tathāgata's desire first to assemble an audience for the purpose of transmitting the sutra. 2) Begins with "[The World-honored One] faced

131

Indra [and the venerable Ānanda]," exhorting them to teach the sutra widely for the benefit of sentient beings. 3) From "Having explained the sutra to them, the Buddha said to Indra": this passage describes the Buddha entrusting the text to Indra for propagation in the heavenly realms. 4) From "[The Buddha] then spoke to Ānanda": this passage describes the Buddha entrusting the text to Ānanda for propagation among the people. Lord Indra is the chief benefactor of the Buddha, and generally requests the Buddha to explain the teachings. Ānanda is a family member who attended the Buddha and regularly listened to the teachings. The sutra was entrusted to these two for transmission.

Propagation of the Teaching 3:
The Sixteen Names for the Sutra

Section three lists the sixteen names that describe the sutra. It has seven subsections. 1) Describes Indra's requesting the name of the sutra from the Buddha. 2) Describes the Tathāgata's praise of the sutra's merits. It begins with "The Buddha told Indra[, 'This sutra has countless and unlimited merits']." 3) Describes the Buddha telling Indra[, here called "Kauśika,"] that he should listen closely to the sutra's names. This subsection begins with "Again, O Kauśika[, you must know that this sutra is profound, subtle, and offers great merits]." 4) Describes Indra and Ānanda respectfully receiving the teaching. This subsection begins with "At that time, Indra [and the venerable Ānanda said to the Buddha, 'Excellent, O World-honored One!']."

19c

5) Lists the sixteen names that describe the sutra. It begins with "The Buddha said, 'This sutra [praises the supreme merits of the truth of the Tathāgata's teaching].'" Since there were fourteen chapter titles listed above for the sutra's main teaching, one might think that these names for the sutra would also total fourteen. But there are two additional names that bring the list to sixteen. One of these names is "The Lion's Roar of Queen Śrīmālā. Uphold it as such." The second name is, "Again, O Kauśika, all doubts are eliminated by explaining this sutra. Have no doubts in regards to the meaning [of this teaching] and enter the path of the One Vehicle." Although these two names are distinct, they point to the same essential teaching. That is, the former uses a person's name to represent the entire teaching, while the latter explains the central principles of the entire sutra.

The fourteen chapters that describe the sutra have individual names and teachings. But they could not be included in the title at the beginning of the sutra, where only two names are used. That is, the [first part of the] sutra's title is "The Lion's Roar of [Queen] Śrīmālā," which is the fifteenth name. "The Correct and Extensive [Sutra Proclaiming] the Great Expedient Means of the One Vehicle," [which also appears at the top of the sutra,] is the sixteenth name.

6) The passage beginning with "O Kauśika, today this [sutra—the Lion's Roar of Queen Śrīmālā—has been entrusted to you,]" refers to the Buddha once again encouraging the sutra's propagation. 7) The next passage reads, "Indra said to the Buddha ['Excellent, O World-honored One! I respectfully receive your sublime teaching']." This passage describes the reception of the teachings of the sutra and the promise to put them into practice.

This constitutes the *Shōmangyō-gisho* in one fascicle.

Notes

1   Shōtoku is referred to by other names, including Umayado (also Umayato), Prince Jōgū, Kamitsumiya (an alternative reading of Jōgū), Dharmarāja ("King of the Dharma"), and King Jōgū, although he never ascended the throne. The collection of three texts attributed to Shōtoku is generally referred to today as the *Sangyō-gisho* (*Commentaries on the Three Sutras*), which includes the *Shōmangyō-gisho,* the *Yuimagyō-gisho* (*Commentary on the Vimalakīrtinirdeśa-sūtra*), and the *Hokke-gisho* (*Commentary on the Lotus Sutra*). The individual works of the *Sangyō-gisho* all appear in the *Taishō shinshū daizōkyō,* the Japanese edition of the Chinese Buddhist canon (Taishō no. 2185, no. 2186, and no. 2187, respectively). All three texts have been digitized and are available for download at the SAT website: http://21dzk.l.utokyo.ac.jp/SAT/index.html.

2   The *Śrīmālā-sūtra* has been translated into English by Alex and Hideko Wayman, working from Chinese and Tibetan translations and Sanskrit fragments. See *The Lion's Roar of Queen Śrīmālā: A Buddhist Scripture on the Tathāgatagarbha Theory* (New York: Columbia University Press, 1974). Diana Paul translated the sutra into English using Guṇabhadra's Chinese translation. See *The Buddhist Feminine Ideal: Queen Śrīmālā and the Tathāgatagarbha* (Missoula, MT: Scholars Press, 1980). Her translation also appears in the BDK Tripiṭaka series, under the title *The Sutra of Queen Śrīmālā of the Lion's Roar* (Berkeley, CA: Numata Center for Buddhist Translation and Research, 2004).

3   Shōtoku was the grandson of Emperor Kimmei (r. 539–571 C.E.), the son of Emperor Yōmei (r. 585–587), and the nephew of Empress Suiko (r. 592–628).

4   Some scholars date his death to 623 C.E.

5   In the preface to his work, Mingkong writes, "This commentary was brought by the monks Kaimyō and Tokusei, who were members of a group of eight emissaries that arrived in the seventh year of Tang Daili (772 C.E.). They brought [the *Shōmangyō-gisho*] and the four-fascicle *Hokke-gisho,* which they presented to the Great Vinaya Master Ajari Lingyou of Longxing Monastery in Yangzhou." Quoted in Minowa Kenryō, "Kaimyō," in *Shōtoku Taishi jiten,* ed. Ishida Hisatoyo (Tokyo: Kashiwa Shobō, 1997), p. 29.

6   See Tsuda Sōkichi, *Nihon jōdai no kenkyū* (Tokyo: Iwanami Shoten, 1930) and *Nihon koten no kenkyū,* vol. 2 (Tokyo: Iwanami Shoten, 1950).

7   Some versions of the *Shōmangyō-gisho* exclude the first two of these three passages. While most versions include the declaration of Shōtoku's authorship, here referred

to as "King Jōgū," most scholars agree that this passage claiming his authorship is
an interpolation into the text.

8   The "outer ordinary" corresponds to stages 1–10 of the fifty-two stages of bodhisattva practice; the "inner ordinary" to stages 11–40; and the "first ground and above"
to stages 41–52.

9   This corresponds to the forty-eighth bodhisattva stage.

10   The text refers to a number of "opening" and "combining" metaphors. The former
is a metaphor that introduces a topic, while the latter is a metaphor that synthesizes
and then concludes the material introduced by the opening metaphor.

11   The text erroneously lists the chapter on the *tathāgatagarbha* as Chapter Two, instead
of Chapter Seven.

12   The text erroneously lists the third of these four chapters as "Chapter Seven: The
Tathāgatagarbha" instead of "Chapter Twelve: The Distorted Truths."

13   This section states the "*Tathāgatagarbha* Chapter," which is an error in the *Shōmangyō-gisho*. It should read "Distorted Truths Chapter."

14   The first observation is erroneously written as having "five senses," omitting the
mind as the sixth sense. If the mind is included, then the realms of observations total
eighteen.

Glossary

affliction (Skt. *kleśa*): That which afflicts the mind, causing one to suffer from negative mental, emotional, and physical states, and that entrap one in the cycle of birth, death, and rebirth (samsara). The Buddhist teachings on ethics (*śīla*), meditation (*dhyāna*), and wisdom (*prajñā*) help eliminate the afflictions and lead one toward nirvana. The afflictions can be divided into the fundamental afflictions (ignorance, craving, pride, etc.) and the secondary afflictions (laziness, stinginess, jealousy, etc.). Also called "defilements" and "mental disturbances." *See also* ethics, meditation, and wisdom; nirvana; samsara.

Ānanda: The Buddha's cousin and close disciple. Said to have a perfect memory, he was called on to recite the Buddha's discourses at the First Council held soon after the Buddha's death, during which the Buddha's teachings were collected. Buddhist sutras begin with the phrase, "Thus I have heard," indicating that the text is a direct recitation of the Buddha's words that had been heard by Ānanda. The introduction to the *Śrīmālā-sūtra* in the *Shōmangyō-gisho* states that these words mean not only that the teaching was heard by Ānanda directly from the Buddha, but also that the transmission is free from error. Ānanda also appears at the end of the sutra when he and Lord Indra are entrusted by the Buddha to transmit it to others. *See also* sutra.

Anāthapiṇḍada: An epithet for the elder Sudatta; literally, "[one who offers] alms (*piṇḍa*) to the unprotected (*anātha*)"; also translated as "feeder of the destitute" and "giver of food to the poor." A wealthy financier from Śrāvastī who became a chief patron of the early Buddhist community. With Prince Jeta, he helped construct a spiritual center in a park not far outside the city that was frequented by the Buddha and his disciples during the rainy season retreat. *See also* Jeta Grove and Anāthapiṇḍada Garden; Prince Jeta; Śrāvastī.

Anavatapta. *See* Lake Anavatapta.

arhat ("one who is worthy [of respect]"): The ideal practitioner in the Theravāda and other Nikāya Buddhist schools. Having eliminated the afflictions and escaped transmigration, the arhat is thus "worthy" (*arhat*) of receiving others' respect and offerings. The arhat as a spiritual ideal is often criticized in Mahayana polemics as a lesser Buddhist path, referred to pejoratively as the Hinayana, or "Small Vehicle." The term arhat can also be rendered as "one who has slain the enemy of birth and death" or "one who has destroyed the enemy of the afflictions." *See also* bodhisattva; Hinayana; two vehicles.

Ayodhyā: An ancient city in the kingdom of Kośala. Modern-day Ayodhyā is located in the north Indian state of Uttar Pradesh. *See also* King Prasenajit; Kośala.

bodhisattva ("enlightenment being"): The ideal practitioner in the Mahayana traditions whose selfless compassion is contrasted to the purported selfishness of the arhat and other followers of the Hinayana, or "Small Vehicle." Having aroused the mind of enlightenment (*bodhicitta*), the bodhisattva compassionately vows to save all other sentient beings before entering final nirvana. The bodhisattva progresses toward buddhahood in a series of stages through the practice and accomplishment of the perfections. *See also* arhat; fifty-two stages; Hinayana; Mahayana; perfections.

buddha-nature: The potential to attain enlightenment that inheres in all sentient beings. It is realized by practicing the Buddhist teachings on ethics, meditation, and wisdom. Buddha-nature developed in conjunction with the concept of the *tathāgata-garbha,* and the two terms are often used as synonyms. Although the buddha-nature doctrine became quite popular in some Buddhist schools, it was criticized by others as positing a form of permanent selfhood that contravenes Buddhist teachings on emptiness (*śūnyatā*). The term *tathāgatagarbha* appears in the *Shōmangyō-gisho* more than fifty times, in contrast to only one reference to buddha-nature. *See also* emptiness; ethics, meditation, and wisdom; sentient beings; *tathāgatagarbha.*

Conditioned Four Noble Truths: One of two types of Noble Truths examined in the *Śrīmālā-sūtra* and elaborated in the *Shōmangyō-gisho.* The conditioned truths are described by Queen Śrīmālā as limited, since they offer only a provisional understanding of reality, and were taught by the Buddha to practitioners of the two vehicles as skillful means. *See also* Eight Noble Truths; skillful means; two vehicles; Unconditioned Four Noble Truths.

deva: A divine or celestial being who abides in one of the six *deva* heavens of the desire realm, or in the higher heavens of the form and formless realms. The *Shōmangyō-gisho* often refers to the "*deva* vehicle," one of the five vehicles, and identifies Brahma and Indra, two *deva*s, by name. *See also* five vehicles; Lord Indra; three realms.

Dharma: The teachings of the Buddha; truth itself; one of the Three Treasures. *See also* Three Treasures.

Dharma body (Skt. *dharmakāya*): One of the three bodies of a buddha. The *dharmakāya* represents the eternally abiding and indestructible truth. It also represents emptiness and reality itself. In some schools of Buddhism, the Dharma body is represented by Vairocana. *See also* enjoyment body; manifestation body; three bodies.

Dharma gate: The Buddha's teachings that serve as the entry into the path of enlightenment. The *Shōmangyō-gisho* describes "eighty-four thousand Dharma gates," a number equal to the delusions of sentient beings.

Dharma Master Fayun (467–529 C.E.): One of the three great Buddhist masters of the Chinese Liang dynasty, along with Sengmin (476–527 C.E.) and Zhizang (458–522 C.E.). Dharma Master Fayun's interpretation of the two types of birth and death is addressed in the *Shōmangyō-gisho. See also* Liang dynasty; two types of birth and death.

diamondlike mind (Skt. *cittavajra*): Refers to the mind of the bodhisattva that is sharp, rare, and indestructible. In particular, the phrase refers to the mental state of a bodhisattva at the level of "virtual enlightenment," the stage just before attaining buddhahood, called the "stage of wonderful enlightenment." Also called the "adamantine mind." *See also* bodhisattva; fifty-two stages.

disciple (Skt. *śrāvaka*): Orginally, this term referred to the disciples of the Buddha who had directly heard him teach. As the Mahayana developed, disciples and self-enlightened ones (Skt. *pratyekabuddhas*) were criticized as followers of the Hinayana ("Small Vehicle"), which focused on individual salvation and was thus described as inferior to the Mahayana ("Great Vehicle") and its ideal of the compassionate and altruistic bodhisattva. *See also* bodhisattva; Hinayana; Mahayana; self-enlightened one; two vehicles.

eightfold path: The teaching given in the last of the Four Noble Truths, each of the eightfold path's elements begins with the word "right" and describes a central Buddhist practice that leads to the cessation of suffering and thus the attainment of enlightenment. The eight spokes of the wheel of Dharma correspond to these eight practices, which are often divided into the three main categories of ethics, meditation, and wisdom (Skt. *śīla, dhyāna, prajñā*). In this division, ethics, or *śīla*, includes right speech, right action, and right livelihood; meditation, or *dhyāna*, includes right effort, right mindfulness, and right concentration; and wisdom, or *prajñā*, includes right view and right thought. *See also* ethics, meditation, and wisdom; Four Noble Truths.

eighth stage: The eighth of the ten highest stages (Skt. *bhūmi*s) of bodhisattva practice, called "immovable" (*acalā*). At this stage the mind is unperturbed and the bodhisattva's compassion for other beings cannot be disrupted by worldly attachments. Upon reaching this stage of the path, retrogression is no longer possible. The *Shōmangyō-gisho* describes this stage as the first stage of "other-practice." *See also* bodhisattva; fifty-two stages; other-practice.

Eight Noble Truths: Two sets of Four Noble Truths are described in the *Śrīmālā-sūtra* and analyzed in detail in the *Shōmangyō-gisho*: The Conditioned Four Noble Truths, representing provisional truth, is associated with the two vehicles; the Unconditioned Four Noble Truths, representing ultimate truth, is the realm of the bodhisattva. *See also* bodhisattva; Conditioned Four Noble Truths; Four Noble Truths; two vehicles; Unconditioned Four Noble Truths.

elements of existence (Skt. *dharma*s): The constituents of the phenomenal world.

emptiness (Skt. *śūnyatā*): The teaching that all the elements of existence are in constant flux, subject to causes and conditions, and empty of inherent self-nature. This principle also applies to the human personality, which is comprised of five temporary aggregates (*skandha*s): form, sensation, conception, volition, and consciousness. The *Shōmangyō-gisho* takes up the subject of emptiness in "Chapter Nine: The Concealed Truth: The Meaning of Emptiness," discussing two types of wisdom regarding emptiness that are possessed by the Buddha alone.

enjoyment body (Skt. *saṃbhogakāya*): One of the three bodies of a buddha, the body that enjoys the fruits of accumulated merit. Also called the "reward body." The manifestation of the enjoyment body is represented in some schools by Buddha Amitābha. *See also* three bodies.

entrenched ignorance: Innate and deeply ingrained ignorance. Distinguished in the *Shō-mangyō-gisho* from the four entrenchments. *See also* four entrenchments.

ethics, meditation, and wisdom (Skt. *śīla, dhyāna, prajñā*): The three aspects of the eight-fold path: ethics (*śīla*) includes right speech, right action, and right livelihood; meditation (*dhyāna*) includes right effort, right mindfulness, and right concentration; and wisdom (*prajñā*) includes right view and right thought. *See also* eightfold path.

Fayun. *See* Dharma Master Fayun.

fifty-two stages: The progressively higher stages of the path to buddhahood attained by Mahayana bodhisattvas through the practice of the perfections. They are subdivided into ten stages of faith, ten abodes, ten practices, ten dedications of merit, ten stages, virtual enlightenment, and wonderful enlightenment. *See also* bodhisattva; eighth stage; Mahayana; perfections; pure stages.

five precepts: The basic ethical principles of the Buddhist path observed by both monastics and lay followers. They are commitments to abstain from killing, stealing, engaging in sexual impropriety, lying, and consuming intoxicants.

five types of storehouses: The *Shōmangyō-gisho* lists these as the storehouses of the *tathāgatagarbha,* all phenomena, the Dharma body, the highest supramundane, and the intrinsically pure.

five vehicles: The vehicles of humans, *deva*s, disciples, self-enlightened ones, and bodhisattvas. *See also* four vehicles; three vehicles; two vehicles.

four distorted views: Seeing the impermanent as permanent, suffering as pleasure, the impure as pure, and non-self as self.

four entrenchments: The entrenchments that arise from attachment to: 1) the form realm, 2) the desire realm, and 3) existence itself, as well as 4) the entrenchment of the unenlightened view that sees all phenomena springing from a single ground. The four entrenchments are distinguished in the *Shōmangyō-gisho* from entrenched ignorance. *See also* entrenched ignorance; three realms.

four evil demons: The demons of the heavens, the afflictions (Skt. *kleśa*s), the aggregates (*skandha*s), and death (often personified as Māra). *See also* affliction; Māra.

Four Noble Truths: A fundamental teaching of the Buddha, taught as part of the first turning of the wheel of Dharma at the Sarnath Deer Park. The truths of suffering, origination, cessation, and the path—existence entails suffering; suffering is caused by desire; nirvana is the realm free from suffering; and the eightfold path leads to nirvana. *See also* Conditioned Four Noble Truths; Eight Noble Truths; Unconditioned Four Noble Truths.

four vehicles: Listed in one passage in the *Shōmangyō-gisho* as the vehicles of humans, *deva*s, disciples, and self-enlightened ones, but in another passage as those of humans and *deva*s, disciples, self-enlightened ones, and bodhisattvas. *See also* five vehicles; three vehicles; two vehicles.

Ganges River: One of the sacred rivers of the Indian subcontinent. The *Śrīmālā-sūtra,* the *Shōmangyō-gisho,* and other Buddhist texts often refer to an inconceivable number with some variation of the phrase "more numerous than the sands of the Ganges River."

Great Sage: An epithet for the Buddha.

Great Vehicle. *See* Mahayana.

Guṇabhadra (394–468 C.E.): An eminent Buddhist scholar-monk from Magādha, one of the sixteen "great countries" (Skt. *mahājanapadas*) located in central India. Born into a brahman family, he traveled to China around 435 C.E. and eventually translated some thirty Buddhist texts, including the *Śrīmālā-sūtra.*

Hinayana ("Small Vehicle"): A pejorative term used in Mahayana Buddhist texts to describe the practice and spiritual goal of followers of the two vehicles, centered on the pursuit of individual enlightenment, as opposed to the altruistic practice of the Mahayana bodhisattva. Hinayana followers generally include disciples, self-enlightened ones, and arhats, although there is variation in usage. *See also* arhat; bodhisattva; disciple; Mahayana; self-enlightened one; Theravāda; two vehicles.

Jeta Grove and Anāthapiṇḍada Garden (Skt. Jetavana Anāthapiṇḍada-ārāma): A park and retreat center located outside the city of Śrāvastī, established by Prince Jeta and the elder Anāthapiṇḍada for the use of the Buddha and his disciples during the rainy season. *See also* Anāthapiṇḍada; Prince Jeta; Śrāvastī.

King Prasenajit: The ruler of the kingdom of Kośala and the father of Queen Śrīmālā. A key early patron of Buddhism. *See also* Kośala; Queen Śrīmālā.

Kośala: One of the sixteen "great countries" (Skt. *mahājanapadas*) of the Indian subcontinent at the time of the Buddha, ruled by King Prasenajit. Ayodhyā and Śrāvastī were two of Kośala's major cities. *See also* Ayodhyā; King Prasenajit; Śrāvastī.

Kunlun Mountains: A mountain range in the western part of modern-day China. Part of the range divides Xinjiang province from the northern part of the Tibetan Autonomous Region.

Lake Anavatapta: The lake that is "devoid of heat" (Skt. *anavatapta*), home to a dragon (*nāga*) king who was converted to Buddhism and became a bodhisattva. In Buddhist cosmology, Lake Anavatapta is described as being at the center of the world, located on the continent of Jambudvīpa to the north of the Himalayas. The *Shōmangyō-gisho* describes it as the source of four great rivers, possibly the Ganges, Indus, Amu, and Tarim Rivers, although scholars have offered other possibilities, such as the Ganges, Brahmaputra, Amu, and Sutlej Rivers.

Liang dynasty (502–557 C.E.): Founded by Xiao Yan (Emperor Wu of Liang; 464–549 C.E.). The third of the Southern dynasties of China, known also as the Southern Liang dynasty. *See also* Liu-Song dynasty.

Liu-Song dynasty (420–479 C.E.): Founded by Liu Yu (Emperor Wu of Liu Song; 363–422 C.E.), also referred to as the Southern Song dynasty to distinguish it from the later Song dynasty (960–1279 C.E.). The first of the four southern dynasties of China. *See also* Liang dynasty.

Lord Indra: Lord of the *deva*s who lives in the Trāyastriṃśa Heaven ("Heaven of the Thirty-three") atop Mount Sumeru. He and Brahma are known as the chief protectors of Buddhism. Also called Śakra, Kauśika, and Śakra Devānām Indra. Indra and Ānanda appear at the end of the sutra, where they are entrusted by the Buddha to transmit the text to others. *See also* Ānanda; *deva.*

Lotus Sutra (*Saddharmapuṇḍarīka-sūtra*): A major Mahayana sutra that employs stories and parables to offer teachings on the One Vehicle, bodhisattva practice, buddhanature, and skillful means, among other themes. The *Lotus Sutra* is the object of exegesis of the *Hokke-gisho,* one of two other Buddhist commentaries attributed to Prince Shōtoku. *See also* bodhisattva; buddha-nature; Mahayana; One Vehicle; Prince Shōtoku; skillful means.

Mahayana ("Great Vehicle"): While the origins and development of the Mahayana remains a subject of scholarly debate, it is commonly held that proto-Mahayana can be traced to an early split in the Buddhist community at the Second Buddhist Council, perhaps arising in a dispute over the rules of the Vinaya, between the Mahāsāṃghika ("Great Assembly") and the Sthaviravāda ("Teaching of the Elders") schools. Another common view has been that the Mahayana developed as a lay-based, devotional movement that venerated stupas, although this view has been challenged by recent scholarship. Regardless of the truth of its origins, the Mahayana developed a distinctive set of texts, tenets (emptiness, buddha-nature, *tathāgatagarbha,* the three buddha bodies, etc.), and practices. As it developed, its adherents came to idealize the selfless compassion of the bodhisattva; indeed, the *Śrīmālāsūtra* and other Mahayana texts often criticize the purported selfishness of the arhat path of the Hinayana ("Small Vehicle"). Mahayana schools, including Chan, Pure Land, Tiantai, and others, are found mainly in the countries to the north and east of modern India. *See also* arhat; bodhisattva; buddha-nature; emptiness; Hinayana; Second Buddhist Council; *tathāgatagarbha;* three bodies; Vinaya.

Mallikā: *See* Queen Mallikā.

manifestation body (Skt. *nirmāṇakāya*): One of the three bodies of a buddha, which manifests in the world to teach and save sentient beings according to their individual capacities. Represented by Śākyamuni Buddha. *See also* three bodies.

Māra ("death"): The "Evil One," the personification of death, the representation of desire and negative mental states. In accounts of the Buddha's enlightenment, Māra appears to attempt to block his progress toward liberation and prevent him from teaching the Dharma to others. *See also* four evil demons.

model text: The *Shōmangyō-gisho* refers to the interpretations of other commentaries, often using a variation of the phrase, "An interpreter states." Except for Dharma Master Fayun, however, these interpreters remain anonymous. Among the anonymous commentaries are twelve references to a "model text" that served as a source for the composition of the *Shōmangyō-gisho*. These references offer short summaries of the model text's interpretation of a particular point. After summarizing the point, the *Shōmangyō-gisho* frequently provides an alternative interpretation. Scholars have debated the identity of the model text and have used it to make arguments regarding the *Shōmangyō-gisho*'s authorship, meaning, and originality. *See also* Dharma Master Fayun.

Mount Sumeru: In Buddhist cosmology, Mount Sumeru is the central and highest mountain of the world, said to rise to a height of eighty thousand *yojana*s (an Indian unit of distance equivalent to 4.5–9 miles). To the south of Mount Sumeru is the continent of Jambudvīpa, the world inhabited by humans.

nirvana: Liberation from the cycle of transmigration (samsara) by extinguishing the clinging to desires that causes one to suffer. The *Śrīmālā-sūtra* and the *Shōmangyō-gisho* distinguish nirvana with remainder from nirvana without remainder. *See also* nirvana with remainder; nirvana without remainder; samsara.

Nirvana Sutra: A group of texts in both the Pāli (Theravāda) and Mahayana canons describing the end of the Buddha's life and his final teaching. The Pāli versions are referred to as the *Mahāparinibbāna-sutta* and the Mahayana versions as the *Mahāparinirvana-sūtra;* both titles can be translated as the *Sutra of the Great Final Nirvana.* The Mahayana versions address the status of the community (sangha) after the Buddha's death and such doctrinal issues as buddha-nature, the *tathāgatagarbha,* and the "great self." The *Shōmangyō-gisho* refers to the *Nirvana Sutra* in its discussion of the sixteen restraints of evil. *See also* buddha-nature; Mahayana; sangha; *tathāgatagarbha;* Theravāda.

nirvana without remainder (Skt. *nirupadhiśeṣa-nirvana*): A state of nirvana that is attained after the death of the physical body. In this form of nirvana both the karmic causes of transmigration and the fruit of past actions (karma) have been eliminated. *See also* nirvana; nirvana with remainder.

nirvana with remainder (Skt. *sopādhiśeṣa-nirvana*): A state of nirvana that is attained while one still experiences embodied existence in the world. In this form of nirvana the causes of transmigration in samsaric existence have been eliminated but the consequences of past actions (karma) still remain to play out. *See also* nirvana; nirvana without remainder.

one great vow: Embracing the true Dharma; a central topic of the *Śrīmālā-sūtra. See also* true Dharma.

One Vehicle (Skt. *ekayāna*): The Buddhist teaching that the various paths of practice taught by the Buddha represent a single teaching—the single Buddhist vehicle that will ultimately lead all beings to enlightenment. According to later Mahayana teachings, the various vehicles (often presented as groups of three, four, or five) and the apparent differences among them were taught by the Buddha as skillful means in order to attract to the Buddhist path those of differing capacities. The doctrine of the One Vehicle is discussed extensively in the *Śrīmālā-sūtra* and in other Mahayana Buddhist texts, such as the *Lotus Sutra*. *See also* Mahayana; skillful means; three vehicles.

other-practice: The *Shōmangyō-gisho* distinguishes "other-practice" (Chapters 4–5 in the *Śrīmālā-sūtra*) from "self-practice" (Chapters 1–3 in the *Śrīmālā-sūtra*). Other-practice, so called because its focus is the altruistic wish to help all suffering sentient beings to liberation, is undertaken by bodhisattvas at the eighth stage and above, while self-practice refers to the practice leading to enlightenment undertaken by bodhisattvas at the seventh stage and below (such as Queen Śrīmālā), with the ultimate goal of eventually progressing through all the fifty-two stages. *See also* bodhisattva; fifty-two stages; self-practice.

perfections (Skt. *pāramitā*s): Mahayana Buddhist practices that are undertaken by the bodhisattva in order to eliminate negative karma (i.e., the results of unwholesome actions), promote compassionate behavior, and bring about peaceful mental states, thereby allowing continual progress on the path toward enlightenment. The six perfections are generosity (*dāna*), ethics (*śīla*), patience (*kṣānti*), diligence (*vīrya*), meditation (*dhyāna*), and wisdom (*prajñā*); an expanded list of ten perfections adds skillful means (*upāya*), determination (*praṇidhāna*), spiritual power (*bala*), and knowledge (*jñāna*). The perfections are discussed in the *Śrīmālā-sūtra* and other major Buddhist sutras, such as the *Lotus Sutra*. *See also* bodhisattva; Mahayana; skillful means; two types of patience.

Prajñāpāramitā sutras: A group of Mahayana sutras that analyze the perfection (Skt. *pāramitā*) of wisdom (*prajñā*), one of the six perfections of Mahayana bodhisattva practice. These texts are generally distinguished by their length: the *Heart Sutra,* the shortest at just fourteen verses (*śloka*s), is said to distill the essential teachings of the entire corpus. Commonly recited in Zen Buddhist temples, the *Heart Sutra* describes Avalokiteśvara, the bodhisattva of compassion, expounding on the emptiness of the elements of existence (*dharma*s) to Śāriputra, one of the Buddha's chief disciples. Another relatively short but popular text in this corpus is the *Diamond Sutra* (*Vajracchedikā-prajñāpāramitā-sūtra*). The longest, the *Śatasāhasrikā-prajñāpāramitā-sūtra,* contains one hundred thousand verses. The *Shōmangyō-gisho* refers to the *Prajñāpāramitā* and the *Vimalakīrtinirdeśa* sutras as examples of Mahayana texts that are distinct from *ekayāna* (One Vehicle) texts. *See also* Mahayana; One Vehicle; perfections.

Prātimokṣa: Lit., "toward liberation," also translated more loosely as "that which causes liberation from suffering" or "liberation from the afflictions." A part of the Vinaya precepts that are meant to help Buddhist monastics eliminate negative and promote positive behavior, and thus progress toward liberation. It includes specific rules for monks (*bhikṣu-prātimokṣa*), which vary in number from two hundred and eighteen to two hundred and sixty-three rules; and from two hundred and seventy-nine to three hundred and eighty rules for nuns (*bhikṣuṇī-prātimokṣa*). *See also* Vinaya.

pratyekabuddha. See self-enlightened one.

Prince Jeta: An early patron of the Buddha. Prince Jeta is known for selling land near the city of Śrāvastī to the elder Anāthapiṇḍada, which became the site of a retreat center for the early sangha and is known as one of the earliest Buddhist monasteries. During the rainy season the Buddha and his disciples frequented this center, known as the Jeta Grove and Anāthapiṇḍada Garden. *See also* Anāthapiṇḍada; Jeta Grove and Anāthapiṇḍada Garden; Śrāvastī.

Prince Shōtoku (574–622): A Japanese prince who is remembered as an adroit politician and revered as the father of Japanese Buddhism. Shōtoku is known by other names, including Umayado (also Umayato), Prince Jōgū, Kamitsumiya, Dharmarāja ("King of the Dharma"), and King Jōgū. He is said to have authored three Buddhist sub-commentaries (the *Hokke-gisho,* on the *Lotus Sutra;* the *Shōmangyō-gisho,* on the *Śrīmālā-sūtra;* and the *Yuimakyō-gisho,* on the *Vimalakīrtinirdeśa-sūtra*), a seventeen-article proto-constitution, and two historical works. His life and works remain the topic of great scholarly and popular interest.

pure stages: A reference in the *Shōmangyō-gisho* to the first through the seventh of the ten stages of bodhisattva practice that precede enlightenment. *See also* bodhisattva; fifty-two stages.

Queen Mallikā: The wife of King Prasenajit, ruler of the kingdom of Kośala, and mother of Śrīmālā. *See also* King Prasenajit; Kośala; Queen Śrīmālā.

Queen Śrīmālā: The protagonist of the *Śrīmālā-sūtra.* Śrīmālā was the daughter of King Prasenajit and Queen Mallikā, the rulers of the kingdom of Kośala. Upon receiving a letter from her parents extolling the virtues of the Mahayana, Śrīmālā uttered the Buddha's name in praise and requested that he appear before her and her court in Ayodhyā. The Buddha grants Queen Śrīmālā great eloquence ("the lion's roar") to expound the teachings of the One Vehicle, the *tathāgatagarbha,* and the Eight Noble Truths, and her discourse is the basis of the text of the *Śrīmālā-sūtra. See also* Eight Noble Truths; Mahayana; One Vehicle; *tathāgatagarbha.*

Śākyamuni ("sage [Skt. *muni*] of the Śākya [clan]"): The historical Buddha who lived in the fifth century B.C.E., although the actual dates of his birth and death are disputed. Said to have been born a prince in Lumbinī, (modern-day) Nepal, Siddhārtha Gautama, through meditative and ascetic practice, became the Buddha ("Awakened One"). The events of his life and his eventual attainment of enlightenment form the basis for the teachings of Buddhism that were put forth and further developed over time by the community of Buddhist followers. There are only two references to

Śākyamuni in the *Shōmangyō-gisho*; more commonly he is referred to as Tathāgata, Buddha, and World-honored One.

sangha: The Buddhist community. Capitalized, the term refers to one of the Three Treasures along with the Buddha and Dharma. *See also* Three Treasures.

samsara: The cycle of birth, death, and rebirth in which beings transmigrate; the world of suffering, distinct from nirvana. *See also* nirvana.

Second Buddhist Council: Held at Vaiśālī about a hundred years after the Buddha's death (although the dates are disputed), the Second Council addressed ten points of debate, one of which concerned varied interpretations of the Vinaya rules regarding the handling of money. This debate led to a split in the Buddhist community between the Mahāsāṃghika ("Great Assembly") and the Sthaviravāda ("Teaching of the Elders"; Pāli: Theravāda) schools. *See also* Mahayana; Theravāda.

"See the sutra": This phrase appears more than forty times in the *Shōmangyō-gisho* and is used to refer the reader to the subject of the commentary itself, the *Śrīmālā-sūtra*, for material that is clearly presented therein and so does not require further comment, or for material that is not central to the main argument but is further elaborated in the sutra.

self-enlightened one (Skt. *pratyekabuddha*): Sometimes also called "solitary realizer," those who have attained enlightenment by direct realization but who live apart from other religious strivers and who do not teach or guide others. One of the paths of the two vehicles criticized in the *Śrīmālā-sūtra* and the *Shōmangyō-gisho* for their lack of altruism and concern with saving others. The path of individual salvation is described as inferior to that of the bodhisattva, since it leads only to a provisional form of enlightenment. *See also* bodhisattva; disciple; two vehicles.

self-practice: The *Shōmangyō-gisho* distinguishes "self-practice" (Chapters 1–3 in the *Śrīmālā-sūtra*) from "other-practice" (Chapters 4–5 in the *Śrīmālā-sūtra*). Self-practice is the realm of bodhisattvas at the seventh stage (such as Queen Śrīmālā) and below, while other-practice refers to those at the eighth stage and above. *See also* bodhisattva; eighth stage; other-practice; seventh stage.

semblance Dharma: The second period of the Buddha's teaching, in which practitioners' capacity for understanding the Dharma has declined, life span has decreased, and few are able to attain liberation. The semblance Dharma lasts for one thousand years and follows the initial five hundred-year period of the true Dharma (in some calculations this period is said to last a thousand years). The period of the semblance Dharma, so called as it offers only a limited semblance of the complete teaching, precedes a period of even greater decline, known as the "end of the Dharma" (Jpn. *mappō;* also rendered as "the latter day of the law [Dharma]"), which is said to last for ten thousand years.

sentient beings: Unenlightened beings who continue to transmigrate in samsara due to the results of their negative actions (karma). They are contrasted to Śākyamuni

Buddha and others who have attained liberation (nirvana) from the cycle of transmigration. Some schools of Buddhism consider even trees, rocks, and other elements of nature to be sentient and thus capable of enlightenment and liberation. *See also* nirvana; samsara.

seventh stage: The seventh stage (Skt. *bhūmi*) of bodhisattva practice, referred to as "far-reaching" (*dūraṃgamā*). The *Shōmangyō-gisho* identifies Queen Śrīmālā as having attained this stage. This is the last stage of self-practice according to the division outlined in the text; the eighth stage, called "immovable" (*acalā*), is the first stage of other-practice. *See also* eighth stage; fifty-two stages; other-practice; self-practice.

seven virtues: The seven virtues of the Buddha that are are not fully developed in followers of the two vehicles: wisdom, elimination of the afflictions, liberation, purity, merit, wisdom based on complete observation of phenomena, and nirvana. *See also* two vehicles.

six principles: These principles are discussed in conjunction with the cause of enlightenment of the two vehicles. They are: 1) The teaching of the Buddha that flourishes, 2) the teaching of the Buddha that declines, 3) embracing virtuous behavior, 4) freeing oneself from evil behavior, 5) taking up the religious life first by leaving home, and 6) taking the precepts. *See also* two vehicles.

skillful means (Skt. *upāya; upāya-kauśalya*): Techniques used by the Buddha and high-level disciples to teach and save sentient beings. Using skillful means suggests careful selection and adaptation of the Dharma to accord with the differing needs and capacities of those receiving a particular teaching.

Small Vehicle. *See* Hinayana.

śrāvaka. See disciple.

Śrāvastī: One of the major cities in the kingdom of Kośala, located about seventy-five miles northeast of modern-day Lucknow, Uttar Pradesh, India. The Jeta Grove and Anāthapiṇḍada Garden was near this ancient city. *See also* Jeta Grove and Anāthapiṇḍada Garden; Kośala.

Śrīmālā-sūtra (Skt. *Śrīmālādevīsiṃhanāda-sūtra*, lit., "The Lion's Roar of Queen Śrīmālā"): One of the early Mahayana sutras that discusses the *tathāgatagarbha*. In the text, Queen Śrīmālā, with the eloquence ("lion's roar") granted her by the Buddha, expounds the *tathāgatagarbha,* the One Vehicle, and the conditioned and unconditioned forms of the Four Noble Truths. The *Śrīmālā-sūtra* is the object of exegesis of the *Shōmangyō-gisho. See also* Four Noble Truths; Mahayana; One Vehicle; Queen Śrīmālā; *tathāgatagarbha.*

sutra: (Skt., lit., "thread"): A Buddhist text, such as the *Śrīmālā-sūtra,* that contains the Buddha's teachings. Sutras originally contained teachings that were directly expounded by the Buddha, preserved in the oral tradition, and later collected and recorded. However, the development of the Mahayana saw the production of numerous texts that are accorded the status of sutras. Capitalized, the term refers to one of the "three baskets" (Tripiṭaka) of the Buddhist canon. *See also* Mahayana; Tripiṭaka.

Tathāgata: An epithet for the Buddha that appears frequently in the *Śrīmālā-sūtra* and the *Shōmangyō-gisho*. Literally, the term means one who has "thus gone" (Skt. *tathā*, "thus"; *gata*, "gone") to the other shore of enlightenment (nirvana), but who has also "thus come" (*tathā; āgata*, "come") back to the world of suffering (samsara) out of compassion for sentient beings in order to teach them and help guide them to liberation. *See also* nirvana; samsara; sentient beings.

tathāgatagarbha: Lit., "storehouse," "womb," or "matrix" (Skt. *garbha*) of the Tathāgata. A central teaching of the *Śrīmālā-sūtra*, the *tathāgatagarbha* is similar to buddha-nature, the inherent potential of all sentient beings to attain enlightenment. *See also* buddha-nature; Tathāgata.

ten great vows: The ten Mahayana ordination vows. Discussed in detail in the *Śrīmālā-sūtra* (in which the text's protagonist, Queen Śrīmālā, receives them) and in the *Shōmangyō-gisho*, these vows are distinguished from the Hinayana precepts. In the sutra, Queen Śrīmālā vows to: 1) not develop an attitude in which one would transgress any of the earlier precepts; 2) show neither pride nor jealousy toward the worthy elders; 3) not hate sentient beings; 4) refrain from being jealous of others' physical appearance and material possessions; 5) refrain from being stingy with her own possessions; 6) not accept material things for her own benefit; 7) not practice solely for her own benefit the four methods of the bodhisattva to help others: giving, loving speech, beneficial acts, and cooperation; 8) offer comfort to those beings who are solitary, struck by illness, and suffering hardship; 9) not forsake those who engage in acts that contravene the teachings; and 10) never forget embracing the true Dharma. *See also* bodhisattva; Hinayana; Mahayana; Queen Śrīmālā; sentient beings; true Dharma.

ten evils: Three evils of the body: killing, stealing, and sexual impropriety; four evils of speech: lying, slander, harsh speech, and gossip; and three evils of the mind: greed, anger, and wrong views.

Theravāda ("Teaching of the Elders"; Skt. Sthaviravāda). One of the two schools of Buddhism that emerged from a split in the early Buddhist community at the Second Buddhist Council. The school sees itself as transmitting the original teachings of the Buddha and sometimes criticizes the Mahayana for distorting those teachings. The Theravāda is prominent in South and Southeast Asia, and its texts are preserved in the Pāli canon. *See also* Hinayana; Mahayana; Second Buddhist Council.

three bodies (Skt. *trikāya*): The three bodies of the Buddha, which became a central teaching in Mahayana Buddhist schools, include the Dharma body (Skt. *dharmakāya*), the enjoyment body (Skt. *saṃbhogakāya*), and the manifestation body (Skt. *nirmāṇakāya*). The *trikāya* developed as a way to explain the relationship between the Buddha and reality itself. Although there are varied interpretations of these bodies, a common understanding is that the Dharma body refers to truth itself, expressing reality as thusness. The enjoyment body, also referred to as the "reward body," refers to the body that enjoys the benefits received from engaging in bodhisattva practice and accumulating good merit. Finally, the manifestation body refers to the body that appears in the world in varied forms to save sentient beings. *See also* Dharma body; enjoyment body; manifestation body.

three great vows: The three great vows taken by Queen Śrīmālā: 1) to bring peace to innumerable sentient beings and attain the wisdom of the true Dharma; 2) to explain the true Dharma for the benefit of all sentient beings with a mind that does not weary; and 3) to be prepared to abandon body, life, and wealth in teaching the true Dharma.

three poisons: Greed, hatred, and ignorance. In Buddhist teachings, these three unwholesome mental states are viewed as the root of the other afflictions (*kleśa*s). *See also* affliction.

three realms: The three realms of existence: the realm of desire (*kāmadhātu*), the realm of form (*rūpadhātu*), and the realm of formlessness (*ārūpyadhātu*). Beings that transmigrate in samsara are part of the desire realm, to which they are bound in varying degrees by the need to gratify sensual desires. The form realm is inhabited by those with subtle physical forms that lack sexual distinctions and are not consumed by sensual desires, and who are invisible to inhabitants of the desire realm. In the formless realm, beings lack material form and occupy levels that correspond to their degree of mastery of the four formless concentrations.

Three Treasures: The Buddha (the teacher), the Dharma (the teachings), and the Sangha (the community of practitioners). The three objects of refuge for Buddhist followers.

three vehicles: The paths of the disciples (*śrāvaka*s), self-enlightened ones (*pratyeka-buddha*s), and bodhisattvas. A central argument of the *Śrīmālā-sūtra* is that the paths of three vehicles are all part of the One Vehicle. *See also* bodhisattva; disciple; One Vehicle; self-enlightened one; two vehicles.

Tripiṭaka (Skt. "three baskets"): The three divisions of the Buddhist canon, consisting of Sutra (the Buddha's teachings), Vinaya (monastic codes of discipline), and Abhidharma (doctrinal treatises).

true Dharma: The true teaching of the Buddha; the ultimate teaching of the Buddha regarding the true nature of reality. Embracing the true Dharma, referred to as the "one great vow," is a central concern of the *Śrīmālā-sūtra*. The true Dharma is distinguished from the provisional teachings of the two vehicles. *See also* two vehicles.

two types of birth and death: The birth and death of limited cyclic existence (samsara) experienced by practitioners of the two vehicles, and the birth and death of inconceivable transformation experienced by advanced bodhisattvas. The *Shōmangyō-gisho* briefly describes two other forms of birth and death: the birth and death of the mid-space between the two realms, and the birth and death associated with the earliest moment of transmigration. *See also* bodhisattva; samsara; two vehicles.

two types of patience: Also known as "two types of endurance" and "two types of for-bearance," the *Shōmangyō-gisho* describes these as the "patience of faith in the Buddha" and the "patience of following the teachings," although there are other pairs, such as "patience with sentient beings under all conditions" and the "patience of those who understand the non-arising of the elements of existence." The *Shō-mangyō-gisho* mentions briefly the latter item as a third type of patience, and Buddhist texts often describe patience (Skt. *kṣānti*), one of the six perfections, in groups of three. For example, "patience under hatred," "patience under physical difficulties," and "patience in the pursuit of faith"; or the "patience of non-retalia-tion," the "patience of enduring trials," and the "patience of resolutely practicing the Dharma." *See also* perfections.

two vehicles: The Buddhist vehicles of the disciples (*śrāvaka*s) and self-enlightened ones (*pratyekabuddha*s). Certain passages in the *Shōmangyō-gisho* describe the two vehicles as those of the arhats and self-enlightened ones. In Mahayana texts, these two groups are often criticized for following the inferior path of the Small Vehicle (Hinayana), which offers only a provisional form of truth, wisdom, and liberation, contrasted to that of the bodhisattva, who follows the teachings of the Great Vehicle that offer ultimate truth, wisdom, and liberation. *See also* arhat; bodhi-sattva; disciple; Hinayana; Mahayana; self-enlightened one.

Unconditioned Four Noble Truths: One of two sets of Noble Truths discussed in the *Śrīmālā-sūtra* and the *Shōmangyō-gisho.* The *Śrīmālā-sūtra* states that the Uncon-ditioned Four Noble Truths were taught by the Buddha as ultimate truth and were intended for Mahayana practitioners; they were not intended for those practicing the provisional teachings of the two vehicles, to whom were taught the Conditioned Four Noble Truths. *See also* Conditioned Four Noble Truths; Four Noble Truths; Mahayana; two vehicles.

Vimalakīrtinirdeśa-sūtra: A Mahayana sutra that expounds the teachings of emptiness and nonduality. Layman Vimalakīrti, the sutra's protagonist, is presented as a supremely skillful practitioner who teaches arhats and bodhisattvas about the Dharma, culminating in the teaching of emptiness. The *Shōmangyō-gisho* refers to the *Vimalakīrtinirdeśa* and the *Prajñāpāramitā* sutras as examples of Mahayana texts that are distinct from *ekayāna* (One Vehicle) texts. The *Vimalakīrtinirdeśa* is the object of exegesis of the *Yuimagyō-gisho,* one of two other Buddhist commentaries attributed to Prince Shōtoku. *See also* arhat; bodhisattva; emptiness; Mahayana; One Vehicle; Prajñāpāramitā sutras; Prince Shōtoku.

Vinaya: Codes of moral discipline followed by members of the Buddhist community, especially by ordained monastics; one of the "three baskets" (Tripiṭaka) of the Buddhist canon. There are a number of Vinaya traditions that vary in the numbers of rules, sphere of geographic influence, etc. *See also Prātimokṣa;* Tripiṭaka.

World-honored One (Skt. *bhagavat*): An epithet for the Buddha that appears frequently in the *Śrīmālā-sūtra,* particularly when Queen Śrīmālā is addressing the Buddha.

Bibliography

Aston, W. G., trans. *Nihongi: Chronicles of Japan from the Earliest Times to A.D. 697.* 1896. Rutland, VT: Charles E. Tuttle Co., 1972, reprint.

Carr, Kevin Gray. *Plotting the Place: Shōtoku Cults and the Mapping of Medieval Japanese Buddhism.* Honolulu: University of Hawai'i Press, 2012.

Chamberlain, Basil Hall, trans. *The Kojiki: Records of Ancient Matters.* Rutland, VT: Charles E. Tuttle Company, 1982.

Como, Michael I. Shōtoku: *Ethnicity, Ritual, and Violence in the Japanese Buddhist Tradition.* Oxford, England: Oxford University Press, 2008.

Deal, William E. "Hagiography and History: The Image of Prince Shōtoku," in *Religions of Japan in Practice,* pp. 316–333. George J. Tanabe, Jr., ed. Princeton, NJ: Princeton University Press, 1999.

de Visser, Marinus Willem. *Ancient Buddhism in Japan: Sūtras and Ceremonies in Use in the Seventh and Eighth Centuries A.D. and Their History in Later Times.* Leiden, The Netherlands: E. J. Brill, 1935.

Fujieda, Akira. *"Shōmangyō-gisho,"* in *Nihon shisō taikei 2: Shōtoku Taishishū (A Survey of Japanese Thought 2: Prince Shōtoku Collection),* pp. 484–544. Ienaga Saburō, et al., eds. Tokyo: Iwanami Shoten, 1975.

Fujii, Kyōkō. *"Shōmangyō-gisho,"* in *Daijō butten Chūgoku Nihonhen 16: Shōtoku Taishi-Ganjin (A Compilation of Chinese and Japanese Mahayana Buddhist Scriptures: Prince Shōtoku and Ganjin),* pp. 5–250. Takasaki Jikidō, ed. Tokyo: Chūō-kōronsha, 1990.

Fukui, Kōjun. *"Sangyō-gisho no seiritsu no gigi"* ("Doubts about [Prince Shōtoku's] Composition of the *Sangyō-gisho"*), in *Kanakura hakushi koki kinen: Indogaku bukkyōgaku ronshū (Collected Essays from Indian and Buddhist Studies: In Commemoration of Dr. Kanakura's Seventieth Birthday),* pp. 457–480. Sakamoto Yukio, ed. Kyoto: Heirakuji shoten, 1966.

Furuya, Myōkaku. "Shōtoku Taishi *Shōmangyō-gisho* no ikkōsatsu" ("An Investigation of Prince Shōtoku's *Shōmangyō-gisho"*), *Nantō bukkyō (Nara Buddhism)* 5 (1958): 14–25.

Guth, Christine. "The Pensive Prince of Chūgūji," in *Maitreya, the Future Buddha,* pp. 191–214. Alan Sponberg and Helen Hardacre, eds. New York: Cambridge University Press, 1988.

Hanayama, Shinshō. *Nihon bukkyō no genryū to shite no "Sangyō-gisho" (The "Sangyō-gisho" as the Source of Japanese Buddhism).* Tokyo: Meiji Shoin, 1940.

—. *"Sangyō-gisho* ni tsuite: Fukui Kyōju no gimon ni sokutō" ("An Immediate Response to Professor Fukui's Doubts about the *Sangyō-gisho"*), *Indogaku Bukkyōgaku Kenkyū (Journal of Indian and Buddhist Studies)* 4–2 (1956): 14–23.

—. *Shōmangyō-gisho.* Tokyo: Iwanami Shoten, 1948.

—. *Shōmangyō-gisho kōyaku (A Revised Translation of the Shōmangyō-gisho).* Tokyo: Yoshikawa Kōbunkan, 1977.

—. *"Shōmangyō-gisho* ni tsuite" ("In Regard to the *Shōmangyō-gisho"*), *Shōtoku Taishi kenkyū (The Journal of Prince Shōtoku Research)* 9–10 (1976): 1–12.

—. *"Shōmangyō-gisho" no Jōgūōsen ni kansuru kenkyū (Research on King Jōgū's Authorship of the "Shōmangyō-gisho").* Tokyo: Iwanami Shoten, 1944.

—. *Shōmangyō-gisho: tuketari kaisetsu hōjiban Shōmangyō-gisho (kagein) (The Shōmangyō-gisho: with Commentary of the Hōji Edition of the Shōmangyō-gisho [a facsimile]).* Tokyo: Yoshikawa Kōbunkan, 1977.

Hayashima, Kyōshō. *Shōmangyō: Shōmangyō-gisho (The Śrīmālā-sūtra and the Shōmangyō-gisho).* Tokyo: Seikai Seiten Kankō Kyōkai, 1999.

Hirakawa, Akira. *"Shōmangyō-gisho* no chūshaku ni okeru Taishi no taidō" ("The Attitude of Prince [Shōtoku] in the *Shōmangyō-gisho* Commentary"), *Shōtoku Taishi kenkyū (The Journal of Prince Shōtoku Research)* 4 (1968): 1–15.

—. *"Shōmangyō-gisho* to Nai 93 to no kankei ni tsuite" ("The Relationship between the *Shōmangyō-gisho* and Nai 93"), in *Shōtoku Taishi ronshū (Collected Essays on Prince Shōtoku),* pp. 207–230. Ishida Mosaku, et al., eds. Kyoto: Heirakuji Shoten, 1971.

Inazu, Kizō. *Jōgū-Shōtoku Taishisen "Shōmangyō-gisho" kaitei shinpan (A Revised Edition of the "Shōmangyō-gisho" Written by Prince Jōgū-Shōtoku).* Tokyo: Sanbō, 1983.

—. *Shōmangyō-gisho,* in *Bukkyō kyōiku hōten (Compendium of Buddhist Education) 2, Shōtoku Taishi-Nantō Bukkyōshū (Anthology of Essays on Prince Shōtoku and Nara Buddhism),* pp. 63–148. Deguchi Jōjun and Hiraoka Sadaumi, eds. Tokyo: Tamagawa Daigaku Shuppanbu, 1962.

Inoue, Mitsusada. *"Sangyō-gisho* seiritsu no kenkyū" ("Research on the Composition of the *Sangyō-gisho"*), in *Zoku nihon kodaishi ronshū (Anthology of Essays on Ancient Japan—A Supplement),* vol. 2, pp. 143–211. Tokyo: Yoshikawa Kōbunkan, 1972. Reprinted in *Shōtoku Taishi to Asuka bukkyō (Prince Shōtoku and Asuka Buddhism),* pp. 263–329. Tamura Enchō and Kawagishi Kōkyō, eds. Tokyo: Yoshikawa Kōbunkan, 1985.

Kamstra, J. H. *Encounter or Syncretism: The Initial Growth of Japanese Buddhism.* Leiden, The Netherlands: E. J. Brill, 1967.

Kanaji, Isamu. "*Hokke-gisho* narabi ni *Shōmangyō-gisho* senjutsu no mondai o megutte (1)" ("On the Problem of the Composition of the *Hokke-gisho* and the *Shōmangyō-gisho*–1"), *Shōtoku Taishi kenkyū* (*The Journal of Prince Shōtoku Research*) 13 (1979): 1–13.

——. "*Hokke-gisho* narabi ni *Shōmangyō-gisho* senjutsu no mondai o megutte (2)" ("On the Problem of the Composition of the *Hokke-gisho* and the *Shōmangyō-gisho*–2"), *Shōtoku Taishi kenkyū* (*The Journal of Prince Shōtoku Research*) 14 (1980): 10–22.

——. "Jikaku to kie: *Shōmangyō-gisho* shikai (ichi)" ("Interpretation of Self-realization and Refuge in the *Shōmangyō-gisho*–1"), *Shitennōji Tandai Kiyō* (*Bulletin of Shitennōji Junior College*) 8 (1966): 1–23.

——. *Jōgūōsen "Sangyō-gisho" no shomondai* (*Problems Concerning King Jōgū's Authorship of the "Sangyō-gisho"*). Kyoto: Hōzōkan, 1985.

——. "Nori no inga (ue): *Shōmangyō-gisho* shikai" ("Interpretation of the *Shōmangyō-gisho:* Cause and Effect in the [Great] Vehicle"), *Shitennōji kiyō* (*Bulletin of Shitennōji*) 10 (1968): 23–42.

——. "*Sangyō-gisho* no seiritsu ni tsuite: Fukui hakase no gigi ni ou" ("A Response to Dr. Fukui's Doubts about the Composition of the *Sangyō-gisho*"), *Shōtoku Taishi kenkyū* (*The Journal of Prince Shōtoku Research*) 4 (1968): 54–92.

——. "Setsuji shōbō: *Shōmangyō-gisho* shikai (ni)" ("Interpretation of Embracing the True Dharma in the *Shōmangyō-gisho*–2"), *Shitennōji Tandai Kiyō* (*Bulletin of Shitennōji Junior College*) 9 (1967): 1–23.

——. "*Shōmangyō-gisho* ni okeru nyoraizō shisō" ("*Tathāgatagarbha* Thought in the *Shōmangyō-gisho*"), *Indogaku Bukkyōgaku Kenkyū* (*Journal of Indian and Buddhist Studies*) 17–1 (1968): 55–59.

——. "*Shōmangyō-gisho* ni okeru shōji no mondai" ("The Problem of Birth and Death in the *Shōmangyō-gisho*"), *Indogaku Bukkyōgaku Kenkyū* (*Journal of Indian and Buddhist Studies*) 16–1 (1967): 346–349.

——. *Shōmangyō-gisho no shisōteki kenkyū* (*Research on the Thought of the Shōmangyō-gisho*). Tokyo: Sankibō Busshorin, 1971.

——. "*Shōmangyō-gisho* no tokushitsu: Shōtoku Taishi ni okeru *Shōmangyō* no haaku" ("The Special Characteristics of the *Shōmangyō-gisho:* Prince Shōtoku's Understanding of the *Śrīmālā-sūtra*"), *Shōtoku Taishi kenkyū* (*The Journal of Prince Shōtoku Research*) 3 (1967): 31–45.

——. "Three Stages in Shōtoku Taishi's Acceptance of Buddhism," *Acta Asiatica* 47 (1985): 31–47.

Kaneko, Daiei. *Sangyō-gisho to Nihon bukkyō* (*The Sangyō-gisho and Japanese Buddhism*). Tokyo: Kyōgaku Kyoku, 1939.

Kaneto, Mamoru. "*Shōmangyō-gisho* hyōgen no mondaiten 1" ("Problematic Expressions in the *Shōmangyō-gisho* 1"), *Shōtoku Taishi kenkyū* (*The Journal of Prince Shōtoku Research*) 2 (1966): 36–46.

——. "*Shōmangyō-gisho* no 'hongi' ni tsuite" ("The 'model text' of the *Shōmangyō-gisho*"), *Shōtoku Taishi kenkyū* (*The Journal of Prince Shōtoku Research*) 7 (1972): 25–38.

Bibliography

—. *"Shōmangyō-gisho* no hyōgen ni tsuite: tonkō hon Nai 93 (Shoi hongi) to no taishō" ("An Examination of Expressions in the *Shōmangyō-gisho* in Light of the Dunhuang Manuscript Nai 93 [the so-called model text]"), *Shōtoku Taishi kenkyū* (*The Journal of Prince Shōtoku Research*) 6 (1971): 17–28.

Kanno, Hiroshi. *"Sangyō-gisho* no shingi mondai ni tsuite" ("The Problem of the Authenticity of the *Sangyō-gisho*"), in *Sōgō kenkyū Asuka bunka* (*Comprehensive Research on Asuka Culture*), pp. 465–502. Ōkura Seishin Bunka Kenkyūjo, ed. Tokyo: Kokusho Kankōkai, 1989.

Katsumata, Shunkyō. *"Shōmangyō-gisho* ni shimesareta nyoraizō shisō" ("*Tathāgatagarbha* Thought in the *Shōmangyō-gisho*"), in *Shōmangyō-gisho Ronshū* (*Collected Essays on the "Shōmangyō-gisho"*), pp. 76–87. Genryū Kenkyūkai (Research Association for the Origins of Japanese Buddhism), ed. Kyoto: Nihon Bukkyō, 1965.

Koizumi, Enjun. "Tonkōhon Shōmangisho hongi" ("The Dunhuang Shōmangisho Model Text"), *Shōtoku Taishi kenkyū* (*The Journal of Prince Shōtoku Research*) 5 (1969): 59–141.

Lee, Kenneth Doo Young. *The Prince and the Monk: Shōtoku Worship in Shinran's Buddhism.* Albany, NY: State University of New York (SUNY) Press, 2007.

Lurie, David Barnett. *Realms of Literacy: Early Japan and the History of Writing.* Cambridge, MA: Harvard University Press, 2011.

Masaki, Akihiko. *"Shōmangyō-gisho* oyobi kankyōso no hikaku kenkyū josetsu: ryōkyo ni mirareru joseikan" ("Preliminary Research Comparing the View of Women in the *Shōmangyō-gisho* and the *Commentary on the Contemplation Sūtra*"), *Shōtoku Taishi kenkyū* (*The Journal of Prince Shōtoku Research*) 3 (1967): 66–75.

Mochizuki, Kazunori. *"Shōmangyō-gisho* ni kansuru ikkōsatsu" ("Reflections on the *Shōmangyō-gisho*"), *Shūkyō Kenkyū* (*Journal of Religious Studies*) 41–194 (1968): 152–153.
—. *"Shōmangyō-gisho* no tokuchō shinshishō ni tsuite" ("Special Characteristics of the *Shōmangyō-gisho* in the True Children [of the Tathāgata Chapter]"), *Indogaku Bukkyōgaku Kenkyū* (*Journal of Indian and Buddhist Studies*) 17–1 (1968): 110–114.

Muranushi, Keikai. *"Shōmangyō-gisho* ni okeru 'setsuju shōbō' ni tsuite" ("'Embracing the True Dharma' in the *Shōmangyō-gisho*"), *Indogaku Bukkyōgaku Kenkyū* (*Journal of Indian and Buddhist Studies*) 5–1 (1957): 243–246.

Nakamura, Hajime. *A History of the Development of Japanese Thought A.D. 592 to 1868.* Tokyo: Kokusai Bunka Shinkōkai, 1969.
—. *Ways of Thinking of Eastern Peoples: India, China, Tibet, Japan.* Honolulu, HI: East-West Center Press, 1964.

Ogura, Toyofumi. "*Sangyō-gisho* Jōgūōsen ni kansuru gigi" ("Doubts Concerning King Jōgū's Composition of the *Sangyō-gisho*"), in *Shōtoku Taishi to Asuka Bukkyō (Prince Shōtoku and Asuka Buddhism)*, pp. 144–167. Tamura Enchō and Kawagishi Kōkyō, eds. Tokyo: Yoshikawa Kōbunkan, 1985.

Ōyama, Seiichi. *Nagayaō mokkan to kinsekibun (The Mokkan and Epigraphy of Prince Nagaya)*. Tokyo: Yoshikawa Kōbunkan, 1998.

—. *Shōtoku Taishi no shinjitsu (The Truth about Prince Shōtoku)*. Tokyo: Heibonsha, 2003.

—. *Shōtoku Taishi no tanjō (The Birth of Prince Shōtoku)*. Tokyo: Yoshikawa Kōbunkan, 1999.

—. *Shōtoku Taishi to Nihonjin (Prince Shōtoku and the Japanese)*. Nagoya: Fūbaisha, 2001.

Paul, Diana M., trans. *The Buddhist Feminine Ideal: Queen Śrīmālā and the Tathāgatagarbha*. Missoula, MT: Scholars Press, American Academy of Religions, 1980. Reprinted in *The Sutra of Queen Śrīmālā of the Lion's Roar*. Berkeley: Numata Center for Buddhist Translation and Research, 2004. http://www.bdkamerica.org/default.aspx?MPID=81.

Pradel, Maria del Rosario. *The Fragments of the Tenjukoku Shūchō Mandara: Reconstruction of the Iconography and the Historical Contexts*. Ph.D. dissertation, University of California Los Angeles (UCLA), 1997.

Saitō, Noriō. "*Sangyō-gisho* Jōgūō seiso no shingi ni tsuite" ("The Truth about King Jōgū's Authorship of the *Sangyō-gisho*"), *Risshō shigaku (Risshō University Journal of Historical Research)* 21.22 (1968): 69–70.

Sakamoto, Tarō. "*Shōmangyō-gisho* no kenkyū ni tsuite" ("Research on the *Shōmangyō-gisho*"), in *Shōtoku Taishi ronshū (Collected Essays on Prince Shōtoku)*, pp. 656–660. Ishida Mosaku, et al., eds. Kyoto: Heirakuji shoten, 1971.

—. "Shōtoku Taishi kenkyū no rekishi" ("The History of Prince Shōtoku Research"), in *Shōtoku Taishi ronshū (Collected Essays on Prince Shōtoku)*, pp. 646–648. Ishida Mosaku, et al., eds. Kyoto: Heirakuji Shoten, 1971.

Seeley, Christopher. *A History of Writing in Japan*. Leiden, The Netherlands: Brill, 1991. Reprinted under the same title, Honolulu, HI: University of Hawai'i Press, 2000.

Shirai, Shigenobu. *Sangyō-gisho no rinrigakuteki kenkyū: Shōtoku Taishi gosen (Research on the Ethics of the "Sangyō-gisho" Written by Prince Shōtoku)*. Kyoto: Hyakkaen, 1970.

Shōtoku Taishi Kenkyūkai (Association of Prince Shōtoku Research), ed. *Shōtoku Taishi butten kōsetsu: "Shōmangyō-gisho" no gendaigoyaku to kenkyū (An Interpretation of the Buddhist Scriptures of Prince Shōtoku: Research and a Modern Translation of the "Shōmangyō-gisho")*. Tokyo: Taimeidō, 1988–1989.

Tsuda, Sōkichi. *Nihon jōdaishi kenkyū (Research on Ancient Japanese History)*. Tokyo: Iwanami Shoten, 1930.

—. *Nihon koten no kenkyū (Research on the Japanese Classics)*, 2 volumes. Tokyo: Iwanami Shoten, 1948.

Watanabe, Kōjun. "*Sangyō-gisho* no shinshin ni tsuite" ("The True Body in the *Sangyō-gisho*"), *Shōtoku Taishi kenkyū (The Journal of Prince Shōtoku Research)* 9–10 (1976): 63–70.

—. "*Sangyō-gisho*" *no tankyū (Research on the "Sangyō-gisho")*. Osaka: Shōtoku Taishikai, 1984.

—. "*Shōmangyō-gisho* no tokuchō ni tsuite" ("The Special Features of the *Shōmangyō-gisho*"), in "*Shōmangyō-gisho*" *ronshū (Collected Essays on the "Shōmangyō-gisho")*, pp. 126–132. Nihon Bukkyo Genryu Kenkyūkai (Research Association for the Origins of Japanese Buddhism), ed. Kyoto: Nihon Bukkyō Genryu Kenkyūkai, 1965.

—. "*Shōmangyō-gisho* sandaiganshō ni okeru gosha ni tsuite" ("Copying Errors in the Three Great Vows of the *Shōmangyō-gisho*"), *Indogaku Bukkyōgaku Kenkyū (Journal of Indian and Buddhist Studies)* 17–1 (1968): 232–235.

—. "*Shōmangyō-gisho* to *Jōgū teisetsu* ni miyuru nehan jōjū goshu busshō no ikku ni tsuite" ("Concerning the Phrase on the Eternally Abiding Nirvana and the Five Types of Buddha Nature in the *Shōmangyō-gisho* and the *Jōgū teisetsu*"), *Indogaku Bukkyōgaku Kenkyū (Journal of Indian and Buddhist Studies)* 5–1 (1957): 236–237.

Watanabe, Shōkō. "*Sangyō-gisho* no sakusha mondai: nihon bukkyō no ayumi" (6) ("The Problem of the Authorship of the *Sangyō-gisho* in Relation to the Development of Japanese Buddhism"), *Daihōrin (The Great Wheel of Dharma)* 24–8 (1957): 148–155.

Wayman, Alex, and Hideko Wayman. *The Lion's Roar of Queen Śrīmālā: A Buddhist Scripture on the Tathāgatagarbha Theory.* New York: Columbia University Press, 1974.

Index

A

affliction(s) (*see also* defilement) xx, 17,
    18, 25, 27, 53, 56, 59, 60, 63, 64–65,
    66, 67, 68, 69, 70–71, 72, 73, 75, 76,
    77, 79, 80, 81, 82, 83–84, 99, 100,
    105, 106, 107, 108, 109, 122, 123,
    124, 125, 129
  active 69, 71, 72, 73, 76, 77, 81, 82, 83,
    84, 105, 123
  demon of (*see also* four demons) 17, 85
  essence and characteristics of 70, 71,
    73, 75, 82, 83
  mental, mind's (*see also* mental distur-
    bances) 14, 16, 17, 53, 63, 64, 70,
    71, 82, 93
  stores of 96, 98, 99, 107, 108
  two types of 70–71, 76, 82, 83, 123
aggregate(s) 17, 71, 105, 106
  demon of (*see also* four demons) 17,
    18, 85
Amaterasu xv
Ānanda 7, 8, 10, 132
Anāthapiṇḍada (*see also* Jeta Grove and
    Anāthapiṇḍada Garden) 8
Aramaki, Noritoshi xx
arhat(s) xiv, 55, 59, 61, 62, 63–64, 65,
    67, 70, 74, 75, 76, 86, 87, 95, 105,
    111, 114, 127
  wisdom of 85, 86, 115
aspiration(s) 27, 28, 29
Avalokiteśvara xvii
Awakening of Mahayana Faith xiii
Ayodhyā xiii, 3, 9, 11

B

Baekje xv
birth and death (*see also* cyclic existence;
    rebirth) 10, 18, 25, 40, 49, 54, 66,
    67–68, 69, 74, 79, 84–87, 100,
    101–102, 117, 118, 119–120,
    121–122
  four types of 67–69
  two types of 17, 63, 66, 69, 70, 76, 82,
    84–86, 100, 101
Bodhidharma xvii
bodhisattva(s) xiv, xix, xx, 8, 9, 13, 23,
    25, 26, 29, 31, 38, 41, 42, 43, 44,
    47, 48, 50, 53, 55, 63, 68, 74, 76,
    97, 111, 125, 126, 128
  at the eighth stage (and above) xix, 13,
    27, 28, 30, 31, 32, 33, 34, 36–37, 38,
    40, 41, 42, 43, 46, 47, 48, 50, 55, 56,
    67, 68, 101, 102, 103, 126
  at the seventh stage (and below) xix,
    13, 27, 28, 30, 32, 33, 46, 50, 51, 55,
    56, 57, 58, 67, 68, 101, 102, 103,
    105, 112
  perfections of (*see also* perfections)
    28, 45
  practice(s) xix, 22, 27, 31, 136
  stage(s) (*see also* stage) 3, 27, 136
  of the tenth stage 3
  vehicle (*see also* vehicle) xiv, 40, 42,
    52
  vows 32, 33
body, speech, and mind 12, 23
buddha(s) 3, 5, 20, 34, 50, 56, 89, 90, 129

BDK English Tripiṭaka
(First Series)

Abbreviations

Ch.: Chinese
Skt.: Sanskrit
Jp.: Japanese
Eng.: Published title

Title	Taishō No.
Ch. Changahanjing (長阿含經) Skt. Dīrghāgama	1
Ch. Zhongahanjing (中阿含經) Skt. Madhyamāgama	26
Ch. Dachengbenshengxindiguanjing (大乘本生心地觀經)	159
Ch. Fosuoxingzan (佛所行讚) Skt. Buddhacarita Eng. *Buddhacarita: In Praise of Buddha's Acts* (2009)	192
Ch. Zabaocangjing (雜寶藏經) Eng. *The Storehouse of Sundry Valuables* (1994)	203
Ch. Fajupiyujing (法句譬喻經) Eng. *The Scriptural Text: Verses of the Doctrine, with Parables* (1999)	211
Ch. Xiaopinbanruoboluomijing (小品般若波羅蜜經) Skt. Aṣṭasāhasrikā-prajñāpāramitā-sūtra	227
Ch. Jingangbanruoboluomijing (金剛般若波羅蜜經) Skt. Vajracchedikā-prajñāpāramitā-sūtra	235
Ch. Daluojingangbukongzhenshisanmoyejing (大樂金剛不空眞實三麼耶經) Skt. Adhyardhaśatikā-prajñāpāramitā-sūtra	243
Ch. Renwangbanruoboluomijing (仁王般若波羅蜜經) Skt. Kāruṇikārājā-prajñāpāramitā-sūtra (?)	245

Title	Taishō No.
Ch. Dabiluzhenachengfoshenbianjiachijing (大毘盧遮那成佛神變加持經) Skt. Mahāvairocanābhisambodhivikurvitādhiṣṭhānavaipulyasūtrendra- rājanāmadharmaparyāya Eng. *The Vairocanābhisaṃbodhi Sutra* (2005)	848
Ch. Jinggangdingyiqierulaizhenshishedachengxianzhengdajiao- wangjing (金剛頂一切如來眞實攝大乘現證大教王經) Skt. Sarvatathāgatatattvasaṃgrahamahāyānābhisamayamahākalparāja Eng. *The Adamantine Pinnacle Sutra* (in *Two Esoteric Sutras,* 2001)	865
Ch. Suxidijieluojing (蘇悉地羯囉經) Skt. Susiddhikaramahātantrasādhanopāyika-paṭala Eng. *The Susiddhikara Sutra* (in *Two Esoteric Sutras,* 2001)	893
Ch. Modengqiejing (摩登伽經) Skt. Mātaṅgī-sūtra (?)	1300
Ch. Mohesengqilü (摩訶僧祇律) Skt. Mahāsāṃghika-vinaya (?)	1425
Ch. Sifenlü (四分律) Skt. Dharmaguptaka-vinaya (?)	1428
Ch. Shanjianlüpiposha (善見律毘婆沙) Pāli Samantapāsādikā	1462
Ch. Fanwangjing (梵網經) Skt. Brahmajāla-sūtra (?)	1484
Ch. Youposaijiejing (優婆塞戒經) Skt. Upāsakaśīla-sūtra (?) Eng. *The Sutra on Upāsaka Precepts* (1994)	1488
Ch. Miaofalianhuajingyoubotishe (妙法蓮華經憂波提舍) Skt. Saddharmapuṇḍarīka-upadeśa	1519
Ch. Shih-chu-pi-pʻo-sha-lun (十住毘婆沙論) Skt. Daśabhūmika-vibhāṣā (?)	1521
Ch. Fodijinglun (佛地經論) Skt. Buddhabhūmisūtra-śāstra (?) Eng. *The Interpretation of the Buddha Land* (2002)	1530
Ch. Apidamojushelun (阿毘達磨俱舍論) Skt. Abhidharmakośa-bhāṣya	1558

Title	Taishō No.
Ch. Zhonglun (中論)	1564
Skt. Madhyamaka-śāstra	
Ch. Yüqieshidilun (瑜伽師地論)	1579
Skt. Yogācārabhūmi	
Ch. Chengweishilun (成唯識論)	1585
Eng. *Demonstration of Consciousness Only* (in *Three Texts on Consciousness Only,* 1999)	
Ch. Weishisanshilunsong (唯識三十論頌)	1586
Skt. Triṃśikā	
Eng. *The Thirty Verses on Consciousness Only* (in *Three Texts on Consciousness Only,* 1999)	
Ch. Weishihershilun (唯識二十論)	1590
Skt. Viṃśatikā	
Eng. *The Treatise in Twenty Verses on Consciousness Only* (in *Three Texts on Consciousness Only,* 1999)	
Ch. Shedachenglun (攝大乘論)	1593
Skt. Mahāyānasaṃgraha	
Eng. *The Summary of the Great Vehicle* (Revised Second Edition, 2003)	
Ch. Bianzhongbianlun (辯中邊論)	1600
Skt. Madhyāntavibhāga	
Ch. Dachengzhuangyanjinglun (大乘莊嚴經論)	1604
Skt. Mahāyānasūtrālaṃkāra	
Ch. Dachengchengyelun (大乘成業論)	1609
Skt. Karmasiddhiprakaraṇa	
Ch. Jiujingyichengbaoxinglun (究竟一乘寶性論)	1611
Skt. Ratnagotravibhāgamahāyānottaratantra-śāstra	
Ch. Yinmingruzhenglilun (因明入正理論)	1630
Skt. Nyāyapraveśa	
Ch. Dachengjipusaxuelun (大乘集菩薩學論)	1636
Skt. Śikṣāsamuccaya	
Ch. Jingangzhenlun (金剛針論)	1642
Skt. Vajrasūcī	
Ch. Zhangsuozhilun (彰所知論)	1645
Eng. *The Treatise on the Elucidation of the Knowable* (2004)	

Title	Taishō No.
Ch. Putixingjing (菩提行經) Skt. Bodhicaryāvatāra	1662
Ch. Jingangdingyuqiezhongfaanouduoluosanmiaosanputixinlun (金剛頂瑜伽中發阿耨多羅三貌三菩提心論)	1665
Ch. Dachengqixinlun (大乘起信論) Skt. Mahāyānaśraddhotpāda-śāstra (?) Eng. *The Awakening of Faith* (2005)	1666
Ch. Shimoheyanlun (釋摩訶衍論)	1668
Ch. Naxianbiqiujing (那先比丘經) Pāli Milindapañhā	1670
Ch. Banruoboluomiduoxinjingyuzan (般若波羅蜜多心經幽賛) Eng. *A Comprehensive Commentary on the Heart Sutra* (*Prajñāpāramitā-hṛdaya-sūtra*) (2001)	1710
Ch. Miaofalianhuajingxuanyi (妙法蓮華經玄義)	1716
Ch. Guanwuliangshoufojingshu (觀無量壽佛經疏)	1753
Ch. Sanlunxuanyi (三論玄義)	1852
Ch. Dachengxuanlun (大乘玄論)	1853
Ch. Zhaolun (肇論)	1858
Ch. Huayanyichengjiaoyifenqizhang (華嚴一乘教義分齊章)	1866
Ch. Yuanrenlun (原人論)	1886
Ch. Mohezhiguan (摩訶止觀)	1911
Ch. Xiuxizhiguanzuochanfayao (修習止觀坐禪法要)	1915
Ch. Tiantaisijiaoyi (天台四教儀)	1931
Ch. Guoqingbailu (國清百録)	1934
Ch. Zhenzhoulinjihuizhaochanshiwulu (鎮州臨濟慧照禪師語録) Eng. *The Recorded Sayings of Linji* (in *Three Chan Classics*, 1999)	1985
Ch. Foguoyuanwuchanshibiyanlu (佛果圜悟禪師碧巖録) Eng. *The Blue Cliff Record* (1998)	2003
Ch. Wumenguan (無門關) Eng. *Wumen's Gate* (in *Three Chan Classics*, 1999)	2005

Title	Taishō No.
Ch. Liuzudashifabaotanjing (六祖大師法寶壇經) Eng. *The Platform Sutra of the Sixth Patriarch* (2000)	2008
Ch. Xinxinming (信心銘) Eng. *The Faith-Mind Maxim* (in *Three Chan Classics*, 1999)	2010
Ch. Huangboshanduanjichanshichuanxinfayao (黄檗山斷際禪師傳心法要) Eng. *Essentials of the Transmission of Mind* (in *Zen Texts*, 2005)	2012A
Ch. Yongjiazhengdaoge (永嘉證道歌)	2014
Ch. Chixiubaizhangqinggui (勅修百丈清規) Eng. *The Baizhang Zen Monastic Regulations* (2007)	2025
Ch. Yibuzonglunlun (異部宗輪論) Skt. Samayabhedoparacanacakra Eng. *The Cycle of the Formation of the Schismatic Doctrines* (2004)	2031
Ch. Ayuwangjing (阿育王經) Skt. Aśokāvadāna Eng. *The Biographical Scripture of King Aśoka* (1993)	2043
Ch. Mamingpusachuan (馬鳴菩薩傳) Eng. *The Life of Aśvaghoṣa Bodhisattva* (in *Lives of Great Monks and Nuns*, 2002)	2046
Ch. Longshupusachuan (龍樹菩薩傳) Eng. *The Life of Nāgārjuna Bodhisattva* (in *Lives of Great Monks and Nuns*, 2002)	2047
Ch. Posoupandoufashichuan (婆藪槃豆法師傳) Eng. *Biography of Dharma Master Vasubandhu* (in *Lives of Great Monks and Nuns*, 2002)	2049
Ch. Datangdaciensisancangfashichuan (大唐大慈恩寺三藏法師傳) Eng. *A Biography of the Tripiṭaka Master of the Great Ci'en* *Monastery of the Great Tang Dynasty* (1995)	2053
Ch. Gaosengchuan (高僧傳)	2059
Ch. Biqiunichuan (比丘尼傳) Eng. *Biographies of Buddhist Nuns* (in *Lives of Great Monks and Nuns*, 2002)	2063

Title	Taishō No.
Ch. Gaosengfaxianchuan (高僧法顯傳)	2085
Eng. *The Journey of the Eminent Monk Faxian* (in *Lives of Great Monks and Nuns,* 2002)	
Ch. Datangxiyuji (大唐西域記)	2087
Eng. *The Great Tang Dynasty Record of the Western Regions* (1996)	
Ch. Youfangjichao: Tangdaheshangdongzhengchuan (遊方記抄: 唐大和上東征傳)	2089-(7)
Ch. Hongmingji (弘明集)	2102
Ch. Fayuanzhulin (法苑珠林)	2122
Ch. Nanhaijiguineifachuan (南海寄歸内法傳)	2125
Eng. *Buddhist Monastic Traditions of Southern Asia* (2000)	
Ch. Fanyuzaming (梵語雜名)	2135
Jp. Shōmangyōgisho (勝鬘經義疏)	2185
Eng. *Prince Shōtoku's Commentary on the Śrīmālā Sutra* (2011)	
Jp. Yuimakyōgisho (維摩經義疏)	2186
Jp. Hokkegisho (法華義疏)	2187
Jp. Hannyashingyōhiken (般若心經秘鍵)	2203
Jp. Daijōhossōkenjinshō (大乘法相研神章)	2309
Jp. Kan-jin-kaku-mu-shō (觀心覺夢鈔)	2312
Jp. Risshūkōyō (律宗綱要)	2348
Eng. *The Essentials of the Vinaya Tradition* (1995)	
Jp. Tendaihokkeshūgishū (天台法華宗義集)	2366
Eng. *The Collected Teachings of the Tendai Lotus School* (1995)	
Jp. Kenkairon (顯戒論)	2376
Jp. Sangegakushōshiki (山家學生式)	2377
Jp. Hizōhōyaku (秘藏寶鑰)	2426
Eng. *The Precious Key to the Secret Treasury* (in *Shingon Texts,* 2004)	
Jp. Benkenmitsunikyōron (辨顯密二教論)	2427
Eng. *On the Differences between the Exoteric and Esoteric Teachings* (in *Shingon Texts,* 2004)	

Title	Taishō No.
Jp. Sokushinjōbutsugi (即身成佛義)	2428
Eng. *The Meaning of Becoming a Buddha in This Very Body* (in *Shingon Texts*, 2004)	
Jp. Shōjijissōgi (聲字實相義)	2429
Eng. *The Meanings of Sound, Sign, and Reality* (in *Shingon Texts*, 2004)	
Jp. Unjigi (吽字義)	2430
Eng. *The Meanings of the Word Hūṃ* (in *Shingon Texts*, 2004)	
Jp. Gorinkujimyōhimitsushaku (五輪九字明秘密釋)	2514
Eng. *The Illuminating Secret Commentary on the Five Cakras and the Nine Syllables* (in *Shingon Texts*, 2004)	
Jp. Mitsugoninhotsurosangemon (密嚴院發露懺悔文)	2527
Eng. *The Mitsugonin Confession* (in *Shingon Texts*, 2004)	
Jp. Kōzengokokuron (興禪護國論)	2543
Eng. *A Treatise on Letting Zen Flourish to Protect the State* (in *Zen Texts*, 2005)	
Jp. Fukanzazengi (普勧坐禪儀)	2580
Eng. *A Universal Recommendation for True Zazen* (in *Zen Texts*, 2005)	
Jp. Shōbōgenzō (正法眼藏)	2582
Eng. *Shōbōgenzō: The True Dharma-eye Treasury* (Volume I, 2007) *Shōbōgenzō: The True Dharma-eye Treasury* (Volume II, 2008) *Shōbōgenzō: The True Dharma-eye Treasury* (Volume III, 2008) *Shōbōgenzō: The True Dharma-eye Treasury* (Volume IV, 2008)	
Jp. Zazenyōjinki (坐禪用心記)	2586
Eng. *Advice on the Practice of Zazen* (in *Zen Texts*, 2005)	
Jp. Senchakuhongannenbutsushū (選擇本願念佛集)	2608
Eng. *Senchaku Hongan Nembutsu Shū: A Collection of Passages on the Nembutsu Chosen in the Original Vow* (1997)	
Jp. Kenjōdoshinjitsukyōgyōshōmonrui (顯淨土眞實教行証文類)	2646
Eng. *Kyōgyōshinshō: On Teaching, Practice, Faith, and Enlightenment* (2003)	
Jp. Tannishō (歎異抄)	2661
Eng. *Tannishō: Passages Deploring Deviations of Faith* (1996)	

Title	Taishō No.
Jp. Rennyoshōninofumi (蓮如上人御文)	2668
Eng. *Rennyo Shōnin Ofumi: The Letters of Rennyo* (1996)	
Jp. Ōjōyōshū (往生要集)	2682
Jp. Risshōankokuron (立正安國論)	2688
Eng. *Risshōankokuron or The Treatise on the Establishment of the Orthodox Teaching and the Peace of the Nation* (in *Two Nichiren Texts*, 2003)	
Jp. Kaimokushō (開目抄)	2689
Eng. *Kaimokushō or Liberation from Blindness* (2000)	
Jp. Kanjinhonzonshō (觀心本尊抄)	2692
Eng. *Kanjinhonzonshō or The Most Venerable One Revealed by Introspecting Our Minds for the First Time at the Beginning of the Fifth of the Five Five Hundred-year Ages* (in *Two Nichiren Texts*, 2003)	
Ch. Fumuenzhongjing (父母恩重經)	2887
Eng. *The Sutra on the Profundity of Filial Love* (in *Apocryphal Scriptures*, 2005)	
Jp. Hasshūkōyō (八宗綱要)	extracanonical
Eng. *The Essentials of the Eight Traditions* (1994)	
Jp. Sangōshīki (三教指帰)	extracanonical
Jp. Mappōtōmyōki (末法燈明記)	extracanonical
Eng. *The Candle of the Latter Dharma* (1994)	
Jp. Jūshichijōkenpō (十七條憲法)	extracanonical